Asian Media Studies

John Nguyet Erni is dedicating this book in memory of his parents, while Siew Keng Chua would like to dedicate it to her mother and in memory of her father.

Asian Media Studies
Politics of Subjectivities

Edited by

John Nguyet Erni
and *Siew Keng Chua*

Blackwell
Publishing

BLACKWELL PUBLISHING
350 Main Street, Malden, MA 02148-5020, USA
108 Cowley Road, Oxford OX4 1JF, UK
550 Swanston Street, Carlton, Victoria 3053, Australia

The right of John Nguyet Erni and Siew Keng Chua to be identified as the
Authors of the Editorial Material in this Work has been asserted in accordance
with the UK Copyright, Designs, and Patents Act 1988.

First published 2005 by Blackwell Publishing Ltd

Library of Congress Cataloging-in-Publication Data

Asian media studies : politics of subjectivities / edited by John Nguyet Erni
and Siew Keng Chua.
p.   cm.
Includes bibliographical references and index.
ISBN 0-631-23498-5 (hardcover : alk. paper)—ISBN 0-631-23499-3
(pbk. : alk.paper)
1. Mass media—Asia   I. Erni, John Nguyet.   II. Chua, Siew Keng.
III. Title.

P92.A7A764   2005
302.23′095—dc22
2004003229

A catalogue record for this title is available from the British Library.

Set in 10.5 on 13 pt Minion
by SNP Best-set Typesetter Ltd., Hong Kong
Printed and bound in the United Kingdom
by TJ International Ltd, Padstow Cornwall

The publisher's policy is to use permanent paper from mills that operate a
sustainable forestry policy, and which has been manufactured from pulp
processed using acid-free and elementary chlorine-free practices. Furthermore,
the publisher ensures that the text paper and cover board used have met
acceptable environmental accreditation standards.

For further information on
Blackwell Publishing, visit our website:
http://www.blackwellpublishing.com

Contents

Contents

Notes on Contributors

Sue Abel is a doctoral student in the Department of Film, Video, and Television Studies at the Faculty of Arts, University of Auckland, New Zealand. She is the author of *Shaping the News: Waitangi Day on Television*. Her research interests include the representation of gender and race, advertising and consumption, news and magazines.

Siew Keng Chua researches and publishes in the fields of Asian media, gender studies, and cultural studies. She has headed research and teaching departments in universities in Australia and Singapore and has held research fellowships at the University of California at Berkeley, University of British Columbia (Vancouver), and City University of Hong Kong. She is currently working on a book on nation and gender in Chinese cinema and a manuscript on a Hong Kong film. At present, she is Adjunct Professor at the School of Communication, Faculty of Arts, Auckland University of Technology, New Zealand.

John Nguyet Erni is Associate Professor of Media and Cultural Studies and Coordinator of Graduate Studies in the Department of English and Communication, City University of Hong Kong. He is author of *Unstable Frontiers: Technomedicine and the Cultural Politics of "Curing" AIDS* (1994), editor of a Special Issue entitled "Becoming (Postcolonial) Hong Kong" for *Cultural Studies* (2001), and co-editor of a new book (with Ackbar Abbas), *Internationalizing Cultural Studies* (Blackwell, 2004). He is currently Chair of the Philosophy of Communication Division of the International Communication Association. His current work includes globalization and public health, *Harry Potter* in China, and youth media and cultural consumption in Hong Kong and Asia.

Kelly Hu is assistant professor in the Department of Communication and Institute of Telecommunications at National Chung Cheng University, Taiwan. She obtained her Ph.D. in Cultural Studies and Sociology from the University of Birmingham in 2001. In her dissertation she explored the meanings of VCDs as an Asian technology in relation to Chinese transnationalism, Asian styles of technoglobalization, and pirate modernity. She has also done research on the significance of modern reflexivity and self-narration in Japanese TV dramas.

Koichi Iwabuchi is Assistant Professor of media and cultural studies at International Christian University, Tokyo, and the author of *Recentering Globalization: Popular Culture and Japanese Transnationalism* (2002).

Vamsee Juluri was born in Hyderabad, India, and is an Assistant Professor in the Department of Media Studies at the University of San Francisco. He received his Ph.D. from the University of Massachusetts at Amherst. He has written about the politics of global audience studies in *Critical Studies in Mass Communication* and the meaning of family ties under liberalization in India in the *European Journal of Cultural Studies*. He is the author of *Becoming a Global Audience: Longing and Belonging in Indian Music Television* (2003).

Afshan Junaid has recently graduated with an MA in Communication Studies at Nanyang Technological University. She is presently pursuing a career in advertising and business.

Myung-koo Kang is a professor of communication studies at Seoul National University, teaching critical communication theories, and media and cultural studies. His recent research interests are the historical formation of Korean consumer culture and post/colonial conditions of knowledge production.

Gaik Cheng Khoo is currently a Postdoctoral Fellow at the Asia Research Institute, Singapore. She is preparing her dissertation for publication and doing research on Malaysian independent film. Her interests range from cultural studies, gender, and film to postcolonial literature.

Notes on Contributors

Keehyeung Lee is currently a lecturer in the Graduate School of Communication and Arts at Yonsei University, Seoul, South Korea. His recent scholarly works include "War, Televisual Images, and the Logistics of Perception" and "Toward an Articulation of Advertising Criticism and Cultural Studies." His research interests lie in the cultural studies of television and popular media, cultural geography, and the politics of memory.

Eric Ma is Head and Associate Professor in the Communication Division of the Graduate School at the Chinese University of Hong Kong. He is the author of *Culture, Politics and Television in Hong Kong* (1999) and *Underground Radicals* (in Chinese, 2001).

Anthony J. Spires is a doctoral candidate in Sociology at Yale University and Assistant Editor of YaleGlobal Online, a publication of the Yale Center for the Study of Globalization. His dissertation explores the changing social status of private business owners in China.

Irene Fang-chih Yang is Assistant Professor teaching cultural studies and media studies in the Department of English, National Dong Hwa University, Taiwan.

Acknowledgments

The editors and publisher gratefully acknowledge the permission granted to reproduce the copyright material in this book:

John Nguyet Erni and Anthony J. Spires, "The Formation of a Queer-Imagined Community in Post-Martial Law Taiwan." An earlier version of this chapter first appeared in *Sexualities*, 4(1), 2001, pp. 25–49, under the title "*G&L Magazine* and 'Tongzhu' Cultural Visibility in Taiwan." Reprinted by permission of Sage Publications Ltd.

Eric Kit-wai Ma, "Re-advertising Hong Kong: Nostalgia Industry and Popular History," in *Positions*, vol. 9, no. 1, pp. 131–59. © 2001 by Duke University Press. All rights reserved. Used by permission of the publisher.

Every effort has been made to trace copyright holders and to obtain their permission for the use of copyright material. The publisher apologizes for any errors or omissions and would be grateful if notified of any corrections that should be incorporated in future reprints or editions of this book.

1

Introduction: Our Asian Media Studies?

John Nguyet Erni and Siew Keng Chua

In this volume, our endeavor is to forge afresh the connection between media practices and the politics about the formation of subject positions found in the transnational Asian context today. We are particularly concerned about the specific local *realpolitik* through which media work takes place; that is, the *real* spaces and processes in political channels across various dominant *imaginations* about "Asias" today – nationalist, regionalist, globalist "Asias" – that attempt to manipulate and control the media, with varying kinds of intended and unwished-for consequences. To appropriate Foucault, we want to look at the "governmentalist" articulation of nationalism, of a specific vision of trans-Asian capital formation, forms of globalization, historical memories, and gender politics in the region's media world, and examine how these formations impinge upon subjectivity, from the conceptions of "audiences" to that of national sentiments in Asia. Thus, our main concern in this volume is to ask: what are the processes, phenomena, events, and discourses that suture "media" and "politics" together in such Asian contexts as Singapore, Hong Kong, Taiwan, Malaysia, India, China? To what extent do various media practices reflect broader political situations and political contestations found in specific Asian locales? It is imperative, therefore, that we have asked our contributors to present their own research projects, and simultaneously to reflect on the political context of their work, to write about the extent to which their projects call into question specific political problems confronted by the local society and culture, and on their projects' value as political interventions.

Other volumes on Asian media studies have provided an uneven attention to such questions. Many important works on the subject have largely been driven by methodological debates, which often means an evaluation of the appropriateness of western methods and knowledge-forms in media research for local contexts. A general situation has existed in the field for over four decades, whereby western methodologies and epistemologies have been largely accepted as a guiding light and "the local" was accepted as the recipient or the context of their glow. For a long time this was the *paradigmatic* predicament of Asian social-scientific research, since it was developed within a much broader historical and geopolitical framework of Third World international development and modernization. Even today, many Asian media studies research communities, associations, and their journals have persisted in conducting their research according to methods and problematics often originally articulated in Euro-American contexts. Interestingly, such persistence has developed alongside a sustaining cry of media imperialism voiced by the same research communities. Thus, the fervent period of growth in Asian media studies from the early 1970s to the early 1990s saw a practice of *skeptical* relay, absorption, and appropriation by many local, but western-trained, scholars *vis-à-vis* Euro-American media theories and methods. What has been generally touted today as the historical development of a postcolonial political consciousness in Asia has not necessarily led to genuinely original theory- or method-building that specifically speaks to media development and critique arising from indigenous political forms, intellectual legacies, or social relations across the region. Lodged in the western framework, local media researchers nonetheless seek ways to "decolonize" their work through adopting the critical impulses of more mainstream Third World political movements in denouncing western cultural imperialism. The reframing of postcolonial politics within media studies in Asia has produced a number of important guiding questions for the region, which can be broadly summarized as follows:

- In what ways has the role of Asian nation-states been reconstituted in the face of transborder flow of media products and practices under the ubiquitous shadow of "globalization"? (See e.g. Gunaratne, 2000; Kang, 2003.)
- In what ways has the whole idea of "domestic" media been challenged, when local media producers themselves have actively sought to emulate, and sometimes create, "cultural pirated versions" of western production codes and programming? (See e.g. Moeran, 2001.)

- Under the political impulse of "cultural resistance," what strategies – through economic production and symbolic reproduction – have been deployed by national media across Asia to defend and bolster national pride, and how have media studies been used to facilitate this putatively defiant stance? (See e.g. Sinha, 2000.)
- What are the consequences of seeing Asian media varieties in the mode of representation only as "case studies," to which western media theories and methods are applied? What is the difference between seeing them as "case studies" as opposed to a more historically informed notion of "contexts"? (See e.g. Curran & Park, 2000.)

It would be misleading to say that only poststructuralist-minded media scholars of recent times were capable of asking these critical questions about our media and media studies practices. In fact, earlier media studies work in the post-Second World War era in Asia, especially in India and China, was implicitly challenging unquestioned adoption of western models of inquiry, despite its need to deploy "accurate methods" steeped in western social sciences in order to gain scholarly legitimacy. Nonetheless, the questions above were asked with a renewed sense of urgency and political acuteness throughout the late 1980s and 1990s by Asian researchers, since they could rely on sufficient legitimate ground in the international media research community, especially through the establishment of such professional institutions and bodies as the Asian Media Information and Communication Center based in Singapore, the Bangalore-based Center for the Study of Society and Culture, the Chinese Communication Association, the Korean Society for Journalism and Communication Studies, and so on. The deeply political project to "decolonize" Asian media and cultural studies was launched through the establishment of the journal *Inter-Asia Cultural Studies*, which saw the most explicit triangulation of Marxist media and cultural critique, the historical critique of "Asia" as a problematic nodal point for various intellectual disciplines, and local decolonization social movements across subnational Asia. In sum, the field of Asian media studies, if we can claim any sense of totality about it, has been constituted by three important (overlapping) moments of development, namely the politics of appropriation for legitimacy (1960s to 1970s), the politics of self-legitimacy through rejecting western cultural imperialism (late 1970s to early 1990s), and the politics of critical legitimacy through deconstructive postcolonial tactics (early 1990s to the present). Moving through this roughly mapped out trajectory, Asia-born media scholars have traveled, shuttled, moved back and forth, and returned across geographical points between Asia and the US, Europe, and Australia. Our own travel and educational histories thus press on our theorization of "Asian media" and of the relevant analytical practices; a not insignificant part of Asian media studies must have to do with the creation and negotiation of *subject positions* as media consumers, producers, and researchers living in, and moving across, the region.

Politics of Subjectivities

In view of the specific essays collected in this volume, we see ourselves as positioned to make explicit the often implied question about subjectivity formations underlying the history of media studies in Asia. The various politics of legitimacy of our own critical sensibility toward our media point to the problematic of subject-positioning as one of important, and recurring, sites of research and cultural politics in the region. Is it any wonder that a visible majority of media research in Asia – as it is in other developing countries – has been audience research?

While audience research does not and cannot answer all questions about the realities and politics of subjectivity, its ethnographic epistemological impulse comes closest to the heart of the matter. In the nonwestern context, the ethnographic episteme indeed has arisen as a pointed opposition to a certain epistemological debate found in western media studies circles, who posited the so-called "impossibility of audience studies" in the face of the (ironically totalizing) postmodern condition. Fractured, fragmented, multiply implicated in a deeply entangled matrix of historical, textual, and sociopolitical factors, and finally unhinged from the rational self, the "audience" is hence positioned (overtheorized?) by western postmodernism. The very political project to dismantle the post-enlightenment legacy has, ironically, threatened to wipe out the non-metropolitan voices that postmodern politics has sought to support. Where media imperialism has long been a critique *shared* by both Third World scholars and progressive researchers in the west, the imperialism of Theory has not been so communal a critique. A reassertion of audience studies – in fact, of the centrality of "subjectivity studies" – in relation to the media thus underwrites many critical projects in Asia, including this present volume.

Two juxtaposing scenarios that conjoin "Asia" and "media" help to illustrate the dynamics of subjecthood that traverse the locus of Asian media studies signposted and examined in this volume.

Love

"For a time, we were on the map."

Karim Bangcola, senior Vice President of the AMA Computer College in urban Manila, uttered those words in reflection of what his infamous student has done on a fateful day. Being "on the map," he implies, puts his country's name in an ambiguous perspective, for the international internet-using community has not forgotten his student's deed so easily. This is a story about media use, more specifically about internet hacking. The fact that it is also about Asia is not incidental. Rather, "Asia" figures in this international incident as a player who loves to be noticed, if only through a cybercrime.

On May 4, 2000, millions of computers around the world were infected with a virus lodged in their email systems. When clicked on, the opened email destroyed files and spread itself to other email accounts. What prompted so many to commit this fatal tap of the finger on their keyboards was the subject heading of the email dreamed up by a soft-spoken young Filipino: "I Love You." Who would refuse this mail, especially when it came anonymously? Who could withstand these knowingly clichéd little words? And who'd think what became known as the Love Bug virus could cause an estimated US$10 billion in damage as it shut down computer systems throughout the world, from corporations to the Pentagon to the British Parliament?

Onel de Guzman's love message to the world could easily be rewritten as "Asia Loves You." "I'm not a hacker who destroys. I don't want to hurt computers. In fact, I want more people to use them," de Guzman said in an interview (Pimentel, 2001). Described as soft spoken and acne-faced, de Guzman is an ordinary Filipino youth hailing from one of the Philippines' poorest provinces on Samar Island. A certain dissatisfaction with using his computer only for playing video games or ICQ apparently led him to begin trying out programming commands, altering codes, and breaking through cybernetic firewalls. Like thousands of other Asian youth, de Guzman wished for a bigger and better life, and like so many in poor locales in the developing world, realized that honing his skills in the computer field was just about the only ticket to international success. Antivirus and computer security experts say that computer attacks such as the "I Love You" virus and its variants are part of the "growing pain" of the internet society found all over the developing world.

The thematic of "I Love You" functions as more than a benign joke; it can, on the one hand, be said to be a kind of subjectivity indicative of the geopsychological fate of "Asia" caught in the disjuncture between economic and political disfranchisement in the still-operative development model in global internet diffusion, and, on the other, the real experience of a tech-novernacular life eminently accessible by and affordable to the Asian multitude. Indeed, the narrative of "Asian rising" must be taken seriously as a locus for understanding the discursive positioning of a media-saturated "Asia" as a point of conflict between Asian (national) assertion, especially of technological prowess, and aspects of Asia-based transgressions, especially in media matters (e.g. media piracy being the most acute and well-publicized problem). The surprising element, however, is that this virus was associated with the Philippines, which has not been conventionally linked to the symbolic production of Asianism as a site of international political dialectic. At any rate, the sentimentalizing trope in the form of a traveling computer virus speaks to an important relationality between Asia and the world over the body of the media, namely that "love" is only a relational term *vis-à-vis* other sentimentalizing tropes, including that of resentment. "Love, The Costliest Bug" was the headline used by the *Seattle Post-Intelligencer* to make explicit the hidden message dreamed up and spread by a modest Asian man to the rest of the world. As a global symbolic production, the virus was inviting enough yet destructive enough to put Asia "on the map." Sporadic but sustained attention to computer viruses abound after this incident, which has only further ambiguated the position of Asia in the international media-use communities. In locales such as the Philippines, India, and Malaysia, the sentiment has been that Asian information technology know-how has become the region's point of pride (if not "revenge"). But as for the developed world, who habitually claim superiority in technologies, the incident has fueled the image of half-literate Third World criminal hackers "tucked away in small bedrooms across the globe" (Elks, 2002) as an addition to the repertoire of terroristic images of the criminal underworld associated with subaltern regions of the world.

If this story about the love bug shows the disjuncture in subjectivity that distinguishes "Asian media use" as a site of geopolitical and psychological violence in the global information society, then another story also about Asian sentimentality will illustrate a convergence of subjectivity hurling "Asian media use" onto a different plane of articulation, a different way of being "on the map." We are referring to the highly visible phenomenon of Asian television idol melodramas. Over the past few years, the flow of these dramas across the region has produced an institutional and broad cultural impetus for transnational media production, distribution, and consumption. The Japanese and more recently Korean TV idol dramas represent another type of love bug that has bitten many devoted fans across Taiwan, Hong Kong, the PRC, and Singapore. They are distinguished from earlier forms of transnational Asian pop such as Hong Kong action films and Cantopop music, and also from parallel contemporary productions such as J-pop and K-pop music videos and CDs. We are interested in the same trope of sentimental love that may be producing new kinds of desiring subjects capable of identifications across historical and cultural boundaries.

Japanese TV idol dramas run through the by-now predictable plot about young lovers in urban Tokyo engaging in complex and subtle romantic hopes and failures, while Korean TV idol dramas place the heart-wrenching, often tragic, stories of young lovers in the Confucian familial framework (see Iwabuchi, 2001; Lin, 2002). The former popular drama highlights the testiness of urban relationships, whereas the latter heightens the conflict arising from family (and familial) duties – but all the while both kinds of TV dramas have a great deal in common. Through interviewing fans of these Japanese idol dramas in other Asian locales, Koichi Iwabuchi (2001) has theorized the complex articulation of "cultural proximity" in terms of models of romantic pursuit among Asian heterosexual youth and young adults, and identification of social and familial forces impinging upon their love affairs. We would add that this cultural proximity has also been articulated through identification of racial proximity in the norms of beauty (male and female), mannerism, styles in clothing, a sense of Asianness in contrast to perceived western outlooks, and so on. The "structure of feeling" is that of a translocal reckoning of moral ideals and practical decision-making not only in terms of matters of youthful sentimentality and sexuality, but also of a syncretic "Asian modernity" capable of enlisting middle-class-based, cross-generational, and western-value sensitized, dialogue and sentiment as a part of the social imaginary for an increasingly regionalized cultural Asia. Here, the triangulation of cultural nationalism, postcolonial sentiments, and the globalist mood in Asian media has found its useful *affective* form for imagining alliances through the televisual field.

The immense popularity of these TV dramas within and across East Asia – interestingly, as carried by the same theme of love – serves as a useful contrast to the incident mentioned earlier about de Guzman and his global love virus. The divergence of "technological Asia" and "cultural Asia" aside, the two "love stories" mark the in-between space for Asian media today with respect to the global media world. The globalist tendency of the computer virus incident contrasts sharply to the more inward-circulating *regionalist imaginary* that underpins the flow of popular TV drama series. We may say that the *centrifugal* politics of self-insertion into the global map of media and information technology and the *centripetal* politics of mutual validation of cultural and emotional proximity through the televisual media, have produced a special environment for Asian media consumption, and more significantly, Asian subjectivity formation (cf. Chan, 2002).

"Context" is the Name of Something We Lack

Returning to the four major questions framed by the postcolonial consciousness in Asian media studies, we can begin to ascertain the complexity of reformation among Asian nation-states who control their media systems to effect new lines of convergence and divergence in order to satisfy both their regionalist and globalist desires as parallel imperatives, if only through discursive representations in the media broadcast near and far. We can also begin to appreciate the kinds of negotiation media producers make in creating programming for a slippery "domestic market" whose tastes and values are sometimes inward-looking and sometimes internationalist in nature (see Moeran, 2001). As for the whole problem of "cultural resistance," the dialectic noted above through the two "love stories" lays bare the complex ambiguities that can be found either at the level of media consumers/audiences or at the level of nation-states. For instance, the love of TV idol dramas in East Asia can be said to mediate against the popularity of American TV dramas of youthful romance and adventures also found in cable channels in Asia (e.g. *Beverly Hills 90210; Felicity*). If we interpret the fans' love of these dramas as cultural "resistance" against media imperialism, then we underestimate the deep influence of American production values and aesthetic packaging on these Asian productions that also form the basis for the Asian fans' enthusiastic reception. It is like ignoring how the Love virus calls attention to the deep-seated need for visibility of Asian information-technology know-how in the global high-tech world.

It is because of all these terms of negotiations that are pushing Asian media – and Asian media studies – to consistently be obsessed with the "nation question," the "political economy of media question," and the "resistance question," that we suggest that "Asia" can no longer be taken as a site for mere "case studies," to which western media theories and methods are applied. Rather, we must see it via the more historically informed notion of "contexts." By showcasing some of the ways in which media studies is conducted by our contributors in this volume, we hope to fill in the details of the context of "Asias." We hope that these fresh works show how the scholars – many of them young scholars, and most Asian by ethnicity – practice their own rigorous cultural analyses and critiques, and in turn, how their politically minded use of western media theories and methods performs its transnational translations. At what we have earlier called the moment of "critical legitimacy" currently confronting Asian media studies, this translation is not only necessary; it is urgent. Given the complex dialectical curves of "centrifugalism" and "centripetalism" criss-crossing the discursive field of Asian media, a longing for context need not be nationalist in impulse or citizenly in force. In fact it is more likely that this desire for context is organized by transnational constituents of subjectivity and experience, and by mobile figures of strategic resistance or excess. Hence, we have organized the essays in this volume by using the trope of movements: "moving in/out" to refer to transnational flow as a dynamic feature of the Asian media world today; "moving backward/forward" to refer to the histories and politics of media, and of media and cultural studies in the region; and "moving between" to refer to varieties of formations of subjectivities (whether they are pressed into formations of audiences is also a point of investigation and theorization by some of the contributors).

Synchronic Mapping of Audiences

The first section of the book articulates the transnational cultural flows in and out of the Asian region. In chapter 2, Iwabuchi explores the intraregional flows of media products and consumption among Japan, Taiwan, and Hong Kong. He notes that the Japanese consumption of Hong Kong popular culture is a "nostalgia for a 'lost' Asian vigor" or a sense of "longing for vanished popular cultural styles and social vigor." At the same time, Taiwanese youths read Japanese drama series to locate "our Asian reality." Iwabuchi sees an ever-increasing volume of regional cultural flows, which are, however, "uneven transnational connections." He sees popular culture connecting audiences within East Asia as a newly articulated form of power relations in the region.

On the other hand, Chua and Junaid (chapter 3) remark on the transnational flow of cultural consumption which moves from the "West" to Asia, specifically to Singapore. This chapter reflects upon a study of very young children's (4- to 6-year-olds') consumption of advertising and fast food. The article shows that media hegemony reflects the wider political economy, which, in the case of very small kids, may not be easy to resist or oppose. The authors note the gap in cultural studies focusing on children's culture and point to the need for this to be addressed in the future.

In yet another turn in transnational cultural flows, Hu (chapter 4) opposes "Asia" to Japan and the west. In her chapter on video compact disk (VCD) technology use and its market, she notes that "VCD signifies Asian technology in a global context." For her, VCD technology use "signifies resistance to Japanese and western technocolonization" and marks "Asia" as different from Japan or the west, or at least a "different type of techno-capitalism." Thus, the Asian VCD phenomenon is seen as "a good example to mobilize the popular idea that the origin of globalization is either located in the west or entirely manipulated by transnational corporations."

The first section, then, generally critiques the uneven transnational cultural flows of media technologies, products, and processes in and out of the region and among locales within the region. The second section of the book lays out, as it were, the historical and political trajectories of media texts and institutions in relation to the constraints on their democratic potential. In chapter 5, Kang sets out the history of the struggle for freedom of the press and its later attainment of hegemonic power. He shows how the "conservative alliance consisting of political power, the bureaucracy, and the conservative press, has played a crucial role in suppressing democratization in civil society in the 1990s." Instead of being a political watchdog, the press "has itself become an organ of power." He examines the relationships between the state, civil society, and the press of South Korea and traces the rise of journalistic power in collusion with a corrupt and conservative political leadership.

In a different example of journalistic collusion with the governing regime, Abel (chapter 6) looks at news presentation to uncover the use of "the discourse of nationalism and looking to the future" to support the political and economic status quo in Singapore. She notes that statist discursive power underlies news presentation strategies to maintain an ideology of control, and constructs the audience as citizens of the nation in "a climate of domestic uncertainty about the fragility of the state and the economy." Abel constructs herself as both an "insider" and "outsider" in Singapore to claim an edge in critical perspective while doing a deconstruction of television news.

In chapter 7, Lee points to the methodological and theoretical crisis in communicational cultural studies in Korea. He looks at a specific community of media analysts, Munhwa Yonku Bunkwa (MYB), and critiques the lack of "empirically rigorous and historicized studies of dominant social discourses and the historically specific forms of domination and opposition." He notes the strong influence of the Birmingham School of cultural studies but laments that this has prevented the MYB scholars from "rigorously engaging with vexed social and political questions in contemporary Korea." For him, communicational cultural studies needs to go "beyond the narrow confines of mass media and cultural texts."

On the other hand, Ma (chapter 8) attempts to map "the nostalgic practices in Hong Kong at a key moment of political transition," through the production and consumption practices relating to a 60-second TV commercial of a major bank in the Special Administrative Region. He refutes the claims that media consumers can find their way out of the hegemonic control "from above." This chapter investigates how "self-claimed 'authentic' coding and encoding of popular meanings can be, in Anthony Giddens's term, structurated within the ideological formation of the political economy at large."

Thus the second section of the book critiques the populist notion that audiences could determine their own subjectivities to a large extent and that the hegemonic power of the media could be challenged from below. If this section delineates a more negative politics of the realities of subject formations in Asian countries, the third section lets in a ray of hope. Each of the following four chapters presents a more upbeat picture of audience formations. In chapter 9, Juluri sees the growing importance of audience studies and asks, "What would make for an 'Indian' media audience studies?" He locates MTV as a pervasive TV genre in India which necessitates "new questions for national/global connection." He envisages a new kind of audience research that is able to deconstruct media power while enabling the "epistemic authority in speaking as viewing subjects – of being an Indian." Juluri's new contemporary cosmopolitans lay claim to a "relational sensibility" which is "the bedrock of global condition" while also being capable of creating "a possibility for an alternative globality."

In the next chapter, Yang comments on the dearth of cultural studies work in communication and media studies in Asian countries. She reiterates the significance of feminist media studies and their interventionist analyses and epistemological styles. At the same time, she sees a possible collision between cultural studies and feminist studies and points to the necessity of inflecting cultural studies with a political-economy approach. Such an approach would locate audience studies within both institutional and production contexts while acknowledging the emergence of audience power. She delineates a changing audience landscape in tandem with the changing nature of media genres. Thus her account of the moral panic accompanying shows featuring female teenage bodies seeks to draw attention to the urgency of change within the Asian media landscape and a rereading of variety shows. At the same time, Yang underscores the epistemic power of feminist analyses in both interventionist and analytical practices.

Moving to Malaysia, we see Khoo's (chapter 11) feminist-inflected cultural studies work on the recuperation of *adat* (custom/performativity) in the the portrayal of female sexuality embedded in the image of the Malay woman (*perempuan*) in films of male Malay directors. For Khoo, this representation of native, female sexuality recuperates an essential "Malayness" or an essentialized ethnicity that is cathected onto the body of the gendered Other. Muslim women cover themselves by wearing headscarves (*tudung*) and the *baju kurung*, a long sleeved, loose-fitting blouse over a long skirt. Khoo critiques this process of reclaiming ethnic roots while resisting a homogeneous global modernity and fundamentalist Islam. For her, privileging ethnicity in this case may mean sacrificing gender politics. Like Yang, Khoo sees feminist analyses as enabling cultural critiques of the media and the positioning of audience subjectivities.

Finally, Erni and Spires, in their chapter on another marginalized group, gays and lesbians in Taiwan in the 1990s, look at "broader questions about what has been called 'weak group' [*roushi tuanti*] identity politics, family life and modernity in Taiwan." They examine the formation of gay and lesbian identities in Taiwan as expressed in their cultural consumption of the popular *G&L Magazine*. Through a deconstruction of "filial piety central to the Taiwanese sociocultural formation and individual subjectivity," they point to the contradictory dynamics of new liberal ideologies and family politics in Taiwan's queer popular culture. In this chapter the authors show the enabling power of marginalized groups to inform their own subjectivities in negotiating between hegemonic societal constructs and the use of the media.

What these analyses show, then, is that there are many Asias not just in terms of geopolitical spaces but also in relation to gender and other cultural spaces. This volume could have been titled "Media in Asia" in many ways, and yet we wish to call into focus what binds Asia as a region in relation to its media while also acknowledging the diversity of the region within each different geopolitical, nationally bounded space.

Postmodernism has valorized polyvocality and diversity in subject positions; however, as our authors show, we still need to enunciate political and critical issues while acknowledging that we can't return to the old metanarratives. Gender, class, ethnicity, age, and national politics are still important concerns. Who enunciates what is as important as how some issues are enunciated. In a region where media control remains largely in the hands of government regimes, many of which are authoritarian in practice, it is important to acknowledge the contestation of meanings in media spaces. Nevertheless, it is still important to critique such contestation and the claim that media audiences can negotiate their own meanings. We wish to ask, to what ends? Can cultural readings as strategies for negotiation activate any form of alternative media and public spaces? How can the valorization of audiences carve out a space from authoritarian control? Does the internet actually free up spaces for activism towards social transformation? When most of Asia's media are under the control of government regimes in conjunction with multinational companies in search of the last big deal, what power do audiences have in getting what they want? Do they know what they want? Is it to be entertained to death?

Synchronic mapping of audiences as a way into understanding how the media works in the Asian region can be salutary. In the past, media scholarship in Asia has tended to look at production and institutional practices. How do we genuinely do media studies from the bottom up? How do audiences – critics, scholars, and lay people – make political meanings out of their textual readings? As Souchou Yao says, "cultural politics in Southeast Asia and elsewhere is about the all-important prerogative to imagine differently, and to 'envision' an alternative political future, a perogative for which lives and limbs have been lost, and personal and civil liberties curtailed" (Yao, 2001: 9).

Shaping Strategies of Scholarship

What sort of political meanings apply across the region? How do we as scholars make sense of what is happening on the ground in relation to media politics? Where are the scholars in this area? Who controls scholarship? Who controls the dissemination of scholarship? How relevant are these "western" strategies such as those that call for resisting the hegemony of "official discourses" (Lyotard, 1984: 140–7), or "unmasking of cultural artifacts as socially symbolic acts" (Jameson, 1981: 20–1), or "reading within the interstices of the discursive regimes" (Foucault, 1980)? These have been influential in shaping strategies for scholars within the region.

Old Marxist metanarratives may no longer be enabling but how enabling are the new poststructuralist tactics? Can we only speak of alignments and tactical approaches or can we carve out space(s) for the articulation of new ways of critiquing and reading the media? How do we translate discourse into action? Feminists of many different positions have always acknowledged the importance of the link between discourse and practice. We wish to re-inflect cultural theory or cultural studies with this perspective and to enunciate the importance of this in the study of "Asian" media. At the same time the politics of place must always be borne in mind. September 11, 2001, played on the global screen but brought home sharply the politics of place, the space of the media for the staging of an ethnic and religious "first-strike" by a group of extremely media-savvy terrorists. And, of course, the Bush administration responded with an equally spectacular media display of beating up the "enemy" by pounding on the Afghan national space and in the process wiping out innumerable innocent, ordinary Afghans while ostensibly at war with terrorism. If this creates a feeling of déjà-vu for those of us in Asia who have lived through the era of the Vietnam wars, it also reaffirms the media as the twenty-first-century gladiatorial arena. The trauma is not just globalized, horrendous as it is, it also specifically displaces the media from its cozy cocoon of "entertainment as news" couch position. Suddenly what is brought home is how relevant "politics" as news is again, at least in the US and Europe. In Asia, ethnic and religious politics have always been part of everyday life. Contestation of meaning has always been played out between authoritarian regimes and fundamentalist ethnic/cultural warriors. The former has more and more displaced the hatred of the colonial, or the ex-colonial, while constructing a culture of fear via the latter to keep the citizens under control. Cultural spaces, in particular, broadcast media spaces, always have this edge of lived politics being strongly in place.

References

Chan, Ching-kiu Stephen (2002). "Mapping the Global Popular: An Analytical Framework for Hong Kong Culture." Paper presented at Lingnan University, Dec. 12.

Curran, James and Park, Myung-Jin, eds. (2000). *De-westernizing Media Studies.* New York: Routledge.

Elks, David (2002). "Think Ahead to Beat the Hackers Who'd Just Love You to Get a Virus." *The Sentinel* 26, May 12.

Foucault, Michel (1980). "Space, Knowledge and Power." In P. Rabinow, ed., *The Foucault Reader.* New York: Pantheon Books, pp. 239–56.

Gunaratne, Shelton A., ed. (2000). *Handbook of the Media in Asia.* New Delhi: Sage.

Heng, Geraldine and Devan, Janadas (1992). "State Fatherhood: The Politics of Nationalism, Sexuality, and Race in Singapore." In A. Parker, ed., *Nationalisms and Sexualities.* New York: Routledge.

Hutcheon, Linda (1988). *A Poetics of Postmodernism: History, Theory, Fiction.* New York: Routledge.

Iwabuchi, Koichi (2001). "Becoming 'Culturally Proximate': The A/scent of Japanese Idol Dramas in Taiwan." In Brian Moeran, ed., *Asian Media Productions.* Surrey: Curzon Press, 54–74.

Kang, Myung-koo (2003). "East Asian Modernities and the Formation of Media and Cultural Studies." Paper presented at the Annual International Communication Conference, San Diego.

Lin, Angel M. Y. (2002). "Modernity and the Self: Explorations of the (Non-)Self-Determining Subject in South Korean TV Dramas." *M/C Journal* 5(5) (Oct.), published on the web: http://www.media-culture.org.au/mc/0210lin.html.

Lyotard, Jean-François (1984). *The Postmodern Condition: A Report on Knowledge,* tr. Geoffrey Bennington and Brian Massumi. Minneapolis: University of Minnesota Press.

Jameson, Fredric (1981). *The Political Unconscious: Narrative as a Socially Symbolic Act.* Ithaca: Cornell University Press.

Jameson, Fredric (1991). *Postmodernism: Or, the Cultural Logic of Late Capitalism.* Durham, NC: Duke University Press.

Moeran, Brian, ed. (2001). *Asian Media Productions.* Surrey: Curzon Press.

Pimentel, Benjamin (2001). Hacker tries to help others, not hurt. *The San Francisco Chronicle,* Feb. 11, p. B1.

Sinha, D. (2000). "Info-age and Indian Intellectuals: An Unfashionable Poser." *Economic and Political Weekly,* 4188–94.

Yao, SouChou (2001). *House of Glass: Culture, Modernity, and the State in Southeast Asia.* Singapore: Institute of Southeast Asian Studies.

Part I

Moving In, Moving Out: Transnational Flows

2

Discrepant Intimacy: Popular Culture Flows in East Asia

Koichi Iwabuchi

The development of communications technologies has facilitated the simultaneous circulation of media information, images, and texts on a global level. In this process, various (national) markets are being penetrated and integrated by powerful global media giants such as News Corp and Disney. However, media globalization does not just mean the spread of the same products of Western (mostly American) origin all over the world through these media conglomerates. Non-Western players also actively collaborate in the production and circulation of global media products. For transnational corporations to maximize the profit, the imperatives are the global selection of new cultural products with an international appeal as well as the establishment of a business tie-up with partners at each level – whether in the form of buy-out or tie-up – to enter simultaneously such various market domains as global, supranational regional, national, and local. In this context of increasing integration, networking, and cooperation among transnational cultural industries, we are witnessing the global circulation of Japanese animation and video games, Hong Kong stars and directors' inroads into Hollywood, and the involvement of Japanese corporations such as Sony in global media conglomeration.

These developments testify to a decentering of capitalist modernity from the West and of the global cultural power structure from the US (Tomlinson, 1997). The unambiguous dominance of Western cultural, political, economic, and military power has constructed a modern world-system covering the whole globe. However, the historical process of globalization has not simply produced a Westernization of the world. Its impact on the constitution of the world is much more heterogeneous and contradictory. The experience of "the forced appropriation of modernity" in the non-West has also produced polymorphic vernacular modernities (Ang & Stratton, 1996). This testifies to the ample incorporation of the Western mode of capitalist modernity into non-Western contexts (Dirlik, 1994). Yet, this ongoing asymmetrical cultural encounter in the course of the spread of Western modernity sheds light on various kinds of similar *and* different experiences of urbanization and modernization in many parts of the world. As Ang and Stratton (1996: 22–4) argue, we have come to live in "a world where all cultures are both (like) 'us' and (not like) 'us'," one where familiar difference and bizarre sameness are simultaneously articulated in multiple ways through the unpredictable dynamic of uneven global cultural encounters.

The proliferation of modernities in the world does not just construct a milieu in which "the Rest" plays a significant role in media globalization. It has also facilitated the capitalization on intraregional cultural resonances with the emergence of regional media and cultural centers such as Brazil, Egypt, Hong Kong, and Japan (e.g., Straubhaar, 1991; Sinclair et al., 1996). In east Asia, intraregional media flows particularly among Japan, Taiwan, Hong Kong, and South Korea are gradually becoming active and constant more than ever. Popular culture circulating in east Asia in most cases unavoidably embodies American origin. Nevertheless, preferred cultural products in the region are not without east Asian flavor, as those are reworked in Asian context by hybridizing various latest fads all over the world; they are inescapably global and (East) Asian at the same time, lucidly representing intertwined composition of global homogenization and heterogenization in east Asian context.

Popular culture flows might promote dialogue as well as asymmetry in Asian regions. This chapter explores how the unevenness of transnational media flows is embedded in the perception of cultural distance, which is in a state of flux under globalization processes. Non-Western countries have tended to face the West to interpret their position and understand the distance from Modernity. The encounter has always been based upon the expectation of difference and time lag. The perception of cultural distance among non-Western nations has tended to be swayed by their relative temporal proximity to Western modernity, the standard by which the developmental ranking of the non-West has been determined (cf. Fabian, 1983). As an apt illustration, such a developmental yardstick was earlier exploited by Japanese imperialist ideology to confirm Japan's superiority to other racially and culturally similar Asian nations and justify the Japanese mission to civilize Asia.

The intensification of media and popular culture flows in east Asia suggests a possibility that the diminishing temporal lag, thanks to shared experience of industrialization, global spread of consumerist lifestyles, and the (simultaneous) transnational circulation of media images and information, (re)activates the sense of spatial affiliation and resonance in the region. While in this context some non-Western modern nations are now facing each other to find their neighbors experiencing and feeling similar things, such as the temporality of east Asian vernacular modernities through media and popular culture flows, the careful analysis of intraregional cultural flows will also underline the newly articulated time–space configurations and asymmetrical cultural power relations. In the following, I will examine how the perception of cultural intimacy and "familiar difference" of cultural neighbors is experienced differently and unevenly as media industries increasingly capitalize on the regional cultural resonance in east Asia through the promotion and consumption of Japanese TV dramas in Taiwan and of Hong Kong stars in Japan.[1]

Japanese TV Dramas in Taiwan

Animation, comics, characters, computer games, fashion, pop music, and TV dramas – a variety of Japanese popular culture has been so well received in east and southeast Asia. Particularly noticeable are Japanese TV dramas attracting young audiences in the regions. According to a 1997 Communication White Paper published by the Japanese Ministry of Posts and Telecommunication, the number of TV programs exported to Asian markets in 1995 amounted to 47 percent of the total export and TV dramas occupied 53 percent of the export to Asia.

The most receptive market to Japanese TV drama is Taiwan, in which there are four cable TV channels solely broadcasting Japanese programs. The Taiwanese government banned the broadcasting of Japanese-language programs when the Japanese government officially reestablished diplomatic relations with China in 1972, but Japanese TV programs have been widely watched through pirated videos/VCDs (video compact disks) and illegal cable channels in Taiwan. After the government removed its ban on broadcasting Japanese-language TV programs and songs around the end of 1993, the spread of Japanese TV dramas in east Asia has come to rest on a far broader consumer base. The increasing presence of Japanese popular culture in Taiwan is not mostly initiated by Japanese cultural industries. Rather, there has been a strong local initiative as local companies have grabbed business opportunities to sell Japanese TV programs during the process of media globalization in Taiwan (see Iwabuchi, 1998). Along with political and economic liberalization, the expansion of the entertainment industry and market in Taiwan has facilitated the influx of Japanese popular culture in Taiwan. This development has exposed the audience in Taiwan to more information about Japanese pop icons, through newspapers, magazines, and television, and given the local industries an incentive to exploit the commercial value of Japanese popular music, encouraging them to invest a large amount of money in promoting it in Taiwan.

In Taiwan, the recent surge of Japanese cultural influence is inevitably discussed in relation to the history of colonial rule. In 1997, a leading weekly newsmagazine in Taiwan had feature articles on Japanese popular culture in Taiwan titled "Watch Out! Your Kids are Becoming Japanese." The journal coined a new Taiwanese phrase, 哈日族 [*harizhu*], to describe young people who adore things Japanese (*The Journalist*, April 13–19, 1997). While Japan was not strongly condemned for "cultural invasion," the spread of Japanese popular culture was associated with the colonial habit of mimicking, which is thought to be sedimented deeply in Taiwanese society (see also *China Times*, March 17, 1997).[2] Undeniably, the historical legacy of Japanese colonization has overdetermined the recent influx of Japanese popular culture. From food and housing to language, examples can easily be found of a lingering Japanese cultural influence in Taiwan. Besides Korea, the number of people speaking Japanese that can be found in Taiwan is by far the largest in the world and many Japanese words and cultural meanings have become indigenized. Older people who were educated during the Japanese occupation still speak fluent Japanese and enjoy Japanese-language books, songs, and TV programs. Many also regard their former colonizers in a relatively positive light, the bitter memories of their rule having diminished by contrast with the repressive and authoritarian rule of the KMT government which moved from mainland China to the island after the Second World War (see Liao, 1997). These conditions surely make Japanese TV programs much more accessible than in other parts of Asia, particularly in stark contrast to South Korea.

Yet avid young consumers of Japanese popular culture hold quite different views of and affinity with Japan. The meaning "Japan" possesses for young Taiwanese, most of whom do not understand Japanese language, is undoubtedly different from that which it holds for their forebears. It is often argued that the younger generations have no special affection for Japanese culture, and the symbolic meaning of "Japan" articulated through Japanese popular culture in Taiwan is marked by superficiality.[3] There is some truth in this postmodernist claim of image consumption in the age of global mass culture (Hall, 1991). Nevertheless this does not sufficiently address the issue of why Japanese popular culture is preferred to those from other parts of the world and what cultural resonances are evoked for east Asians by it. In the next section, focusing on the reception of TV dramas, I will consider if and how the ascent of Japanese popular culture is associated with the ascent of transnational regional modernity in Taiwan.

East Asian Modernities and Japanese TV Dramas

One of the most popular daily newspapers, *The China Times*, started an interactive column on Japanese dramas in February 1996. A reporter writing on Japanese dramas for a newspaper informed me that: "Most high school and university students who watch Japanese dramas discuss the storyline with their friends. It is the most common topic for them just as Taiwan prime-time dramas [8 p.m. in the evening] used to be." Japanese dramas have become indispensable for everyday gossip in the younger generation.

There are many things that the audience wants to talk about in watching Japanese dramas. One of the main reasons why people watch Japanese drama in Taiwan is that they feature good-looking Japanese idols. Food, fashion, consumer goods, and music are also popular topics. However, Taiwanese audiences talk most eagerly about the story and the characters in the drama. Japanese dramas are diverse in terms of storylines, setting, and topics, but the dramas that become popular in Taiwan are stories featuring younger people's love affairs and lives in an urban setting. According to my interview with undergraduate students in Taiwan, one of the attractions of Japanese TV drama is its new style of portraying love, work, and women's position in society. These are all issues which young people are facing in urban areas in Taiwan, but which Taiwan TV dramas until recently did not offer to audiences. It seems to be this void that makes Japanese dramas popular texts to be talked about in everyday life.

For example, the popularity of *Tokyo Love Story*, the story of a couple in their early twenties, which sparked off the popularity and recognition of the quality of Japanese dramas in Taiwan and Hong Kong in the early 1990s, has much to do with (female) audiences' identification with the story and the heroine, Akana Rika. Rika is an unusually expressive and positive Japanese woman. A famous phrase uttered to her boyfriend which characterizes Rika symbolically is "Kanchi, let's have a sex!" Rika's single-minded pursuit of love and her frank expression of feelings is the object of admiration and emulation. My interviewees often expressed two seemingly contradictory statements about her. While on the one hand they would observe that "I have a strong feeling that she is exactly what I want to be," they would also remark that "I would not be able to become as brave and open as Rika." It was thus Rika's role as an ideal model that many women considered particularly appealing: she is what one could never quite become but someone one wants to be. Satomi, in contrast, served as Rika's foil. She was the embodiment of the traditional woman – dependent, submissive, domestic, and passive. It may be the case that audiences find Satomi more empirically realistic in the Taiwanese context. As such she was an object of aversion for all of my interviewees. The juxtaposition of Rika and Satomi brings Rika's attractiveness into sharp relief.

The attractiveness of *Tokyo Love Story* does not reside simply in making audiences feel that something different from the present can be imagined and dreamed of. Emotional involvement in the drama is facilitated by its depiction of a sentiment that the audience thinks and feels desirable but not unrealistic. It is not just a dream of tomorrow but a (possible) picture of today. Things happening in *Tokyo Love Story* also seem to be realistic or at least accessible to most of its young audiences. The same things could happen in their own everyday lives. On his home page, a young Hong Kong man explained why he liked the drama in these terms: "The twenty-something urban professionals of the series face a tightrope of coping that young people in many Asian cities have faced, but rarely more sympathetically. The major attraction of *Tokyo Love Story* to me is that it is not a story about somebody else. It is a story about our generation, about us, about myself. I can easily identify shadows of Rika or Kanchi among my peer group, even in myself" ("Kevin's Home," http://home.ust.hk/~kwtse).

This sense of the series being a "story about us" was strongly shared by the Taiwanese fans. More than 60 percent of 61 university students surveyed by Li et al. (1995) – and 75 percent of the female subjects – replied that love affairs such as those portrayed in *Tokyo Love Story* could happen around them. However, like the realism of Rika's character discussed before, this should not be straightforwardly read as evidence of the objective, empirical realism of *Tokyo Love Story*, with which audiences identify. As Ang (1985: 44–5) argues concerning audiences' identification with *Dallas*, "the concrete situations and complications are rather regarded as symbolic representations of more general experiences: rows, intrigues, problems, happiness and misery. And it is precisely in this sense that these letter-writers find *Dallas* realistic. In other words, at a connotative level they ascribe mainly emotional meanings to Dallas." What audiences find "realistic" in viewing *Tokyo Love Story* is thus not that an identical love affair would actually happen or that anyone can become like Rika. Li et al. (1995) suggest that one of the attractions of *Tokyo Love Story* for university students in Taiwan is its new style of portraying love, work, and women's position in society. These are all issues which young people are actually facing in urban areas in Taiwan, but which American or Taiwanese TV dramas have never sympathetically dealt with. It is at this more generalized level of meaning concerning love affairs and human relations represented in *Tokyo Love Story* that audiences in Taiwan perceive it as "our" story.

In my research in Taiwan, I often heard Taiwanese young viewers say that Japanese dramas represent favorable realism that cannot be gained from Western/American dramas or from Taiwan dramas. An early twenties informant told me that the lifestyle and love affairs in an American drama such as *Beverley Hills 90210* are something she enjoys watching, but she found Japanese love stories more realistic and easier to relate to. A 17-year-old high school student also told me that "Japanese dramas better reflect our reality. Yeah, *Beverley Hills 90210* is too exciting [to be realistic]. Boy always meets girl. But it is neither our reality nor dream."

Many people tended to associate Japanese drama's "realism" with cultural similarities between Taiwan and Japan. Japanese dramas are consciously watched as foreign, but Japanese culture is perceived as closer to Taiwan while physical appearance and skin color are quite similar to the American counterpart. "Japan is not quite but much like us," as two early twenties females said, "the distance we feel to Japan is comfortable, while Americans are complete strangers"; "I've never seen such dramas which perfectly express my feeling . . . the West is so far away from us, so I cannot relate to American dramas." They said that the ways of expressing love in Japanese dramas which were delicate and elegant were much more culturally acceptable than those of American dramas, and human relations between family and lovers also looked culturally closer to Taiwan, so much so that Taiwanese audiences could relate to Japanese dramas more easily.

This seems to correspond with a finding that audiences tend to prefer watching TV programs from countries which are supposed to be culturally proximate to their own (cf. Straubhaar, 1991; Sinclair et al., 1996). Yet the perception of "cultural proximity" here should not be conceived in an essentialist manner. There might be some similar cultural values concerning family and individualism between Taiwan and Japan, but the attractiveness of such values is newly articulated by particular programs under a specific historical context. Rika's forward-looking and independent attitude depicted in *Tokyo Love Story*, for example, was perceived as a desirable image of "modern" or "new age" woman in Taiwan. Taiwanese viewers told me that Rika's attitude to love in *Tokyo Love Story* is different both from that of the characters of American dramas like *Beverley Hills 90210* which is too open and not single-minded, and from that of Taiwan dramas which are very passive and submissive. Taiwanese dramas often emphasize a traditional value: "fidelity" of women (Chan, 1996). Young audiences do not relate to it, but they favorably identify Rika's active and "modern" single-mindedness. Conversely, Rika may be too open to emulate, but her single-mindedness is different from American openness. It still represents "our" (Asian) reality and is therefore something to which the audience in Taiwan can emotionally relate. However, what is at stake here is not fidelity or single-mindedness in general or essentialized terms but a specific kind of single-mindedness as it is represented in *Tokyo Love Story*. In other words, this single-mindedness has been articulated through a Japanese (at the site of production) and Taiwanese (at the site of consumption) reworking of cultural modernity in the particular media text. Only through these dynamic processes has it come to embody an attractive single-mindedness, which is perceived to illustrate "New Age woman" in that it is at once implicated in the global (in the sense of "American" in this instance) and situated in east Asian contexts. To engage with the complexity of audience identification with Rika's attractive character in Taiwan, we thus need to consider it in a wider sociocultural context of the 1990s in which cultural modernity is reworked in east Asia.

Becoming Culturally Proximate

In non-Western countries, America has long been closely associated with images of being modern. Whenever American popular culture is consumed, people also enjoy a yearning for the American way of life. As Mike Featherstone (1996: 8) argues regarding the symbolic power of McDonald's, "It is a product from a superior global center, which has long represented itself as the center. For those on the periphery it offers the possibility of the psychological benefits of identifying with the powerful." Indeed, I clearly remember that I ate Kentucky Fried Chicken in the late 1970s in Tokyo, feeling that I was becoming an American. But such a stage is over. In Japan in 1995 I saw a 7-year-old boy express his amazement at seeing a Kentucky Fried Chicken shop in the United States on TV: "Wow there is a Kentucky in America as well." "American dreams" have been indigenized in some modernized non-Western countries (cf. Watson, 1997).

To some Taiwanese audiences for whom modernity is no longer just dreams, images, and yearnings of affluence, but reality, that is, the material conditions in which people live, Japanese popular culture offers what can be called an "operational realism"; American dreams are concretized into something ready for use. A manager of a Japanese cable channel explains this astutely.

> When Taiwan was still a poor country, we had just a dream of a modern lifestyle. It was an American dream. But now that we have become rich, we no longer have a dream but it is time to put the dream into practice. Not American dream but Japanese reality is a good object to emulate for this practical purpose.

It should be noted here that even for those who delight in watching Japanese TV dramas, "Japan" does not attain the status as an object of yearning that "America" once did. Although the recent influx of Japanese popular culture in Taiwan is undoubtedly overdetermined by the legacy of Japanese colonial rule, and the cultural flows between Japan and Taiwan are unambiguously uneven, the popularity of Japanese television dramas in Taiwan does not suggest that the relationship between Japan and Taiwan is straightforwardly conceived to be one of center–periphery. It is not the pleasure of "identifying with the powerful" but rather a sense of living in the same temporality, a sense of being equal, that sustains Japanese cultural presence in Taiwan. As Fabian (1983: 23) argues in his discussion of how the Western denial of recognizing the sharing of the same temporality with non-Western cultural others has been institutionalized in anthropological research, the term "coevalness" connotes two interrelated meanings: synchronicity and contemporaneity. The development of global communication technologies and networks may further the denial of "contemporaneity" of the periphery through the facilitation of "synchronicity." To illustrate, Mark Liechty (1995: 194) elucidated the Nepalese experience of modernity as "the ever growing gap between imagination and reality, becoming and being." The disappearance of a time lag in the distribution of cultural products in many parts of the world has left wide political, economic, and cultural gaps intact, so much so that they facilitate the feeling in non-Western countries that "'catching up' is never really possible" (Morley & Robins, 1995: 226–7).

In Taiwan, as the gap in terms of material conditions narrows or even is disappearing, the meaning of "becoming" also changes from abstract to practical. An early twenties female who has long been a fan of Japanese popular culture said that:

Taiwan used to follow Japan, always be a "Japan" of ten years ago. But now we are living in the same age. There is no time lag between Taiwan and Japan. I think since this sense of living in the same age emerged three or four years ago, more people have become interested in things in Japan.

Seen in this way, cultural proximity should not be conceived in terms of a static attribute of "being" but a dynamic process of "becoming." Cultural proximity in the consumption of media texts is thus being articulated and made conscious under homogenizing forces of "modernization" and "globalization." There is an ever-narrowing gap between Japan and Taiwan in terms of material conditions, the urban consumerism of an expanding middle class, the changing role of women in society, the development of communication technologies and media industries, the reworking of local cultural values, and the reterritorialization of images diffused by American popular culture. Historically overdetermined by Japanese colonization, under simultaneously homogenizing and heterogenizing forces of modernization, Americanization, and globalization, all elements complicatedly interact to articulate Japanese cultural power in the form of the cultural resonance of Japanese TV dramas for some Taiwanese viewers who synchronously and contemporaneously experience "Asian modernity" in mid-1990s east Asia, which American popular culture could never have presented.

Consuming Hong Kong Popular Culture in Japan

In Japan, however, popular culture from other Asian nations does not necessarily signify the same perception of cultural similarity and of living in the synchronous temporality as for Taiwanese viewers of Japanese TV dramas. Japanese consumption of Asian popular music and culture displays a rather different time–space configuration. The ever-increasing intraregional cultural flows within Asia and the narrowing economic gap between Japan and some Asian countries have activated a nostalgic longing for modernized/modernizing Asia, which strongly reflects Japan's colonial legacy in the region.

Since the early 1990s, as the Japanese media industry extended their activities to other (mainly east) Asian markets (Iwabuchi, 1998), the lively east Asian music scenes have captured wide media attention in Japanese male magazines. Particularly conspicuous in the mid-1990s was the heavy promotion of Hong Kong popular culture by the Japanese media industry (see *Nikkei Entertainment*, Dec. 1997: 50–7). On the one hand, the main strategy of Japanese media industries is to sell "modern" and "fashionable" images of Hong Kong to a public more used to viewing the city as backward and dowdy. An example of a firm that pursued this tactic was Purénon H, a small film-distribution company. To improve the image of Hong Kong films, Purénon H organized a Hong Kong film fan club, Honkon Yamucha Kurabu, and established a Hong Kong film shop, "Cine City Hong Kong," in a trendy spot in Tokyo, where many young people enjoy window-shopping in an elegantly decorated space. Purénon H distributed Wong Kar-wai's *Chungking Express* in Japan in 1995, which became a phenomenal hit. It was admired because it was the first Asian movie that refrained from playing upon Hong Kong's alleged exoticism and, instead, made it look like any other major European city (say, Paris) (Edagawa, 1997). Apart from this quality of the film, the director of Purénon H has striven to overcome Hong Kong film's dominant image of kung fu or (vulgar) slapstick comedy. The company chose the Japanese title *Koisuru Wakusei* ('A Loving Planet'), totally unrelated to the original title, *Chungking Express*, from more than 2,000 possibilities, so that the film could sound modern and accessible to wider audiences (*Nikkei Entertainment*, Dec. 1997: 53).

The success of Wong Kar-wai's stylish collage films, as well as the upsurge of Japanese media industries' promotion in the lead-up to the return of Hong Kong to China in July 1997, further fanned the flames of interest in "modern" Hong Kong popular culture in Japan. Especially keenly promoted by Japanese media industries are Hong Kong male stars such as Jacky Cheung, Andy Lau, Leslie Cheung, and Kaneshiro Takeshi,[4] all of whom have performed in Wong Kar-wai's films. Japanese production companies have contracted those stars for media appearances in Japan (*Nikkei Trendy*, June 1997: 97–104). Since December 1995, Hong Kong's "four heavenly kings" have held concerts in Japan and increased their appearances in the Japanese media.[5]

Nevertheless, the growing interest in Asia is never free from Japan's historically constituted haughty conception of "behind-the-times Asia." This is readily discerned in the representation of "Asia" in Japanese media texts in the 1990s, which were marked by nostalgia for Asia. Here, modernizing Asian nations are nostalgically seen to embody a social vigor and optimism for the future which Japan allegedly is losing or has lost. The appreciation of cultural modernity of other parts of Asia tends to be discussed and judged via economic developmental terms. This perception, revealing as it does Japan's disavowal of any possibility of it sharing the same temporality as other Asian nations, displays the asymmetrical flow of intraregional cultural consumption in east Asia.

Similarly, the consumption of Hong Kong popular culture also smacks of the nostalgic yearning for Asia's modern vigor, which is fueled by a deep sense of disillusionment and discontent with Japanese society. The attraction of the films and performers, again, tends to be linked to the loss of energy and power of Japanese society in general, as women in their late twenties and late thirties told me: "Japanese TV dramas do not have dreams or passions. I sometimes enjoy watching them, but still feel [compared with Hong Kong actors] Japanese young actors lack a basic power and hunger for life"; "Wong Kar-wai's films always tell me how human beings are wonderful creatures and how love and affection for others are important for us to live. All of those are, I think, what Japan has lost and forgotten." The consumption of Hong Kong popular culture in Japan has made Japanese fans feel like regaining the vigor and hope they have lost in their daily lives. As a woman in her mid-twenties remarked: "I think people in Hong Kong really have a positive attitude to life. My image is that even if they know they are dying soon, they would not be pessimistic. This is in sharp contrast to present-day Japan. I can become vigorous when watching Hong Kong films and pop stars on video. Hong Kong and its films are the source of my vitality."

Ambivalent Nostalgia for Asian Modernity

The associations of present-day Hong Kong with Japan's loss, it can be argued, testify to the effortless consumption of an idealized Asian other which smacks of refusal to consider it as dwelling in the same temporality. However, as I listened carefully to these fans, I came to think that the sense of longing for vanished popular-cultural styles and social vigor does not exclusively attest to the perception of a time lag. It also manifests the Japanese fans' appreciation for the difference between Japanese and Hong Kong cultural modernity. Here we can see an ambivalence in Japan's nostalgia for a different Asian modernity: the conflation of a nostalgic longing for "what Japan has lost" and a longing for "what Japanese modernity has never achieved." What matters is Japan's lack as well as Japan's loss.

Here, the ever-increasing intraregional cultural flows within east Asia and the narrowing economic gap between Japan and Hong Kong display a rather different time–space configuration in the consumption of Hong Kong popular culture in Japan. Almost all Japanese interviewees also told me that they, like Taiwanese audiences of Japanese TV dramas, can more easily relate to Hong Kong stars and films than to Western ones due to perceived cultural and physical similarities. Western popular culture looks too remote from their everyday lives. However, unlike Taiwanese audiences of Japanese TV dramas, the sense of cultural and bodily proximity tends to simultaneously strengthen the Japanese fans' perception of cultural difference between Japan and Hong Kong. What is crucial here is that such perception is facilitated by recognition of the disappearance of temporal distance between Japan and Hong Kong. As a female in her late twenties told me: "I think that Hong Kong films are powerful and energetic. Hong Kong is apparently similar to Japan in terms of physical appearances, but I realized that its culture is actually completely different from us. [This is clearly shown by the fact that] Hong Kong has also achieved a high economic development, but still retains the vitality that Japan has lost." Although acknowledging Japanese economic superiority to Hong Kong, this Japanese female fan does not assume that Hong Kong is also losing something important, becoming like "us," precisely because Hong Kong has already achieved the same degree of economic growth and modernization as "ours." What sets Hong Kong apart is neither solely attributed to some primordial cultural difference nor to some developmental difference. Rather, the difference between Hong Kong and Japan has become evident in the course of modernization, especially through the way in which Western cultural influence is negotiated.

The Japanese representation and consumption of Hong Kong in the 1990s shows that many Japanese are attempting to recuperate something they think their country allegedly either is losing or has lost. Whether Japan ever had the social vigor projected on Asian popular culture is highly debatable – and ultimately irrelevant. The object of nostalgia is not necessarily some "real" past – the things that used to be[6]; the important point is that nostalgia arises out of a sense of insecurity and anguish in the present and of the present.

In the face of rapid modernization and globalization, nostalgia has played a significant role in the imagining of Japan's cultural authenticity and identity. These processes have intensified the country's cultural encounters with the West, and these, in turn, have generated a nostalgic desire in Japan, "a longing for a pre-modernity, a time before the West, before the catastrophic imprint of westernization" (Ivy, 1995: 241). A similar longing for the purity and authenticity of primordial life underpins Japanese media representations of, and backpacking trips to, "premodern" Asia. However, in the Japanese reception of Hong Kong popular culture, nostalgia is projected onto a more recent past, not before but after the West, or, more precisely, one in conjunction with the West. This nostalgia for a modern Asia is not fed by a nationalistic impulse to get rid of Western influence or to recuperate an "authentic" Japan. Rather, the issue at stake is how to live with Western-induced capitalist modernity, how to make life in actual, modern Japan more promising and humane.

This sense of urgency explains, if partly, why the object of nostalgia is directed to Asia's present. Japan's newly imagined "Asia" serves as a contraposition to their own society – one which is commonly regarded as suffocating, closed, and rigidly structured as well as worn down by a pessimism about the future, instilled by a prolonged economic recession. Here, "Asia" is not simply idealized as the way things were in Japan. Some people in Japan also appreciate it, for the purpose of self-reformation, as representing an alternative, more uplifting cultural modernity.

While it shows the possibility of transcending Japan's denial of coevalness with Hong Kong, the Japanese appreciation of Hong Kong's cultural modernity at the same time reproduces a "backward" Asia. Being critical of the Japanese mode of negotiation with the West nonetheless affirms Western-dominated capitalist modernity. As Morris-Suzuki (1998: 20) argues, the new Asianism in Japan "no longer implies rejection of material wealth and economic success, but rather represents a yearning for a wealth and success which will be somehow *different*" (emphasis in original). The fans' armchair engagement with "Hong Kong" modernity depends crucially on its imagined capitalist sophistication as opposed to the lack thereof in "Asia."

Many Japanese fans of Hong Kong popular culture emphasize the difference between "Hong Kong" and "Asia." This, on the one hand, looks a promising corrective to the construction of an abstract, totalizing conception of "Asia." These Japanese fans reject the dominant media's tendency to use the term "Asia" to refer to Hong Kong male stars.[7] It is in their encounter with a concretized Asia (e.g., appreciating Wong Kar-wai or Leslie Cheung, not Asian film or music in general) that we can detect self-reflexive voices and the realization that Japanese must meet other Asians on equal terms. However, in such a conception, other Asian nations are still reduced to entities that are undifferentiatedly represented by urban middle-class strata, the main players of consumerism. Moreover, the demarcation between Hong Kong and Asia is imperative for many fans, as the latter is predominantly associated with the image of backwardness. I have often heard interviewees remark that premodern China would corrupt Hong Kong's charm: "I am afraid that Hong Kong might be more Sinicized after the return to China. Hong Kong is losing a liberal atmosphere of 'anything goes' by political self-restriction and is influenced by more traditional mainland Chinese culture which is definitely old-fashioned"; "The British presence has made Hong

Kong sophisticated and something special. But I think Hong Kong is becoming dirtier and losing its vigor after its return to China."

China is threatening to destroy the cosmopolitan attraction of Hong Kong not only because of its rigid communist policy, as pointed out by Japanese commentators (e.g., Edagawa, 1997), but because of its "premodern" Chineseness. The imagining of a modern, intimate Asian identity is still based upon the reconstruction of an oriental Orientalism. As observed in the depiction of Asian male stars in *Elle Japon*, "Asian guys are becoming more and more stunning and beautiful with economic development in the region." A certain degree of economic development is thus a minimum condition for other Asian cultures to enter "our" realm of modernity. "Premodern" Asia never occupies a coeval space with capitalist Asia but represents a place and a time that some Japanese fans of Hong Kong popular culture have no desire to identify with. It is not temporally proximate enough to evoke a nostalgic longing for a (different) Asian modernity.

Unevenness Embedded in Intraregional Cultural Flows in East Asia

As we enter the new century, intraregional media and popular culture flows have been increasingly activated. We are observing more co-production and mutual promotion, and the rise of a new player – the popularity of Korean TV dramas and pop music in east Asian markets. My brief research in Taiwan in March 2002 showed that Taiwanese viewers now perceive Korean TV dramas, which subtly depict youth's love affairs in connection with family matters, as "ours" even more than Japanese TV dramas. Popular culture is connecting people at a great distance in east Asia; however, as I have shown in this chapter, the cultural immediacy which the intensifying cultural flows in east Asia evoke does not necessarily lead to cultural dialogue on equal terms. A close look at intraregional cultural flows and consumption highlights the newly articulated asymmetrical power relations in the region, not just in terms of quantity of media import/export, but also in terms of the perception of temporality manifest in the consumption of the media products of cultural neighbors.

Neither should we uncritically deal with the transnational regional flow of a highly commercialized materialistic consumer culture. The connections forged by media and popular culture is mostly between urban areas, especially between Tokyo, Hong Kong, Taipei, Seoul, Singapore, Shanghai, Bangkok, etc.; and many economically deprived people in these areas are still excluded from the shared experience of feeling vernacular modernities in the region. The active construction of meanings takes place under the system of global capitalism in which Japan has a major role. This point became acute at the beginning of the twenty-first century, especially after September 11, 2001, as we were compelled to recognize, through sudden, massive media attention on a hitherto forgotten country, Afghanistan, how the disparity between the haves and have-nots had been greatly widening, and how the disparity itself had been left out of global concern. The development of communication technologies and the intensification of media and cultural flows that simultaneously interconnect many parts of the world have also brought forward global indifference towards many deprived people and regions.

A series of event since September 11 has highlighted anew American economic and military supremacy, and a view that equates globalization with Americanization has accordingly regained momentum. However, I would suggest that such a view is misleading, as it conceals the fact that the unevenness in transnational connections is intensified not solely by the American command but by the various kinds of collusive alliances among the developed countries under the patronage of the dominant American military power. It cannot be emphasized enough that the decentering process of globalization has not dissolved global power structures: the latter has been subtly diffused and even solidified, unceasingly producing asymmetry and indifference on a global scale.

To be critically engaged with those issues, we should take intraregional dynamics in east Asia seriously. No armchair speculation – be it optimistic or pessimistic – would be able to fully capture the contradictory and unforeseeable processes. Empirically and rigorously attending to the way in which transnational popular culture flows connect east Asia is imperative in the study of the globalization of culture, which has heretofore been highly biased towards the ubiquity of Western media and popular culture and has tended to neglect intraregional interactions.

Notes

1   This chapter is a condensed version of some chapters of my book, *Recentering Globalization: Popular Culture and Japanese Transnationalism* (Durham, NC: Duke University Press, 2002). Some parts also appeared in "Becoming Culturally Proximate: A/Scent of Japanese Idol Dramas in Taiwan," in B. Moeran, ed., *Asian Media Productions* (London: Curzon, 2001, 54–74) and "Nostalgia for Asian Modernities: Media Consumption of 'Asia' in Japan," *Positions: East Asia Cultures Critique* 10(3) (2002). Field research was conducted in Tokyo in

mid-January to late February in 1997 and from mid-March to late April 1998, and in Taipei from mid-December 1996 to mid-January and late May in 1997. I conducted informal depth interviews with 18 young female and 3 male viewers (age ranging from 17 to late twenties) of Japanese TV dramas in Taipei, and with 24 female "fans" (age ranging from early twenties to fifties) of Hong Kong film and pop singers in Tokyo.

2   In May 1997 I witnessed the occurrence of two incidents in Taiwan which, when juxtaposed, nicely illustrate that country's complicated relationship with Japan. The first was an anti-Japanese demonstration over the issue of Japan's possession of the Diaoyu Islands. The other was a rock concert by popular Japanese artists such as Globe and Amuro Namie which attracted much media attention as well as young audiences (see also *The Journalist*, June 1–7, 1997). This juxtaposition of "anti-" and "pro-" Japanese sentiment articulates a new generational divide.

3   Wu Nianzhen, the film director of *Dosan: A Borrowed Life* (1994), comments on the popularity of Japanese culture among the younger generation in Taiwan, "[m]y generation and my father's generation have a deep love-and-hate feeling towards Japan, though in quite different ways. But the younger generations have no special affection for Japanese culture, as there is no difference between Japan, America and Europe for them. Japan is just one option among many. I think the relationship between Taiwan and Japan will be more superficial in terms of affective feelings while deepened materially" (quoted in *Views*, Feb. 1996: 42). Like other Asian nations, Wu suggests, the symbolic meaning of "Japan" articulated through Japanese popular culture in Taiwan is marked by a waning affection for it.

4   Kaneshiro is Taiwanese-Japanese, but Hong Kong film has been his main field of activities.

5   Following the successful concerts in Japan of Jacky Cheung in 1995 and Andy Lau in 1996, Leslie Cheung and Aaron Kwok also held concerts in 1997.

6   Stewart (1993: 26) argues: "Nostalgia, like any form of narrative, is always ideological: the past it seeks has never existed except as narrative, and hence, always absent, that past continually threatens to reproduce itself as a felt lack."

7   E.g. *Nikkei Entertainment* (Dec. 1997); *Elle Japon* (Nov. 1997).

References

Ang, Ien (1985). *Watching Dallas: Soap Opera and the Melodramatic Imagination*. London: Methuen.

Ang, Ien and Stratton, Jon (1996). "Asianizing Australia: Notes toward a Critical Transnationalism in Cultural Studies." *Cultural Studies* 10(1): 16–36.

Chan, Joseph Man (1996). "Television in Greater China: Structure, Exports, and Market Formation." In J. Sinclair et al., eds., *New Patterns in Global Television: Peripheral Vision*. New York: Oxford University Press, 126–60.

Dirlik, Arlif (1994). *After the Revolution: Waking to Global Capitalism.* Hanover: Wesleyan University Press.

Edagawa, Koichi (1997). *Hong Kong 24:00* [Honkon 24ji : Konton toshi no shitataka na hitobito]. Tokyo: Magazin Hausu.

Fabian, Johannes (1983). *Time and the Other: How Anthropology Makes Its Object.* New York: Columbia University Press.

Featherstone, Mike (1996). *Undoing Culture: Globalization, Postmodernism and Identity.* London: Sage.

Hall, Stuart (1991). "The Local and the Global: Globalization and Ethnicity." In A. King, ed., *Culture, Globalization, and the World-System.* London: Macmillan, 19–39.

Ivy, Marilyn (1995). *Discourses of the Vanishing: Modernity, Phantasm, Japan.* Chicago: University of Chicago Press.

Iwabuchi, Koichi (1998). "Marketing 'Japan': Japanese Cultural Presence under a Global Gaze." *Japanese Studies* 18(2): 165–80.

Iwabuchi, Koichi (2001). "Uses of Japanese Popular Culture: Media Globalization and Postcolonial Desire for 'Asia'." *Emergences: Journal of Media and Composite Cultures* 11(2): 197–220.

Li, Zhen-Yi, Peng, Zhen-Ling, Li-Qing, and Zhang, Jia-Qi (1995). *Tokyo Love Story: A Study on the Reason of the Popularity and Audience Motivations in Taiwan.* Unpublished undergraduate research paper of National University of Politics, Taiwan. (In Chinese.)

Liao, Chaoyang (1997). "Borrowed Modernity: History and the Subject in "A Borrowed Life." *boundary 2* 24(3): 225–45.

Liechty, Mark (1995). "Media, Markets and Modernization: Youth Identities and the Experience of Modernity in Katmandu, Nepal." In V. Amit-Talai and H. Wulff, eds., *Youth Culture: A Cross-cultural Perspective.* London: Routledge, 166–201.

Morley, David and Robins, Kevin (1995). *Spaces of Identities: Global Media, Electronic Landscapes and Cultural Boundaries.* London: Routledge.

Morris-Suzuki, Tessa (1998). "Invisible Countries: Japan and the Asian Dream." *Asian Studies Review* 22(1): 5–22.

Sinclair, John, Jacka, Elizabeth, and Cunningham, Stuart, eds. (1996). *New Patterns in Global Television: Peripheral Vision.* Oxford: Oxford University Press.

Straubhaar, J. (1991). "Beyond Media Imperialism: Asymmetrical Interdependence and Cultural Proximity." *Critical Studies in Mass Communication* 8(1): 39–59.

Tomlinson, John (1997). "Cultural Globalization and Cultural Imperialism." In A. Mohammadi, ed., *International Communication and Globalization: A Critical Introduction.* London: Sage, 170–90.

Watson, James L., ed. (1997). *Golden Arches East: McDonald's in East Asia.* Stanford: Stanford University Press.

3

Hook 'em Young: McAdvertising and Kids in Singapore

Siew Keng Chua and Afshan Junaid

Globalization has increasingly impinged upon kids' culture, but there are few studies that devote cultural analyses to kids' cultural consumption practices and everyday life. The consumption culture (both material and symbolic) of kids has been globally exploited by multinational companies' marketing strategies for at least two decades since the 1980s.

McDonald's, the ubiquitous fast food synonymous with kids' eating habits, has very early on spread its cover over the young. Globalization has meant that the consumption of Western culture starts in infancy. McDonald's has clearly capitalized on this and it does so by the incorporation of local with the global – the phenomenon called "glocalization" by some scholars (see Robertson, 1992). In this way, while the very young are being socialized into their own local culture, they are also exposed to the "global" culture. Multinational companies have used advertising strategies to commodify children's viewing practices as early as 4 years old, or even younger.

McDonald's can be said to use the media "to invade the most private spheres of our everyday lives, commodifying our national identifications, desires, human needs, for the purposes of commerce" (Giroux, 1994). The child is influenced greatly by advertisers in learning to establish consumption-relation values, priorities, and aspirations (Unnikrishnan & Bajpai, 1998; Lasn, 1999; Schlosser, 2001). The strategies used by McDonald's have successfully helped it to create brand loyalty among very young children. The popularity of McDonald's among many kids all over the world, including Singapore, signifies such loyalty. Singaporeans are among "the largest consumer of McDonald's burgers per capita in the world" (Chua, 2000: 184–96). Supporting evidence for McDonald's' popularity is reflected in a study by Junaid (2002) through the positive responses of some children towards "McAdvertising," its icons, food, promotional items (toys), ambience, representations, identification, and other such intangible entities sold in the advertisements. The children who liked McDonald's advertisements generated a wide range of meanings for the same advertisement, some of which appear to be "a joint collaborative effort on the part of maker and consumer," as O'Barr (1994) puts it.

Junaid's study used ethnographic in-depth interviews of a group of 36 small children to look into the culture and reception of television by children aged 4 to 6 years belonging to two Singaporean schools. Seventeen kids interviewed were from a government school (of which 10 were boys and 7 were girls) and 19 belonged to a private school (of which 13 were boys and 6 were girls). Keeping in view the age range and language skills of the children, a survey of their parents was conducted for additional background information on the children. A total of 34 parents were surveyed using a self-administered questionnaire (2 of them did not participate in the survey). Seventeen parents participating in the survey were those of the government-school children and 17 parents were those of private-school children. The study established "McDonald's" to be a popular choice in fast food for most kids, and hence McDonald's advertisements on television were chosen for the study. Although parents agreed to participate in the survey, they were all reluctant to be interviewed.

An analysis of the data showed that 75 percent (i.e. 27 children) were Chinese, 5.6 percent (2 kids) were Indian, 5.6 percent (2 children) were Malay, 2.8 percent (1 child) was of Caucasian/Eurasian (Australian) origin, and 5.6 percent (2 kids) belonged to other races (Thai and Nepalese). This ethnic constitution of the children under study, except for Malays (who constitute 14 percent of Singapore's population), largely reflects the ethnic demographics of Singapore.

Cross-tabulations of television viewing on weekends from the parents' survey and the children's interviews revealed that most children (from both the schools) watched 2 hours or more of television. Eight parents from the government school reported that their child watched more than 4 hours of television on weekends (1 from private school). Seven parents reported that their child watched less than 2 hours of television on weekends (1 parent from the government school). None of them said that they watched no television on weekends. This meant that all children from this study watched television on weekends.

The themes from children's culture have been borrowed by advertising agencies that redefine them with a focus on consumer culture (Seiter, 1993; Kincheloe, 1997). Television plays a role in the formation of a separate children's consumer culture, giving them a common means of identification and thus communication with other kids (Kincheloe, 1997). It provides children with a shared repository of images, characters, plots and themes, the basis of conversation and play, and it does this on a "national" even "global scale" (Seiter, 1993). Rather than directly exploiting the power of the child's purse the manufacturers exploit the power inherent in the conceptual gulf between the cultures of the adult and the child. "The industry has crucial economic and socializing functions in creating consumer demand, shaping behavior, and inducing people to participate in and thus reproduce consumer society" (Eadie et al., 1999: 331). McDonald's' Singapore TV advertisements literally cash in on the cultural gulf between adults and children to create consumer demand in children, according to Kincheloe (1997). The name "McDonald's" itself is children-friendly, with its evocation of "Old McDonald had a farm, E-I-E-I-O." The company's television depiction of itself to children as a happy place "where what you want is what you get" is very appealing to the young audience (Garfield, 1992). Thus, by the time children reach elementary school they are often zealous devotees of McDonald's, insisting on "McDonaldland" birthday celebrations and surprise dinners. McDonald's advertisers are obviously doing something right, as they induce a phenomenal number of kids to pester their parents for Big Macs and fries.

> McDonald's and other fast-food advertisers have discovered an enormous and previously overlooked children's market. Every month nineteen out of every twenty kids, aged six to eleven, visit a fast food restaurant. In a typical McDonald's promotion where toys like "Hot Wheels" or "Barbies" accompany kid's meals, company officials can expect to sell 30 million to child customers. By the time the child reaches the age of three, more than four out of five know that McDonald's sells hamburgers. (Kincheloe, 1997: 255)

Advertisers target children using cross-marketing strategies (Wicks, 2001). In the case of McDonald's, these strategies include selling of "food, folks, and fun" as the "commodity" for sale in the advertisements (Caputo, 1998); successful use of the icon Ronald McDonald; toys as promotional items accompanying the kids meals; arrangement of birthday parties at McDonald's; creating an appealing environment for children in the ads as well as at the food outlets; localization strategies (especially those in south-east Asia); and of course, the selling of food items that appeal to children. Aaker (1996) aptly sums up the advertising blitz used by McDonald's:

> The kids/fun/family associations are supported by and consistent with Ronald McDonald, McDonald's birthday-party experiences, McDonaldland games, Happy Meals, and McDonald's dolls and toys. A set of social involvement associations includes Ronald MacDonald House. Finally, there is a set of functional associations organized around the concepts of service, value, and meals. The "golden arches" provide a linking function as well as representing the whole identity. (Aaker, 1996: 93)

Television has been used as a baby-sitter for many families where both parents go out to work, and this is very common in Singapore even when the household has a domestic help, usually a foreign worker from the Philippines, Sri Lanka, Indonesia, or other Asian countries. Because the "maids" have household chores such as cooking, cleaning, and washing, very often infants are parked in front of the television while their minders are occupied with their chores. Thus television viewing becomes one of the earliest modes whereby kids are socialized into the culture. In the case of Singapore, because the kids are looked after by someone from a very different culture and also class background, they learn cultural differences in their acculturation from a very early age. McDonald's advertising strategies, precisely because they are spread throughout the region, also become a link between the child and the "maid." McDonald's cuts across class and to some extent ethnic background. Kids are often taken to eat at McDonald's because such restaurants are kid-friendly and "maid"-friendly. The "maids" are often fans of McDonalds in the countries where they come from. What we see then is a symbiotic link between consumption of images and material goods and, literally, consuming viewing culture and viewing consuming culture.

At the same time, we see that McDonald's is not only plugging into the kids' culture by appealing to their sense of fun and desire for toys, but also into the "host" culture by introducing icons which are very much part of that culture, such as television stars and local places of interest to children. In Singapore the McDonald's commercials on television usually have a strong "Singaporean touch" (Yuyi, 1998; Chua, 2000), making it easy for the kids to identify with their own social contexts. For example, these commercials feature Singapore skyscrapers in the Zoe Tay (a local television and film star) commercial and the recent McCrispy campaign (where the two popular McDonald's superheroes – "Fast" and "Steam" – save the day by helping a girl in trouble); "Liang Po Po" (a popular and funny fictional character from a hit Singapore television series and movie) buying food at McDonald's; row over the "best chicken in Singapore" advertisement (appropriating the popular contemporary local movie "Chicken Rice War"); shaking HDB buildings (Housing and Development Board is the public housing where 85 percent of Singaporeans reside) waking up to the morning alarm for a McDonald's breakfast; 3 out of 4 Singaporeans (the corporation includes at least one sleeping child in the images) drooling in their sleep over mouth-watering McDonald's breakfasts. These images all clearly link the Singaporean culture of McDonald's advertising with the company's global marketing.

McDonald's also embeds their advertisements with representations of the "ideal family," "fun," "break from routine," and "happiness," which are also seen in the case of advertisements by the corporation in other countries (Goldman 1992; Seiter, 1993; Love, 1995; Watson, 1997; Yan, 1997; Tierney, 1998; Yuyi, 1998; Caputo, 1998; Chua, 2000; Schlosser, 2001). In many McDonald's commercials on Singapore television, the complete picture of family and fun is shown. Lyrics such "the price so right [...] Oh! Mummy take me there [...] That's my McDonald's!" and montages of "fun with the family"-related images, such as kite flying and a picnic at McDonald's, along with a toddler (who can barely walk) going towards McDonald's, represent the values of family and fun. At the same time, they reinforce the belief by Ray Kroc (McDonald's founding father) that "the child who loves McDonald's TV commercials brings his/her family giving the corporation more customers" (Schlosser, 2001: 41).

McAdvertisements on television are also coupled with ongoing McDonald's promotions. For example, the "Best smiles" advertisement was coupled with McDonald's' best smiles contest held in Singapore, when "Fun boxes" were installed at many McDonald's restaurants in June and July 2001. Su (1999) has suggested that children may be creative in the way they enjoy and derive meaning from television. They interact with television (Cupit, 1987). McDonald's advertisements evoke a series of pleasing images in a youngster's mind: bright colors, a playground, a toy, a clown. In a study of the responses of 34 children (aged 4–6) to McDonald's advertisements by Junaid (2002), over 60 percent of the children liked more McDonald's advertisements on Singapore television. Some children liked the advertisements because they showed people dancing, had music which they enjoyed. The following are some comments made by the children interviewed for the study:

Singing, dancing. Like it because they are very fun. [*What?*] Dancing. (Child A)

Because its very funny. (Child B)

Very funny and cute. (Child C)

It was very funny. Because they are always laughing. (Child D)

McAdvertising strategies hook kids while they are still very young (as early as 2 years old) and suggest the tobacco companies' strategy to hook nonsmokers at a tender age. The preschoolers studied by Junaid (2002) are creative, thoughtful, critical consumers of fast food advertisements, and active meaning producers of such media outputs. Parents and children seem to be embedded in their own distinct cultures. The advertisements tell stories to these children by captalizing on their culture. Some of the kids studied are as attracted to the fast-food advertisements as the women (soap opera viewers) studied by Ang (1985). It has been observed through Junaid's study that despite their limited language ability the preschoolers exhibited very good visual and televisual literacy, as is clearly evident from their responses. The study has illustrated that some preschoolers disliked the McDonald's advertisement shown to them although they liked the fast food at McDonald's, while others grew out of eating the fast food and yet derived feelings of "nostalgia" from the advertisement. There were some preschoolers (in the group studied) who thought that the McDonald's advertisement shown to them was "real." Others simply found it "funny" (by which the children meant "full of fun"). A small number of the children in the study disliked the McDonald's advertisement on television as well as disliked the fast food there. However, the study has shown that a large number of the preschoolers studied (more than 60 percent) liked McDonald's fast food because they liked its television advertisements. Others liked the fast food at McDonald's and hence liked to see it in the McDonald's advertisement on television. Thus it may be said that the preschoolers studied derive pleasure or displeasure from the McDonald's advertisement on television shown to them in a symbiotic relationship which exists between the fast food advertisements on television and eating of fast food by these children. Media globalization has reinforced the material globalization of McDonald's, as the ubiquitous presence of the fast-food restaurants in Singapore shows. The fast-food giant gained a foothold in the tiny nation in the 1970s, and McDonald's restaurants spread rapidly throughout the island in the 1980s. By the 1990s, their overwhelming presence had at least rivaled, if not outstripped, that of the hawker stalls as Singaporeans' popular food haunts.

McDonald's advertisements paint a picture of fun and happiness. They project "nostalgic, sentimentalized, conflict-free, happy family" images (Kincheloe, 1997). Ang (1985) has noted that "the structure of the text (which employs rhetorical strategies) itself plays an important role in stimulating the involvement of viewers." The selling of "happiness along with the food" aspect of the McDonald's advertisements (Schlosser, 2001; Caputo, 1998; Seiter, 1993; Goldman, 1992) appeals to kids who find the advertisements full of fun and likable.

These children have their own "culture" quite separate from the adults. Junaid's study shows the children liked the advertisements because of the element of "fun." Kincheloe (1997) notes that today's postmodern children's culture is created by adults and dispersed via television for the purpose of inducing children to consume. McDonald's advertisements are able to plug into the kinderculture and thus attract the children towards them. Many of the McDonald's advertisements use "toys" in "Happy Meals" to connect with children (Schlosser, 2001; Love, 1995). The excerpt below of the children's responses (from Junaid's study) shows this clearly:

Nice. The toy . . . The toy one. (Child F)

I want . . . I like children one got toys I like children one. KFC toy one because can play I got. Now I got the couples can stick together [*describes the promotional toy*] because I like. Some are . . . some McDonald's I like. Pizza Hut don't have toys. (Child G)

Inside the car got a lot of Hello Kitty. [*Do you like Hello Kitty?*] Yes. [*Why?*] Because Hello Kitty is cute. [*Why?*] Because Hello Kitty don't have mouth. (Child H).

Because McDonald's have something . . . what . . . Toys . . . McChicken have for me. (Child I)

The commodification of children's culture sets the stage for advertising pitches that stress "the incomparable pleasure of making children happy by presenting them with toys" (Seiter, 1993). Many children associate happiness with owning or possessing a toy or simply being indulged. Unnkrishnan and Bajpai (1998) in their study on children and television advertising in India note that "advertising, when it targets the child (say, into eating McDonald's or buying a promotional toy), powerfully promotes a consumer culture and values associated with it." One such promotional toy at McDonald's, called "Hello Kitty" (a Japanese animation character), resulted in a buying frenzy in Singapore in 2001. So toys are also sold to the children along with the food by "appealing to the youngster's desire to be the first, the best, the most popular, and so forth." Advertising has highlighted the family appeal of McDonald's, and promotions which feature giveaways to children, ever since the corporation discovered "children" as their new market (Love, 1995). McDonald's advertisements on children's television channels such as "Kids Central" in Singapore tend to mostly feature its promotional toys which attract the children. Again, the responses of the children (below) support this:

No I see the toy McDonald's ones. See the toy McDonald. A lot, because the food is very nice and they have toys. [*Do you like the toys there?*] Hm. [*The food?*] It's good because they have toys there and have delicious food. (Child I)

Yes [*sees McDonald's ads on TV*] and KFC. [*Do you like that?*] Yes [*Why?*] Because KFC got the toy. [*McDonald's*] Also got like Snoopy. Yes [*Likes toys*] because it is very likable, can play. (Child J)

Because have lots of Pooh [*"Pooh Bear" is a Disney character sold as a promotional item at McDonald's with its meals*]. (Child K)

These responses confirm that before approximately 6 years of age, children are "interested in accumulating lots of toys or other fun objects just for the sheer number and mass that this represents" (Acuff & Reiher, 1997: 15). Children are fond of the toys accompanying their meals (as promotional items) at fast food outlets such as McDonald's. These toys are the reason for the gravitation of these kids to the fast-food joints.

Most of McDonald's' images also reinforce gender stereotyping of children; girls with kitty dolls, boys with soccer balls. However, Junaid's study showed that among the 4- to 6-year-old audience members there was not any marked preference for stereotypical gendering of activities in the images presented to them. Most did not express a preference in relation to gendered images, while a few did so. This suggests that children of this age were not overwhelmingly different in their gender preferences for gendered icons such as dolls or soccer balls.

McDonald's also allows the kids to plug into kinderculture where they appropriate consuming images and products to assert their own identity in a process of self-formation to distinguish themselves from their parents. Even before they are aware of ethnic differences, these kids differentiate between their own and their parents' cultures. What kinds of meanings do kids make out of their own cultural consumption? The children's reaction to the question "what do you think about McDonald's advertising on television?" shows a great fondness for the advertisements in Junaid's (2002) study. Some children like them because of their familiarity, while others because they think they see the people who make the food they like on television. Some children don't yet know the word "advertisement" and call it the "McDonald's show." One child likes to see the "show" with his brother. Another child likes the advertisement because she thinks it is "real." Mankeiwicz (cited in Fowles, 1992: 213) says that youngsters "are enticed into believing that what they see on television is what they'll get in real life." Lang and Lang (1991) suggest that "as long as the meanings read into the content are real, they are . . . real in their consequences. They become part of the culturally enshrined symbolic environment." Yet another child finds that the food that is shown in the advertisement exists in real life, and she enjoys this "reality" aspect. She believes what she sees in the advertisement "is real also." "Real" according to Ang (1985), is "the socio-cultural background of the realistic illusion." She feels that "precisely this constructed illusion of reality is the basis for pleasure" (Ang, 1985: 40) and "any form of pleasure is constructed and functions in a specific social and historical context" (ibid.: 19). An element of pleasure is involved in watching the fast-food advertisements. However, pleasure is neither definable nor quantifiable.

> Pleasure is something uncertain and precarious, being something in life regarded as self-evident, which people don't think about. The socio-psychological constitution of television viewers (individuals, i.e. the child in this case) implies a functionalist conception of pleasure in which its essence is regarded as the experience of satisfaction whenever a certain pre-existent need is fulfilled. Pleasure must be conceived of as not so much the automatic result of some "satisfaction of needs," but rather as the effect of a certain productivity of a cultural artifact. Pleasure is primarily generated during the process of watching, in the actual confrontation between the viewer and the programme. (Ang, 1985: 9)

The kids are also able to identify themselves in some way with the scenes depicted in the advertisements. One child talks about the last scene in the McDonald's advertisement. When describing the advertisement the child suggests that he likes the last scene where the father is carrying a baby and they eat McDonald's french fries together. He says that he likes the scene as it reminds him of the time that he was younger and his father carried him and they had french fries together. His response suggests that "child viewers can identify greatly with other children on television" (Goonsekara et al., 2000). This child is 6 years of age and is not too fond of McDonald's food any more, but still likes a part of the advertisement:

> The people are . . . they are singing a song sing and song then a later last one the daddy carry the baby then they eat the french fries. Because the dad . . . last time I small . . . I small I use . . . my daddy also do like this carry me . . . a gi . . . buy French fries and eat. [*So you like to see that?*] Hm.

The scene, which lasts less than three seconds on television, shows an idealized vision of childhood that prompts the child viewers to compare their own experiences with this memorable image. The scene's structure invites viewers to interpret the ad in terms of the past (Goldman, 1992: 95) in the context of another McDonald's advertisement. This scene of an infant and father bonding together over McDonald's french fries reflects "the parent and child are bound together in an apparent mutually satisfying process of consumption, where the valuation of children (and their relationship to parents) receives expression in terms of commodities" (Goldman, 1992: 103).

Thus McDonald's also appropriates kids' "nostalgia" and their sentimental bonds with their parents as commodifiable products, symbolically identified with the fast food and embedded into the narrative of parental love.

> One does not just recognize oneself in the ascribed characteristics of an isolated fictional character. . . . Identification with a character only becomes possible within the framework of the whole structure of the narrative. Moreover, the involvement of viewers cannot be described exclusively in terms of an imaginary identification with one or more characters. (Ang, 1985: 29)

The response of the child quoted earlier reflects this sense of nostalgia. "Nostalgia," a "longing of the past, a yearning for yesterday, or a fondness for possessions and activities associated with days of yore" (cited in Hoch & Meyer, 2000), is constructed through a cultural process, a "nostalgic" intertextuality, the link of film or TV to the consumer's earlier life or nostalgic past. "Nostalgia for past pleasures plays a significant role in young people's growth towards adulthood" (Nava, 1997; Davies et al., 2003). What appeals to the viewers is that the program is connected with their individual life histories and social situations they are in (Ang, 1985, referring to women viewing soap operas). The McDonald's advertisement features a nostalgia, a sentimentalized, conflict-free history of the family (Kincheloe, 1997). The advertisers hope that "nostalgic childhood memories of a brand will lead to a lifetime of purchase," since the advertisers realize that brand loyalty may begin as early as the age of two. Market research has found children to recognize a brand logo before they can recognize their own names (Schlosser, 2001: 43).

The McAdvertising strategies used in television in Singapore for targeting preschoolers can be compared to "tobacco marketing" (see Eadie et al., 1999, on the role of tobacco companies and young people smoking). "McAdvertising," like cigarette advertising, thrives on "tapping the psycho-sociological insecurities of the child viewers" (Downing et al., 1995). Such advertising is not "selling products" but rather "selling something intangible" (Schlosser, 2001), such as the "food, folks, fun" strategy of McDonald's. A study by Wimmer and Dominick (1994) described the effectiveness of such strategies used by one tobacco company. They found the company ran advertisements featuring cartoon characters that encourage young people to smoke cigarettes. "Old Joe," a cartoon character used by Camel cigarettes, was an effective weapon in Camel's marketing arsenal. One study reported that that 12- and 13-year-olds had the highest recognition of the character and that Camel's market share among 12- to 17-year-old boys was twice that of Camel's market share among 18- to 24-year-old men. Another study found that "Old Joe" was as well known among 9-year-olds as Mickey Mouse (Wimmer & Dominick, 1994: 362). Schlosser (2001) concluded that the "Old Joe" Camel ad campaign which used a hip cartoon character to sell cigarettes showed how easily children could be persuaded by the right corporate mascot.

In the case of McDonald's, a similar phenomenon is the successful use of the company icon, Ronald McDonald, the clown, who is immensely popular with very young children, exhorting kids to consume McDonald's fast food. "Children as young as two years old often pay attention to television because they want to understand it" (Wicks, 2001: 125), and it is simple for them to believe in the McDonald's advertisements that evoke a series of pleasing images in the youngster's mind. It is easy for the kids to view "McDonald's restaurants as social centers and nurturing institutions, locales of conviviality, providers of food and drink in never-ending abundance" (Cross, 1996). For this reason, children are considered the "future of the corporation's survival" (Yan, 1997: 39–96). McDonald's invests heavily in television advertising aimed specifically at children, and makes a point of cultivating this market (see Watson, 1997). Terms such as "leverage," "the nudge factor," and "pester power" are now used by marketers, and "the aim of most children's advertising is straightforward: get the kids to nag their parents and nag them well" (Schlosser, 2001: 43).

Studies have shown that in a consumer society, parent and child are bound together "in an apparent mutually satisfying process of consumption, where the valuation of children (and their relationship to parents) receives expression in terms of commodities" (Goldman, 1992: 103). The advertisements for commodities create needs for consumption. Williamson

(1978) notes that advertisements "lose whatever simple qualities they may have had and become instead texts about production and consumption in the consumer society, about the place of commodities in social life, and about the creation of needs to service an economic system that must sell what has been produced. . . . McDonald's corporation (as an economic institution) reflects or echoes ongoing state policies of Singapore from time to time in its advertisements on television" (cited in O'Barr, 1994: 5).

It is precisely because McDonald's allow a more persuasive semiotics than direct instructions such as those that the kids face in Singapore kindergartens from adults, that these kids react favourably to the ads. At the same time, resistance to the ads is also reflected in the reactions of a small number of other kids who actually "disliked" or "dissociated" themselves from the same advertisements, thus reflecting how the audience "work" or "resist" the economic forces (Gandy, 1995) and subvert the dominant or hegemonic meanings offered by the mass media (McQuail, 1997). These kids were, thus, "making critical/oppositional readings of dominant cultural forms, perceiving ideological messages selectively/subversively" (see Morley, 1992, in another context). These support Ang's claim for the contestation of meaning construction to some extent. But the bulk of the children studied confirm the success of brand advertising strategies used in McAdvertising, though the reception of these advertisements could not be generalized uniformly to all the children. Moreover, some children grew out of watching McDonald's food advertisements and even found the advertisements annoying, while the majority expressed a very clear liking for the McDonald's advertisements and the food.

Junaid's study found the young children to be a "lively audience, far from passive." A substantial number derived a great deal of pleasure from viewing the fast-food advertisements. Many children could not clearly explain the reasons for liking the advertisements, probably because "people do not really give thought to why a particular thing is pleasurable to them" (Ang, 1985: 9). These kids could make visible their identifications with those more ephemeral objects of consumer culture – television advertisements in this case. Such kids could identify greatly with other children on television, as seen in the case of the child who identified himself with the baby in the advertisement carried by the father in the last scene of the advertisement screened in Junaid's study.

This study also indicates a gulf between the culture of the children studied and their parents. A notable number of the children expressed a liking for certain television programs disliked by their parents.

Hook 'em Young

One doesn't have to look far (try any middle-class home) to find that children's enthusiasm for certain television shows, toys, and food isolates them from their parents. Drawing on this isolation, children turn it into a form of power – they finally know something that dad doesn't. How many dads or moms understand the relationship between Mayor McCheese and French Fry Guys? Battle lines begin to be drawn between children and parents, as kids want to purchase McDonald's hamburgers or action toys. (Kincheloe, 1997: 256)

When it comes to television viewing, this conflict takes the shape of what Cupit (1984) calls the "politics of the living room." James's (1982) conception of the "child's relationship to adult culture" is extremely appropriate to children's television advertisements. James (1982) and Seiter (1993) observe that adults often despise the things liked by children, and so a cultural conflict exists among parents and kids. The responses by some children studied by Junaid support their contention of a cultural difference between adults and children in their reception of television. We may not go as far as Seiter (1993) in her claim that, if the food forms most prized by children are held by adults to be repulsive, inedible "trash" or "junk," it is a sign that children's culture inverts and confuses the rules of adult culture. At the same time, we note that McAdvertising capitalizes on the strategy of adult–kid differences to draw in the kids. Fast food is often categorized as "junk food" by many adults (this "junk food is one of the most frequently advertised products on television," according to Lasn, 1999: 174), although, as can be seen in some of the responses of kids studied, it is well liked by many children. Seiter's (1993) view – that by confusing the adult order children create for themselves considerable room for movement within the limits imposed upon them by adult society – seems to be understood by McDonald's, which has capitalized on it as a promotional strategy. For these children, eating McDonald's or other fast food and enjoying their television advertisements may be a way of trying to break free from adult authority and creating space for themselves and their discrete culture.

The study of television audiences has witnessed major conceptual and theoretical shifts over the last two decades. The heterogeneous ways in which audiences receive the media have been dependent on their social, cultural, economic, political, and ethnic situations; and, of course, age. In this article we attempt to address a lack in cultural theory which has looked extensively at youth pop culture but has not, so far, given the same focus to the culture of young children. By focusing on a study of 36 very young

Singaporean children, we see how very young audiences respond to advertising and, simultaneously, how McAdvertising makes use of the cultural capital of these very young kids to appeal to their target audiences. For these tiny tots the world of McDonald's valorizes their own culture of toys, fun, bonding, and play.

When faced with advertising's armory of pleasurable appeals and material promotions, these young kids may not be political enough to resist the appeals. This chapter has suggested that media hegemony reflects the wider political economy, which, in the case of very small kids, may not be easy to resist or oppose. At the same time, these young children can't be viewed merely as passive consumers, since they do interact with the ads and try to influence their minders and parents in order to attain their desire for the products. Moreover, they take pleasure in viewing the ads. Thus, as adults and youths get more politically savvy about ads, ads try to get there early, and foster in very young kids a habit of consumption which may be hard to kick when they grow old. However, more research needs to be done on kids' culture to explore this.

References

http://www.mcdonalds.com/countries/singapore/careers/careers.html

http://www.mcdonalds.com/countries/singapore/corporate/corporate.html

Aaker, D. A. (1996). *Building Strong Brands*. New York: Singapore.

Aaker, J. L. (1997). "Dimensions of Brand Personality." *Journal of Marketing Research* 34: 347–55.

Acker, S. and Tiemens, R. (1981). "Children's Perception of Changes in Size of TV Images." *Human Communication Research* 7(4), 340–6.

Acuff, D. S. and Reiher, R. H. (1997). *What Kids Buy and Why: The Psychology of Marketing to Kids*. New York: The Free Press.

Ang, I. (1985). *Watching "Dallas" Soap Opera and the Melodramatic Imagination*. London: Routledge.

Ang, I. (1989). "Wanted: Audiences." In E. Seiter, H. Borchers, G. Kreutzner, and E. Warth, eds., *Remote Control: Television, Audiences, and Cultural Power*. London: Routledge.

Ang, I. (1991). *Desperately Seeking the Audience*. London: Routledge.

Ang, I. (1995). "The Nature of the Audience." In J. Downing, A. Mohammadi, and A. S. Mohammadi, eds., *Questioning the Media*, 2nd ed. Thousand Oaks, CA: Sage.

Ang, I. (1996). "Culture and Communication: Towards Ethnographic Critique of Media Consumption in the Transnational Media System." In J. Storey, ed., *What is Cultural Studies?: A Reader*. London: Arnold.

Atkin, C. and Block, M. (1983). "Effectiveness of Celebrity Endorsers." *Journal of Advertising Research* 23(1): 57–62.

Atkin, C., Hocking, J., and Block, M. (1984). "Teenage Drinking: Does Advertising Make a Difference?" *Journal of Communication* 34(2): 157–67.

Caputo, J. S. (1998). "The Rhetoric of McDonalization: A Social Semiotic Perspective." In M. Alfino, Caputo, J. S., and Wynyard, R., eds., *McDonalization Revisited – Critical Essays on Consumer Culture*. Westport, CT and London: Praeger.

Chua, B. H. (2000). "Singaporeans Ingesting McDonald's." *Consumption in Asia Lifestyles and Identities*. London: Routledge.

Chua, L. H. (2000). "Singapore: Take a Cue from McDonald's Good PR." Singapore *Straits Times*, Feb. 9.

M. Cross. (1996). *Advertising and Culture: Theoretical Perspectives*. Westport, CT: Praeger.

Cupit, C. G. (1987). *The Child Audience*. North Sydney: Australian Broadcasting Tribunal.

Davies, H., Buckingham, D., and Kelley, P. (2003). "In the Worst Possible Taste: Children, Television and Cultural Value." In R. C. Allen and A. Hill, eds., *The Television Studies Reader*. London: Routledge.

Davies, M. M. (1989). *Television is Good for Your Kids*. London: Hilary Shipman.

Downing, J., Mohammadi, A., and Mohammadi, A. S., eds. (1995). *Questioning the Media*, 2nd ed. Thousand Oaks, CA: Sage.

Eadie, D., Hastings, G., Stead, M., and MacKintosh, A. M. (1999). "Branding: Could it Hold the Key to Future Tobacco Reduction Policy?" *Heath Education* 3: 103–10.

Featherstone, M., Lash, S., and Robertson, R. (1995). *Global Modernities*. London: Sage.

Fischer, P., et al. (1991). "Brand Logo Recognition by Children Aged 3 to 6 Years." *Journal of the American Medical Association* 266(22): 3145–8.

Fiske, J. (1987). *Television Culture*. New York: Routledge.

Fowles, J. (1992). *Why Viewers Watch: A Reappraisal of Television's Effects*. Newbury Park, CA: Sage.

Friedlander, B. Z., Wetstone, H. S., and Scott, C. S. (1974). "Suburban Preschool Children's Comprehension of an Age Appropriate Informational Television Program." *Child Development* 45: 561–5.

Gandy, O. H., Jr. (1995). "Tracking the Audience: Personal Information and Privacy." In J. Downing, A. Mohammadi, and A. S. Mohammadi, eds., *Questioning the Media*, 2nd ed. Thousand Oaks, CA: Sage.

Gardner, B. B. and Levy, S. J. (1995). "The Product and the Brand." *Harvard Business Review* March–April.

Garfield, B. (1992). "Nice ads, but that theme is not what you want." *Advertising Age* 63(8): 53.

Giroux, H. (1988). *Teachers as Intellectuals: Toward a Critical Pedagogy of Learning*. Granby, MA: Bergin and Garvey.

Goldman, R. (1992). *Reading Ads Socially*. New York: Routledge.

Goonsekara, A., et al. (2000). *Growing Up with TV – Asian Children's Experience.* Singapore: AMIC.

Gray, A. (1999). "Audience and Reception Research in Retrospect." In P. Alasuutari, ed., *The Media Audience.* London: Sage.

Hall, S. (1993). "Encoding, Decoding." In S. During, ed., *The Cultural Studies Reader.* London: Routledge.

Halliday, M. A. K. (1975). *Learning How to Mean: Explorations in the Development of Language.* London: Edward Arnold; repr. 1986.

Halpern, W. (1975). "Turned-on Toddlers." *Journal of Communication* 25: 66–70.

Hoch, S. J. and Meyer, R. J., eds. (2000). *Advances in Consumer Research* 27. Provo, UT: Association for Consumer Research.

Hoover's Inc. (2001). "Hoover's Company Profile Database – American Public Companies – McDonald's Corporation." Austin, TX: Hoover Inc. Lexis–Nexis Academic Universe: Singapore, Oct. 8.

Huizinga, J. (1955). *Homo Ludens: A Study of the Play Element in Culture.* Boston: Beacon Press.

James, A. (1982). "Confections, Concoctions, and Conceptions." *Journal of the Anthropological Society of Oxford* 10(2): 83–95.

Junaid, A. (2002). "McAdvertising and Children: Fast Food Television Advertisement Strategies and Reception by Preschoolers." Unpublished Masters' dissertation, Nanyang Technological University, Singapore.

Kellner, D. (1995). "Advertising and Consumer Culture." In J. Downing, A. Mohammadi, and A. S. Mohammadi, eds., *Questioning the Media*, 2nd ed. Thousand Oaks, CA: Sage.

Kellner, D. (1998). "Foreword: McDonalization and its Discontents." In P. Kotler, *Marketing Management: Analysis, Planning, Implementation and Control.* Upper Saddle River, NJ: Prentice-Hall.

Kincheloe, J. L. (1997). "Ronald McDonald (aka Ray Kroc) Does It All For You." In S. R Steinberg and J. L. Kincheloe, eds., *Kinderculture: The Corporate Construction of Childhood: McDonald's, Power, and Children.* Boulder, CO: Westview.

Ko, P. S. and Ho, W. K., eds. (1992). *Growing Up in Singapore: The Pre-school Years.* Singapore: Longman Singapore Publishers.

Koh, T. T. B. (1993, December 14). "Ten Values that Help East Asia's Economic Progress, Prosperity." *The Straits Times*, Singapore, Dec. 14.

Kopp, C. B. and Krakow, J. B. (1982). *The Child: Development in a Social Context.* Redding, MA: Addison-Wesley.

Lang, K. and Lang, G. E. (1991). "Theory Development: Studying Events in their Natural Settings." In K. B. Jensen and N. W. Jankowski, eds., *A Handbook of Qualitative Methodologies for Mass Communication Research.* London: Routledge.

Lasn, K. (1999). *Culture Jam: The Uncooling of America^{TM}.* New York: Eagle Brook.

Leymore, V. L. (1975). *Hidden Myth: Structure and Symbolism in Advertising.* New York: Basic Books.

Love, J. F. (1995). *McDonald's: Behind the Arches.* New York: Bantam Books.

Low, I. (1992). "This Clown Needs Help: McDonald's Advertise for Mascot Assistant." *The Business Times*, Singapore, Aug. 20.

Lull, J. (1990). *Inside Family Viewing: Ethnographic Research on Television Audiences.* London: Routledge.

Macklin, M. C. (1985). "Do Younger Children Understand the Selling Intent of Commercials?" *Journal of Consumer Affairs*, 19(2): 293–304.

Mahbubani, K. (1994). "Pacific Community: Fusion of East and West." *The Straits Times*, Singapore, Sept. 17.

McDonald's Restaurants Pte. Ltd. (2000). *Corporate Factsheet – Singapore.* Singapore, July.

McDonald's Restaurants Pte. Ltd. (2001). *Corporate Factsheet – Singapore.* Singapore, Oct.

McNeal, J. U. (1992). *Kids as Consumers: A Handbook of Marketing to Children.* New York: Lexington Books.

McQuail, D. (1997). *Audience Analysis.* Thousand Oaks, CA: Sage.

Meenaghan, T. (1995). "The Role of Advertising in Brand Image Development." *Journal of Product and Brand Management* 4(4): 23–33.

Morley, D. (1992). *Television, Audiences and Cultural Studies.* London: Routledge.

Moschis, G. P. and Linda, G. M. (1986). "Television Advertising and Interpersonal Influences on Teenagers' Participation in Family Consumer Decisions." *Advances in Consumer Research* 13: 181–6.

Nava, M., Blake, A., MacRury, I., and Richards, B. (1997). *Buy This Book: Studies in Advertising and Consumption.* New York and London: Routledge.

Nelson, J. E. (1978). "Children as Information Sources in Family Decision to Eat Out." *Advances in Consumer Research* 6: 419–23.

Noble, G. (1975). *Children in Front of the Small Screen.* Beverly Hills, CA: Sage.

O'Barr, W. M. (1994). *Culture and the Ad: Exploring Otherness in the World of Advertising.* Boulder, CO: Westview Press.

Palmer, P. (1986). *The Lively Audience: A Study of Children Around the TV Set.* Sydney: Allen and Unwin.

Palmer, P. (1988). "The Social Nature of Children's Television Viewing." In P. Drummond and R. Paterson, eds., *Television and its Audience: International Research Perspectives.* London: British Film Institute.

Paul, W. (1994). *Laughing and Screaming: Modern Hollywood Horror and Comedy.* New York: Columbia University Press.

Piaget, J. (1962). *Play, Dreams and Imitation in Childhood.* New York: Norton.

Ritzer, G. (1996). *McDonaldization of Society.* Thousand Oaks, CA: Pine Forge Press.

Robertson, R. (1992). *Globalization: Social Theory and Global Culture.* London: Sage.

Schlosser, E. (2001). *Fast Food Nation: The Dark Side of the All-American Meal.* Boston: Houghton Mifflin.

Seiter, E. (1993). *Sold Separately: Parents and Children in Consumer Culture.* New Brunswick, NJ: Rutgers University Press.

Seiter, E. (1999). *Television and New Media Audiences.* Oxford: Clarendon Press.

Seiter, E., Borchers, H., Kreutzner, G., and Warth, E. M. (1989). " 'Don't treat us like we're so stupid and naïve': Towards an Ethnography of Soap Opera Viewers." In E. Seiter, H. Borchers, G. Kreutzner, and E. Warth, eds., *Remote Control: Television, Audiences, and Cultural Power.* London: Routledge.

Singer, J. L. and Singer D. G. (1981). *Television, Imagination, and Aggression: A Study of Preschoolers.* New Jersey: Lawrence Erlbaum Associates.

Soldow, G. (1983). "The Processing of Information in the Young Consumer." *Journal of Advertising Research* 12(3): 4–14.

Stutts, M. A., and Hunnicutt, G. G. (1987). "Can Young Children Understand Disclaimers in Television Commercials?" *Journal of Advertising* 16(1): 41–6.

Su, H. (1999). "All Things Japanese: Children's TV Viewing and Spending on Imported Cultural Goods in Taiwan." *Asian Journal of Communication* 9(2).

The Sunday Times (2001). June 10. Singapore: Singapore Press Holdings, p. 21.

Tierney, E. O. (1998). "McDonald's in Japan: Changing Manners and Etiquette." In J. L. Watson, ed., *Golden Arches East: McDonald's in East Asia.* Stanford: Stanford University Press.

Unnikrishnan, N. and Bajpai, S. (1998). *The Impact of Television on Children.* New Delhi: Sage.

Wackman, D., Wartella, E., and Ward, S. (1979). *Children's Information Processing of Television Advertising.* Washington, DC: National Science Foundation.

Wartella, E. (1980). "Children and Television: The Development of Child's Understanding of the Medium." In G. Wilhoit and H. deBock, eds., *Mass Communication Review Yearbook.* Beverley Hills, CA: Sage.

Wartella, E. and Ettema, J. (1974). "A Cognitive Developmental Study of Children's Attention to Television Commercials." *Communication Research* 1: 69–89.

Watson, James. L., ed. (1997). *Golden Arches East: McDonald's in East Asia.* Stanford: Stanford University Press.

Wicks, R. H. (2001). *Understanding Audiences: Learning to Use the Media Constructively.* New Jersey and London: Lawrence Erlbaum Associates.

Williamson, J. (1978). *Decoding Advertisements: Ideology and Meaning in Advertising.* London: Marion Boyars.

Wimmer, R. D. and Dominick, J. R. (1994). *Mass Media Research: An Introduction,* 4th ed. Belmont, CA: Wadsworth.

Wong, S. (1991). "Local Flavor for McDonald's Television Image Spots." *Business Times,* Singapore, Oct. 24.

Yan, Y. (1997). "McDonald's in Beijing: The Localization of Americana." In James L. Watson, ed., *Golden Arches East: McDonalds in East Asia.* Stanford: Stanford University Press.

Yuyi, J. W. (1998). "McDonald's in Singapore: Consumption and Meanings." Master's dissertation, Dept. of Sociology, National University of Singapore, 1998.

4

Techno-Orientalization: The Asian VCD Experience

Kelly Hu

Introduction

This chapter applies a case-study approach to the VCD (video compact disk) to bring out the questions of Asian technology, culture, and geography in terms of power relations between the East and the West in the age of globalization. It aims to highlight what Mike Featherstone has well-expressed as follows: "we are becoming aware that the 'orientalization of the world' is a distinct global process – although the task of unpacking the range of cultural associations summoned up by this concept, and their place in the continuing struggles to define the global cultural order, has yet to begin" (Featherstone, 1990: 12). The present survey on VCD is inspired by a concern for the possibilities of orientalization as a global trend, seeking to grasp the diverse trajectories of techno-orientalization of VCDs. Indeed, in what way, to what extent, and how effectively can we map the formation of the orientalization which forms part of globalization? "The decentralization of capitalism from the West" refers to the fact that globalization is basically part of capitalist expansion and thus is not a Western privilege and will not be loyal to the West alone (Tomlinson, 1997: 140). Apart from high-tech Japan, the rise of the "Four Asian tigers" (Taiwan, Hong Kong, Singapore, and South Korea) is frequently proposed as a sign that global capitalism is not located in the West, but something occurring elsewhere in Asia (Tomlinson, 1999: 27; Morley, 1996: 333).

However, Asia is still regarded as an ambiguous area: it may be promising in terms of economic development, but certainly not in its power of cultural capital in a global arena. Fredric Jameson offers the argument that economic power must be associated with the control of cultural production, which is essential to the success of the globalization of American culture (1998: 67). Even though Japan is so well known for its technological and economic power, it never seems explicitly to promote and package its own cultural elements into its products in the world market. "A dominant image of Japan is of a faceless economic superpower with a disproportionate lack of cultural influence upon the world" (Iwabuchi 1998: 65). Thus, how can we understand the fact that the rest of Asia, which holds even less economic capital than the West and Japan, can make its technological culture global?

This chapter outlines the scenarios of techno-orientalization through various practices of Asian VCDs. The VCD, as a peculiarly Asian phenomenon, has largely bypassed the rest of world, thereby complicating the way in which it is culturally signified/marketed in the global context. To see how this has happened, firstly, I will mainly educe my research into the material through the internet site maps that track down the global distribution/circulation of Asian VCDs, so as to understand the interesting encounter of Asian VCDs in the world, particularly with Western countries, in the form of techno-orientalism. To search for VCDs on the internet is to discover the "Asianness" of the VCD in its global representation. In addition, a brief ethnographic portrait of the pirating of VCDs in Hong Kong will call for attention to the pirating reproduction of the digital form from the Asian perspective. I hope that this chapter can effect a useful political strategy of being "off-center" from the West and Japan in order to comprehend the modern Asian mass culture of technological use.

The process of exploring the VCD is a process of seeking a silenced and suppressed Asian identity, in an attempt to provide an alternative to the dominant models of Western-Japanese centered globalization and technological colonization/modernization. It may be best to begin by exploring the internet to find data on Asian VCDs.

Voyaging Through the Internet: Mapping VCDs' "Asianness"

The research materials of this section mostly come from an internet search on VCDs made in 1999. When "VCD" and "Video CD" was put under the classifying system of American Yahoo, it was identified with such keywords as "shopping and services," "retailer," "countries, culture, and group," "Asia"/

"Asian," "Hong Kong"/"Taiwan"/"Japan."[1] Apparently, VCDs had been specified as an "Asian" commodity sold online, but not a universal audio-visual format. Though Yahoo cannot be defined as a truly global search engine, it at least is a way of going beyond Chinese-language cyberspace, bearing in mind that English is a compulsory global language.

The global distribution and visibility of VCD in this survey may appear to construct encounters among countries in the West, rather than among those in Latin America/the Middle East/Africa, in terms of geotechnological/cultural struggles. The method of search for global VCDs on the internet cannot avoid making use of a global cyberspace in English, which, by ignoring other languages of the world, appears to discriminate in favor of users who have English ability. However, such a limitation in my research exactly points out the inequality which still exists between the West and the rest in the process of globalization. It also reveals that the global traveling of VCDs may have had earlier contact with the West, especially North America, due to the relatively larger diasporic Asian populations there. The internet still admits that Asian ethnic minorities in the West have a global presence in the trading of VCDs. A few cyberbusinesses with global marketing appeal provide entries describing what a VCD is, how to use VCDs, and why VCD technology can be categorized as "Asian." For example, in "setting up a VCD Info Center," coolvcd.com introduces the VCD as "a compact disc that plays movies instead of music." A single disk can play for up to 74 minutes, "so a typical movie will be held in two compact discs that are packaged in a single jewel case." The "VCD Info Center" indicates that VCDs can be played on VCD players which are popular only in Asia. However, the alternatives are a PC with proper CD-ROM/DVD-ROM equipment, and DVD players, though not all DVD players are compatible with VCDs.

In addition, the "VCD Info Center" also functions as the Asian cultural tour guide for unfamiliar Western consumers. It reports that people living in Western countries can obtain VCDs in Chinatown or computer fairs. Many VCDs are Asian imports with subtitles in Chinese, Thai, or Malay, but care is required since it seems that many of them are bootlegged. Here the Asian images of the VCD are clearly affirmed, as they are closely associated with the landmark of Chinatowns, Asian languages, and the notorious Asian piracy practices.

Another VCD cybershop, simplyvcd.com, claims that VCDs are very popular in Asia, while they are in the ascendant in the US, Europe, and Australia because of the transnational interest in Hong Kong movies.[2] I had email contact with Russil Wong,[3] the web maintainer of both Video CD

FAQ and Video CD Q&A Forum.[4] He told me that his fascination with Hong Kong movies drove him to collect materials about VCDs and to create two web stations, as mentioned above, to deal with questions about VCDs. Video CD FAQ has provided several links to internet websites which sell Hong Kong VCD movies. Wong admits that information for the site Video CD FAQ is mostly directed towards Hong Kong movie fans outside Asia who have no easy access to Hong Kong movies. It reveals that the VCD cannot escape from the category of being "Asian," since part of the global attraction of VCDs is their Asian movie content.

The establishment of Video CD FAQ and Video CD Q&A Forum by Wong, a Canadian-born Chinese, further implies that, on the one hand, VCD has become associated with diasporic Chinese audiences and the global dispersal of Hong Kong VCD movies; on the other hand, Asians who have become used to abundant VCDs around them do not seem eager to build up knowledge and power over VCDs in cyberspace in English. In contrast, DVD FAQ on the internet claims to be an official website since it is in a form of an authority with links to various countries and translations. Jim Taylor, who maintains it, told me from his base in America that "it has been approved by the news.answers_moderators as an FAQ for the DVD newsgroups."[5]

It is interesting to see that the cybermapping of VCD more or less reflects that VCDs, though invented by Sony, Panasonic, and Philips in 1993, are indeed ignored in the West. Launched in early 1997, DVD received strong and widespread support from leading consumer electronics giants, Hollywood home video studios, and music video markets. For instance, a "Los Angeles-based, industry funded non-profit corporation" named "the DVD Video Group" aimed at marketing the DVD Video format as "the next generation of home entertainment in North America."[6] DVD in particular, endowed with antipiracy and zone locks functions, is a more advanced audiovisual technology with higher picture quality than VCD, which remains unregulated.[7] With a quite different development from DVDs, the emergence of VCDs in Asia since the mid-1990s has been a historical process which was not initiated by a well-planned global marketing project. Instead, it unexpectedly coincided as an irresistible tendency, pushed by the new wave of local audiovisual companies' interests in the cost-effectiveness of VCD and the burgeoning VCD-pirating industry in Asia.

The operation offices of online VCD stores mentioned earlier – coolvcd.com and simplyvcd.com – are both based in Penang, Malaysia. According to the survey in 1999, some of the online VCD stores come from

Asia, while others are established in America. Besides, my email contacts, including a few online VCD retailers and sources of VCD shopping information offered by Russil Wong's Video CD FAQ, indicate that the online VCD markets are mostly dominated by Asians, especially ethnic Chinese.[8] Most of them are Chinese living in America who have close business connections with Chinese people in Asia.

The cyber VCD shops have global shipping services for global consumers. VCDs sold online usually are not limited to Asian content; Hollywood VCD movies made in Asia with Asian subtitles removed can be alternative attractions, considering that they cost less than DVDs. "Our customer profile is about 60% Asian, 70% of whom are in the domestic US," says Paul Cheung, a Chinese American from Sasa_VCD.com, the site of one of the online VCD stores based in Los Angeles that promotes audiovisual products from Taiwan, Hong Kong, and China.[9] It seems that diasporic Asian audiences, particularly those who have stayed in America, are mainly targeted, but there are a certain number of non-Asian audiences.

In the case study of online VCD shops, VCD is connected to Asia through Asian business links, working through the global interconnections of transnational consumption. In line with Asian audiovisual products and as an Asian technology, VCDs spread out through the movements of Asian populations. Like the global penetration of Hong Kong videos in David Bordwell's observation, the movement of VCDs can be traced along similar routes – from the tiny Chinese VCD shops, Chinese restaurants, Chinese food stores, and even Chinese beauty salons (2000: 83). Moreover, it is reported that most Hong Kong video stores in America always stock both "licensed and pirated videos with few objections from consumers regarding quality and legality" (Wong, 1999: 96). Thus it is not too hard to see how pirated VCDs, due to their miniaturization and lightness, could be more easily disseminated than pirated videos. In my personal experience while studying in the University of Birmingham from 1997 to 2001, ethnic Chinese students from Taiwan, Hong Kong, China, Singapore, and Malaysia constantly exchanged imported pirated and legal VCDs from Asia. It appears that pirated VCDs, together with legal ones, are circulating in both commercial and private systems among Asians all over the world.

The concept of "marginal imperialism" proposed by Ding Tzann Lii (1998) and applied in the capitalist expansion of Hong Kong movies may be helpful to our understanding of the global distribution of VCDs. Marginal imperialism "emerges at the margins of the world system, and occurs primarily within third world countries" (ibid.: 125). Lii points out that Hong Kong movies can be an example of marginal imperialism – they do not, as Hollywood movies do, represent a kind of Western capitalist hegemony which has overall power in the world system.

> I contend that periphery media, exemplified by Hong Kong movies, serve to regionalize and to localize, not to continue the global expansion of capitalism. The process of localization (Asianization) and regionalization here mainly derives from Hong Kong's marginality in being a colony and a periphery country. (Lii, 1998: 135)

By denying Hong Kong's ability to be globally imperial like the West, Lii almost equates the idea of marginal imperialism with local and regional Asianization of the Hong Kong film industry. From this perspective it is difficult to recognize it as "global." Sun Ge also points out that Asia's marginal situation makes it hard to see it as a legitimate part of the history of globalization:

> Undeniably, in the narration of globalization carried out from the perspectives of the West today, the idealistic nature narrating Asia is being concealed, and its position in the world history is not clear. (Sun 2000: 336)

Thus, how can Asia be (re)discovered as participating in contemporary globalization? The "normalization" of VCD consumption takes highly specific and "otherly" forms: through Asian networking, volatile medium/small-size retailers/wholesalers, and underground piracy. That is, such a global expansion of Asian VCDs can be differentiated from the Western type of powerful transnational corporatism, authorized legality, and the nonnecessity of ethnic operations.

The Ambiguities of Techno Self-Orientalism

The fact that VCDs dominate the market in Asia has not apparently gained much attention from the rest of world. However, a North American-based internet company, Query, tried to promote VCDs by fighting against DVDs. It was the time when VCDs were overwhelming many Asian countries, while DVDs, backed mainly by America, had gradually penetrated into the global market. Query is a company which promotes their specific software, enabling VCDs to be automatically connected to the internet. Query spares no effort in advertising VCDs for audiovisual business presentations instead of movie entertainment. It seeks to persuade "professional video production houses, advertising agencies, web designers, corporations, governments and anyone else who wants to communicate with their clients, effectively and inexpensively."[10] Query makes it clear that they aggressively oppose the DVDs favored by North America, listing 45 reasons against them. The company may be afraid that conditions for marketing at DVD standard seem to be buoyant in North America, so that the acceptance of DVDs, including computer DVD-ROMs, for various kinds of uses will be strengthened. They state that "DVD is OVERKILL as a digital corporate communications medium."[11]

Even though Query no longer exists in 2003, its emergence marks a specific moment in the history of contemporary audiovisual consumer technologies, with its fragmentation and differentiation through which VCD is introduced to the West as a popular Asian technology (even though it was not conventionally and initially launched in the West). The following promotional texts by Query may reveal the way in which the West comprehends an oriental technology such as VCD.

Video CD is massive in Asia[12]
The middle classes in China and India are now massively embracing Video CD 2.0[13] because of its ease of use and cost-effectiveness. Video CD technology has leap-frogged VHS and Audio CD technology in these countries. The economies of scale in producing electronic equipment for these two countries are overwhelming, making Video CD extremely cost-effective in the developed world. In fact, the installed base of Video CD players worldwide is approaching 55 million. In China alone, there were 15 million Video CD players sold in 1997 and projections are 40 million for 1998.

Why Haven't You Seen Video CD 2.0 in North America Yet?
There are only 300 million people in North America. What we buy is irrelevant from *a global perspective.*[14]

*   *   *

Microsoft's VENUS project in China links VCD and Super VCD,[15] not DVD; with Windows CE "Web-TV type" device control for sale into the largest consumer market in the world that is China. – Strike 14[16]

India, China, Indonesia and other Asian countries with over 1/2 the world's population are massively buying Video CD and they are now setting the new *global* digital format standards. They can afford VCD. They can't afford DVD. – Strike 18[17]

The economic crisis in Asia has made DVD-video players and DVD production equipment a very difficult sale. – Strike 43

As Query emphasizes, since 1999, Microsoft in partnership with some Chinese computer technology companies has been promoting the cheaper "Web TV" named the "Venus project," which is designed exclusively for China, by incorporating VCD, SVCD, TV watching, and internet as part of its multiple functions. This is a good moment, as the advertisement implies, to learn from Microsoft by associating VCD and SVCD with possible business benefits from Asia. In addition, the Asian economic crisis in the late 1990s makes it very difficult for Asians to purchase the more expensive DVDs and DVD players, which suggests that VCD will be the preferred choice for the Asian markets.

Query's online advertising discourses typify the way in which the West is imagining Asia through VCD, constructing what the West sees as a techno-orientalism targeted at Asia beyond Japan. The review of "Techno-Orientalism: Japanese Panic" written by David Morley and Kevin Robins will be the basis for a further configuration of a different kind of techno-orientalism implied in Query's advertising texts (1995: 147–53). Morley and Robins' article addresses the contradiction and opposition between the West as the master and Japan as the Orient/the Other. The West always considers itself as the privileged forerunner of modernity and technology. Japan's triumph in economically and technologically dominating the world triggered the West's anxiety and resentment towards Japan.

Through various examples, Morley and Robins show how the West attempts to relegate, mystify, and orientalize Japan. The West perceives that Japanese electronics transnational companies, such as Sony and Matsushita, are involved in the Hollywood entertainment industries with the purpose of controlling both the technological software and the hardware markets. Hollywood self-defensively claims that American values are multicultural and open-minded, while Japanese culture is looked down on as being conservative, homogenous, and not global enough from the "self-centered" American perspective. The aim of such oriental discourse is to avert Japanese capitalist investment which might influence Hollywood movie-making decisions and damage American culture.

Further, the recognition of Japanese high-tech portrays Japan as a figure of "cold, impersonal and machine-like" technological power (1995: 169). Marilyn Ivy also describes the way in which Japan is perceived with an oriental intention in America: "the news presents a repetitive and reconfirming scenario of Japan as a sign of impossible, dehumanized productivity, of dystopic capitalism" (1989: 21). That is, in its fear of losing its leading role, the West must deny Japan by constructing it as alien and abnormal in order to sustain its accustomed legitimacy.

Though I agree with most of Morley and Robins' conclusions, I think that the authors perhaps are unconsciously trapped in a stereotypical Western scenario – the "Orient," the "Other" as a counterpart to the technological supremacy of the West, which has not yet gone beyond the category of "Japan." According to Morley and Robins' critique, the narrative structure of techno-orientalism leaves no room for anything other than Japan and the West. What the West can see is only Japan, while the rest of world, including Asia, is not considered as its equivalent. To some extent, Morley and Robins' accounts of techno-orientalism confirms that in the area of audiovisual high-tech, Japan and the West are the two biggest players in competition.

Query's advertisement proposing an Asian version of techno-orientalism challenges the "Japan-only" model of techno-orientalism. As a North American company promoting VCD technology, Query does not necessarily act like a typical chauvinistic techno-orientalist who deliberately debases Oriental technologies. Query at least acknowledges that VCD is a cheap, low-cost, and convenient technology which is embraced by Asia – this is why Query promoted VCD as a good format for business communication for North Americans.

The link between Asia and VCD follows a different trajectory from the conceptualization of Japan and high-tech. We can see how Query's tactics of associating VCD with Asia in a form of orientalism are intricately entangled with the feelings of evaluation and degradation. Query attempts to persuade North Americans to take up the Asian practice of developing cost-effective forms of Asian technology, of which VCDs are the convenient, cheap, profitable, and prolific choice. The short note under the topic "Haven't You Seen Video CD 2.0 in North America Yet?" suggests that the notion of the "global" displaced by the huge population of Asia risks subverting and weakening the dominant role of North America. North Americans should be aware of the possibility that the developing populous Asian countries such as China, India, and Indonesia could "[set] global digital format standards" exactly because of their huge population.

Paradoxically, such recognition of the global position of VCD and Asia arouses a mixture of threats and hidden imperial capitalist ambitions. In the first place, the advertising discourses seem to tease North Americans, who are in danger of being excluded from the global trends of VCDs in Asia, where they will be bought by the largest consumer populations in the world. At the same time, they remind North American businessmen who deal with information/audiovisual consumer technology of the advantages of adopting VCD as their software if they want to extend their transnational capital connections to Asia. Acknowledging VCD as an Asian technology embedded in the Western imperialistic mind is realistically helpful in the exploitation of big Asian consumer markets.

Query's Asian version of techno-orientalism reveals the ambiguous power relations between the West and the East. The West is still privileged to stand in a higher position to devalue the Orient and the technology which it adopts. Query emphasizes the need to come to terms with the profitable economic reality of Asian VCD mass culture, constituted by the large population, though this does not mean that Asia has gained supremacy over global technological capital. To the contrary, what is highlighted is the debased impression that Asia, stricken by economic storms, cannot afford expensive and high-tech DVD. The global status which Asia and VCD have in mind is not the capital of technological innovations ruled by wealthy Japanese/Western-integrated transnational corporations, but the capital of local-regional production and consumerism depending on low-cost economies and even pirate capitalism. Asia is still an incomprehensible and unidentifiable Oriental Other, which is abruptly reduced to masses of populations relevant to a productive birth-rate but not the production of high-tech inventions. Asia and VCDs are mildly threatening, but are not yet as assertively imperialistic and competitive as Japan is, nor do they evoke as much revulsion in the Western psyche.

Morley and Robins' reflections on Western techno-orientalism make use of Japan to criticize Western knowledge which legitimates the West as the only agent which can take modernity forward. Their criticism is significant in that it questions Western modernity, which is generally considered as a universalized paradigm by revealing to us how Japan has been twisted by the West. It is a pity that in their article Morley and Robins do not further develop what they have to say about the uniqueness of Japanese high-tech modernity. That is, Japan becomes for the writers an object with which to defy Western hegemony, but they have not yet surveyed it in its subjectivity. The Asian VCD experiences shown in the present chapter in a sense attempt to avoid treating Asia as an empty object without a grounded study.

In the next section, I will discuss the logic of pirate VCD consumption in Hong Kong, which may provide a clearer picture of the uses of technology in Asia. Nevertheless, it should be noted here that the Hong Kong VCD phenomenon is not meant to be extended to a comprehensive account of the Asian VCD phenomenon, since there is probably diversity in the local meaning-making of VCD consumption in different Asian societies.

In an Age of Digital Overproduction:
The Hong Kong Perspectives

Being more mobile and convenient, and less expensive and heavy, than video is, the VCD demonstrates the coming of a new age of digital reproduction. Unlike DVD, which is endowed with a strict antipiracy corporate purpose, VCD is basically anarchic, lending itself to being copied either at home or by the pirate market. The rampant VCD piracy in Asia reinforces the irrational and abundant translocal/transnational flow of VCDs. Of course, this does not mean that Asia does not have legal VCD markets as well. Taking Hong Kong and Taiwan as instances, VCDs are also sold in local, legitimate VCD/DVD shops.

The pervasiveness of unruly VCDs in Asia leads to a question about the way in which digital reproduction reinvents a new space of mass cultural consumption with a different artistic value of judgment. During my stay in Hong Kong from October 1998 to June 1999, I experienced the most turbulent time of VCD piracy. Despite the pressures from crackdown by the Hong Kong government on VCD piracy, piracy in Hong Kong at that time can be regarded as a revolutionary process, which stimulated the legal VCD market structure to achieve a fair price standard and quick releases in order to compete with pirate sales. In Hong Kong, pirated VCDs have gradually disappeared since 2000, and legal VCDs have become normalized, with reasonable prices (averaging US$2 to $7 each). Even though VCD piracy in Hong Kong is no longer at a boiling point, pirated VCD consumption still needs to be closely examined, as it has transformed both the commodity and the cultural value of audiovisual products in digital form.

The majority of pirated VCDs in Hong Kong include movies, Japanese TV dramas, and Japanese adult videos. Here I will concentrate on a discussion of VCD movies in general. In the Hong Kong pirated VCD market, it is not too difficult to find bad-quality pirated VCDs, though some pirated VCDs are sophisticated enough. A theater copy of a VCD movie is made when someone sneaks a camcorder into the theater or the projectionist films the movie. The screen in a theater copy of a VCD movie usually looks shaky, carrying the shadows of the heads or bodies of the audience. In the worst cases there is even excessive audience noise, including laughter, coughs, and speech. Since the possibility of buying a low-quality VCD movie is high, can we attach any significance to the extreme tolerance of pirated VCD consumers in Hong Kong?

Centering on the topic of daily VCD consumption, I held many conversations with working staff and students in their early twenties to thirties in the Department of Cinema and TV, Hong Kong Baptist University, and some of my Hong Kong friends from late 1998 to mid-1999. Sara, an undergraduate student, told me that she did not care if she got a low-quality VCD since it cost too little to worry about or she could always ask for another copy. She noted that Hong Kong people are always keen on high speed, which confirms one aspect of Hong Kong metropolitan culture. Like Sara, Ellis, a young technician, echoed the idea that being "quick" and "cheap" are two compulsive reasons for Hong Kong devotees to embrace pirated VCDs. Tong, a cultural critic and a friend of mine, also indicated that the picture quality of pirated VCDs is not a big issue for consumers deciding whether to buy, since consumers would not be too fastidious in light of the low price. If the movie was one which people knew they wanted to watch, they would do so in a movie theater. In addition, the Asian economic crisis in the late 1990s deeply depressed the morale of the Hong Kong economy. Pirated VCDs offered low-cost entertainment which consumers were happy with.

Pirated VCDs meet the tastes/requirements of the audiences for movies and lure them to buy satisfaction with their lower price. Pirated VCDs also provide an alternative to the expensive movie ticket, which has reshaped the audience's calculation of the value of a movie, and in a subversive sense it does empower them to reject the legal channels of movie releases at higher cost. On the one hand, pirated VCDs upset the monopoly of the film/video distribution industries, especially with Hong Kong's resistance to the high price of a movie ticket. On the other hand, they reinforce the crippling power of pirated organizations over VCD consumers. As a result, people are locked into being contented with banal movies with banal images exploited by pirated VCD businessmen. Consequently, VCD movies are debased to the point of being disposable because of their cheapness and superabundance.

Nearly a century ago Walter Benjamin developed a profound perception of the changing nature of art as it encountered the emergence of mechanical reproductions at the time. Benjamin raised important issues about the association between technological reproduction and the rise of mass culture. He observed that the "uniqueness" and "permanence" in the aura of traditional art was declining and gradually being replaced by the "transitoriness" and "reproducibility" of mass cultural products (Benjamin, 1970: 225). In the early twentieth century, Western modernity exploiting the technology of mass reproduction inspired Benjamin to reach these insights. Today the digital duplications of VCDs in Asia continue to bring up challenging issues which impel us to pay attention to the development of Asian modernity in an age of digital overproduction.

Distorted versions of various pirated VCDs cannot even be categorized as mechanical reproduction of art "of the kind which at least makes monotonous and standard copies" (Benjamin, 1970: 223), leaving aside the "authenticity" or mysterious "aura" which Benjamin says traditional art possesses. "Piracy calls attention to the truncated life of the entertainment commodity" (Yau, 2000). Indeed digital technology strengthens pirated productions, which makes the images exceedingly uncontrolled and ephemeral. In addition, the consumption of pirated VCDs in Hong Kong shows that there is no guarantee that the technological revolution will necessarily make enough "progress" on the part of mass culture to pursue a better quality of image. In fact it, in turn, interrogates the significance of the legitimate version of image. The primary need of the Hong Kong audience is not an original image made according to a professional standard through lavish high-tech audiovisual equipment and setting – whether the product is authentic or superior, in the first place, is simply not considered.

The general criticisms of the "low taste" of pirated VCDs in Hong Kong public space were made in formal and official demonstrations, which did not upset or threaten the consumers' fondness for pirated VCDs. Whether the consumption of pirated VCDs is an act of low taste or not is not a significant issue to be seriously concerned about. Instead low price, convenience, instant availability, and fluidity are the priorities. The eradication of the pirated VCD organizations by Hong Kong customs and the consequent price-cutting in the legal VCD market are the only means to effectively stop consumers from buying pirated VCDs. Such a populist mentality in accepting pirated VCDs signifies that "careless viewing" and "not-so-serious attitudes" towards the image are reinforced in the impulse to pirate digital duplications. Evidently Hong Kong people need cinematic distractions but do not feel like cherishing the art of the movie; they wish only to pay the least.

Conclusion: The Implications of Techno-Orientalization

This chapter has traveled from the global to the local, in the hope of providing a contextual understanding of Asian VCD experiences. The techno-orientalization exemplified in the development of the VCD proves to be embodied in the process of globalization and modernization in Asia. The global images and representations of Asia and VCDs are very much bound by Asian styles and practices, such as Asian diasporic connections, crimes, piracy, Chinatowns, massive population, and low-cost technology.

How to make sense of the situation? First of all, this has something to do with geographic-cultural-economic power struggles between the West and the East. The particularity of the Orient is constructed through difference, in contrast with the West, under the condition that Western knowledge and practices operate as if they were universal. For example, the need to add a brief explanation of VCD technology in an article of this kind, written in English for international readers, has exposed the global status of the VCD as relatively unknown and exotic. Nowadays Hollywood DVD movies can exist permanently in comparatively rich Asian societies such as Taiwan, Hong Kong, Singapore, and the big cities of China, without having to rely heavily on ethnic links for promotion. They can legitimately and safely be displayed in the transnational Blockbusters/HMV chain stores, rather than having to be harbored with VCDs in the guerrilla types of cyber-retailer business.

Secondly, this VCD survey should not be mistaken for the result of self-orientalization, but rather as a reminder of the Asian way of capitalist production and consumption, operating with its own distinctive kind of cultural logic, which should not be underestimated. As Aihwa Ong indicates, "many Asian countries are not interested in colonialism or post-colonialism" and "are in the process of constructing alternative modernities based on relations with their populations, with capital and with the West" (1999: 35). The Asian VCD experiences can be seen as a way in which Asians are exercising "flexibility" to "accumulate power and capital" and "to react fluidly and opportunistically" (ibid.: 6).

The fact that VCD technology is self-sustaining in the Asian region, but is alien to people living in the non-Asian area, questions the concept of globalization that reduces the rest of the world to having to "establish its position relative to the capitalistic West – to use Robertson's term, [having to] . . . relativize itself" (Walters, 1995: 3). The VCD stores in Asia have given warning – we should not be trapped in a globalization theory which is "a predominantly white/First World take on things" (Massey, 1994: 165). The Asian VCD phenomenon is a good example to challenge the popular idea that the origin of globalization of any kind is either from the West or entirely manipulated by legitimate transnational corporations.

But what do Asia and the VCD matter, if most local Asians are not aware of the image of Asia implied by VCDs? My intention here is not to set up a collective Asian identity for VCDs which Asians could recognize, or to demonstrate the triumph of Asia to non-Asians. Rather I think it significant to bridge the gap in sensibility and mutual understanding of the VCD between Asians and non-Asians, and I want to offer a wider angle for rethinking inter- and intra-technocultural flows at an international level. Proposing the VCD as an Asian technology was meant to invite attention to the ways in which Asian countries are undergoing constant and intimate exchanges based on local-regional transnational capitalism and shared cost-effective consumer technologies/cultures.

The geographical and spatial separation of VCD uses in Asia from those in the rest of the world reveals contradictions, uncertainty, and unevenness, as a consequence of diversifying globalizing imperatives. Efforts are made in VCD research to unveil an Asian mentality and its mechanisms, as a contrast with those of the West, which "may effectively help to put the other, and the sense of a global circumstance, on the agenda" (Featherstone, 1991: 127). It is hoped that this brief study of VCDs can generate reflections on the real practices of globalization and consumerism in and from Asia, and that these reflections will alter the traditional ways of invoking Asia as an object without its own (necessarily fractured) subjectivities.

Notes

1 Retrieved Oct. 19, 1999, from http://www.yahoo.com/. "VCD" and "Video CD" in American Yahoo.

2 Retrieved July 3, 2003, from http://www.simplyvcd.com/faqs.htm.

3 Personal email contact with Russil Wvong, April 13, 1999.

4 Video CD FAQ, retrieved July 3, 2003, from http://www.geocities.com/Athens/Forum/2496/vcdfaq.html; Video CD Q&A Forum retrieved July 3, 2003, from http://www.greenspun.com/bboard/q-and-a.tcl?topic=Video%20CD.

5 Personal email contact with Jim Taylor, April 23, 1999. DVD FAQ was retrieved July 3, 2003, from http://www.thedigitalbits.com/officialfaq.html.

6 Retrieved April 18, 1999, from http://www.dvdvideogroup.com/group/index.html.

7 Retrieved May 3, 1999, from http://www.unik.no/~robert/hifi/dvd/survey/. According to this website, DVD zone-locking "is a feature proposed by the movie industry that makes it impossible to play movies, music or computer software released in one country or 'zone' on a player in another country." There are 8 DVD code zones in the world. However, the DVD zone lock does not effectively achieve its corporate purpose, as many countries currently sell multizone VD players.

8 On October 19, 1999, searching under the category "VCD" revealed that 40 sites relevant to "VCD" were available in cyberspace. However, only 18 websites met my objective of being VCD-related businesses. Currently (July 28, 2003) there are 2,160,000 results in the survey of "VCD." Thus it becomes hard to track down the VCD-related websites one by one. However, if one searches

by "VCD store," the results are reduced to 154,000. The trading of VCDs seems to be expanding surprisingly throughout cyberspace.

9 Personal email contact with Paul Cheung, Sept. 4, 1999.

10 Retrieved July 23, 1999, from http://www.videocd2.com.

11 Retrieved July 23, 1999, from http://www.videocd2.com.

12 "Video CD is Massive in Asia" and "Why Have You Seen Video CD 2.0 in North America Yet?" in "Where is Video CD 2.0?" retrieved July 23, 1999, from http://www.videocd2.com/videocd_2/where_is_vcd.html.

13 Video CD 2.0 was introduced in 1995; it has greater picture quality and works more smoothly than Video CD 1.1, which was first launched in 1993.

14 Italics added for the purpose of emphasis.

15 According to Jukka Aho, "*Super Video CD* (aka *SVCD*, *Super VCD* or *Chaoji VCD*) is an enhancement to Video CD that was developed by a Chinese government-backed committee of manufacturers and researchers, partly to sidestep DVD technology royalties and partly to create pressure for lower DVD player and disc prices in China." Retrieved May 21, 2001, from http://www.uwasa.fi/~f76998/video/svcd/overview/#history. SVCD was invented in 1998 and inspired by the success of VCD in China.

16 "Strike 14" was retrieved from http://www.videocd2.com/dvd/dvd.html, July 23, 1999. It and the following 2 items, "Strike 18" and "Strike 43," all come from "45 Reasons Against DVD."

17 Italics added for the purpose of emphasis.

References

Benjamin, W. (1970). *Illuminations.* London: Collins/Fontana.

Bordwell, D. (2000). *Planet Hong Kong: Popular Cinema and the Art of Entertainment.* Cambridge, MA: Harvard University Press.

Featherstone, M. (1990). *Global Culture: Nationalism, Globalization and Modernity.* London: Sage.

Featherstone, M. (1991). *Consumer Culture and Postmodernism.* London: Sage.

Iwabuchi, K. (1998). "Marketing 'Japan': Japanese Cultural Presence under a Global Gaze." *Japanese Studies* 18(2): 165–80.

Ivy, M. (1989). "Critical Texts, Mass Artifacts: The Consumption of Knowledge in Postmodern Japan." In M. Miyoshi and H. D. Harrotunian, eds., *Postmodernism and Japan.* Durham and London: Duke University Press.

Jameson, F. (1998). "Notes on Globalization as a Philosophical Issue." In F. Jameson and M. Miyoshi, eds., *The Cultures of Globalization.* Durham and London: Duke University Press, 54–77.

Lii, D.-T. (1998). "A Colonized Empire: Reflections on the Expansion of Hong Kong Films in Asian Countries." In K.-H. Chen, ed., *Trajectories: Inter-Asia Cultural Studies.* London and New York: Routledge, 122–41.

Massey, D. (1994). *Space, Place and Gender*. Cambridge: Polity.

Morley, D. (1996). "EurAm, Modernity, Reason and Alternity or, Postmodernism, the Highest Stage of Cultural Imperialism?" In D. Morley and K.-H. Chen, eds., *Stuart Hall: Critical Dialogues in Cultural Studies*. London and New York: Routledge, 326–60.

Morley, D. and Robins, K. (1995). *Spaces of Identity: Global Media, Electronic Landscapes and Cultural Boundaries*. London and New York: Routledge.

Ong, A. (1999). *Flexible Citizenship: The Cultural Logics of Transnationality*. Durham and London: Duke University Press.

Sun, G. (2000). "How does Asia Mean? (Part 1)," tr. S.-L. Hui and K. Lau. *Inter-Asia Cultural Studies* 1(1): 13–47.

Tomlinson, J. (1997). "Internationalism, Globalization and Cultural Imperialism." In K. Thompson, ed., *Media and Cultural Regulation*. London: Sage, 117–53.

Tomlinson, J. (1999). "Globalized Culture: The Triumph of the West?" In T. Skelton and T. Allen, eds., *Culture and Global Change*. London: Sage, 22–9.

Walters, M. (1995). *Globalization*. London: Routledge.

Wong, C. (1999). "Cities, Cultures and Cassettes: Hong Kong Cinema and Transnational Audiences." *Postscript* 19(1): 87–106.

Yau, E. (2000). "The Young and the Dangerous: Re-viewing Hong Kong Cinema." A paper presented at the conference "Year 2000 and Beyond: History, Technology and Future of Transnational Chinese Film and Television," Hong Kong Baptist University, April 19–22.

Part II

Moving Backward,
Moving Forward:
Histories and Politics

5

The Struggle for Press Freedom and Emergence of "Unelected" Media Power in South Korea

Myung-koo Kang

Introduction

Over 50 years after liberation from Japanese colonial rule (1945), South Korean society today faces the two following major tasks: the realization of national reunification and a democratic political order as the completion of a modern society; and the rectification of economic inequality as the material basis for the accomplishment of a modern national community. South Korean society's efforts to solve these national problems, however, are being suppressed or distorted internally by the control strategy of those with vested political and economic rights and externally by changes in international conditions including the emergence of neoconservatism and the global expansion of the movement of capital.

For long, the civil society was subsumed in the sphere of the state, which had grown excessively following the Liberation. It finally seemed to acquire autonomy, with the Democratization Struggle of June 1987 as the opportunity. Due to the alliance between the state and capital and to the desertion of the civil society by the conservative middle class, however, democratization in South Korean society is lagging behind, without having established democratic institutions and practices. Moreover, with economic crisis, the social proposition that South Korean democracy must be strengthened has been forgotten and the social 20/80 divide of well off versus poor has worsened. Consequently, while the general public feels that it must fend solely for itself, the government and the press are responding to such sentiments with neoliberal policies.

Economic power (formed during a state-driven modernization period with corrupt politicians and conglomerates [*chaebul*] as key players), through a premodern collusion of politics and economics, has seized the social decision-making process and suppressed and distorted increasing demands for political and economic democratization. The middle class of South Korean civil society, who had been the main actors in the Democratization Struggle (Rim, 1994; Rim & Song, 1993), have downgraded themselves to bystanders in an antidemocratic political order by contentedly settling down as the passive supporters of the ruling class (Sohn, 1999). In this situation, it is meaningless merely to describe delayed democratization and the middle class's degradation as bystanders in the civil society. Rather, it is more meaningful to ask why circumstances have changed thus. In other words, it is important to examine why the South Korean middle class since 1987 have concurred with the ruling class in amending political and economic crisis and contentedly settled down within the existing order. Regarding such questions, the present chapter claims that: (1) a conservative alliance consisting of political power, the bureaucracy, and the conservative press has played a crucial role in suppressing democratization in the civil society in the 1990s; and (2) the press, instead of monitoring political power, has itself become an organ of power.

In South Korean society, the press occupies a truly peculiar position. Of course in any society the press forms an order of words and writing with different forms and contents, depending on the relationship between the state and the civil society. In the formation of the modern society, however, newspapers, broadcasting, and journalism in South Korea occupy a position that is both peculiar and distinct from that in Western and Asian societies. In the West, the American press has greater social influence than does the European press. This is because, in Europe, the degree to which the conflict between citizens' interests and various interest groups in society converges through party politics is greater than it is in the United States; this lacuna is filled by the press in the latter.

While it is largely closer to the American model, the press in South Korea is increasingly reigning over the civil society together with corrupt and conservative politicians, instead of focusing the various interests and conflicts in the civil society and linking them to the political society. This aspect of the South Korean press may be called a history of struggle for the freedom of the press from the Liberation to 1987, and one of the press's transformation into an organ of power since then. This chapter will examine that change through an examination of the relationships among the state, civil society, and the press of South Korea; and, through an analysis of the role played by the press in the process through which democracy has come to be consolidated in South Korean society, explicate the rise of journalistic power.

The Place of the Press in the Relationship between the State and the Civil Society

Under Japanese colonial rule, the Korean press resisted and collaborated with the authorities at the same time. As the colonial masters, the Japanese imperialists founded newspapers and magazines according to their own needs, and sought to win over as collaborators in colonial rule the nationalist press established by Koreans (Kim, 1999). On the other hand, the nationalist press, as a tool of Korean resistance for the recovery national independence, was active both on the peninsula and abroad. The press in colonial Korea therefore had a history of oppression by the colonial masters, collaboration with the Japanese authorities, and struggle for the Korean people (Kim, 1978; Jung, 1985).

The partition and occupation of the peninsula by the United States and the Soviet Union and the consequent conflict between right-wing and left-wing Koreans following the Liberation served to distort the normal growth of the press in the process of the formation of a modern nation-state in postcolonial Korea. With the national division, the left-wing press all but disappeared in South Korea. From then on, North Korea forged the press as a tool of a powerful socialist system, while South Korea, now ideologically one-sided, saw the establishment of a distorted form of commercial press as an institution in the formation of a postcolonial, modern nation-state. As long as the national division continues, the bulk of studies on the history of the press in modern Korea will have to deal with the South Korean press alone.

Due to the anticommunist policy of the US Army Military Government in Korea (USAMGIK), the nationalist and socialist press disappeared from South Korea. With the subsequent establishment of Syngman Rhee's regime, which was based on former pro-Japanese collaborators, the South Korean press lost its chance to liquidate pro-Japanese remnants. Moreover, journalists who had struggled for national liberation had nowhere to go. With the outbreak of the Korean War (1950–3), pro-Japanese elements in the press ceased to be a problem. With the foundation in 1951 of the Hankook Ilbo as the starting point, Korean newspapers became commercialized. (See table 5.1 for a summary of the history of the South Korean press.)

Table 5.1: Changes in the social characteristics of the South Korean press following the Liberation

Period	Relationship	Nature of journalism	Journalist's role
1910–45	Pro-Japanese colonial press and the resistance of the nationalist press	Means of both colonial rule and anticolonial struggle	Anticolonial nationalistic activist and pro-colonial collaborator
1945–60	Extinction of the leftist press and the emergence of the commercial press	Formation of modern, postcolonial journalism	Collaborator in the formation of a modern nation-state
1960–72	Mouthpiece of modernization	Development journalism	Educator of modernization
1972–86	Mouthpiece of dictatorship	Propaganda journalism	Propagandist of dictatorship
1987–92	Mouthpiece of dictatorship	Propaganda journalism	Propagandist of authoritarian regimes
1993 to present	Collusion of the state and journalistic capital	Populist mobilization of public opinion	Populist opinion leader

With the April 19 Student Revolution of 1960, South Korean society momentarily regained freedom of the press. The strategy of economic modernization implemented by the May 16 Military Revolution of 1961 and the subsequent military regime, however, demanded that the press serve as a mouthpiece of modernization. In the last years of the Chosun Dynasty, the press had likewise been required to play the role of modernist educator. In this era of new (economic) modernization, radio and television broadcasting were especially dependable tools. As the military elite, who had strongly proceeded with economic modernization, became corrupt, and as the Park Chung Hee regime established a *generalissimo* system through the Revitalizing Reforms of October 1972, the press lost its autonomous sphere and came to be subsumed in the state apparatus as a mouthpiece of military dictatorship. The fact that the press was thus subsumed in the state apparatus as an institution is significant. Under Rhee and Park, prior to the Revitalizing Reforms, the press had existed outside the state apparatus and served as a cooperator in the formation of a modern nation-state in Korea and as the educator of economic modernization. Following the Revitalizing Reforms, however, the South Korean press became what amounted to private enterprise and, in spite of the façade of public broadcasting, came to serve as a *de facto* government organ in the promotion of the state apparatus. Thus institutionalized as a mouthpiece, newspaper companies grew as enterprises and journalists faithfully fulfilled their role as *de facto* bureaucrats in the advertisement of the current regime (Kim, 1994).

The so-called amalgamation of the press, which was forcibly implemented by the military regime in 1980, signaled not merely the oppression of the freedom of the press but a process through which the state institutionalized the press as its mouthpiece and expelled any journalists who resisted the measure. Consequently, with the Revitalizing Reforms and the instatement of General Chun Doo Hwan as the President, the South Korean press came to acquire political power and to accumulate capital in much the same way that the Ministry of Information (the present Government Information Agency) did. (See figure 5.1.)

The political change accomplished through the Democratization Struggle served as an opportunity for the expansion of the civil society, which hitherto had been subsumed in the authoritarian state. However, its nature was defined from the Third Republic (1963–72) to the Sixth Republic (1981–7), during which the state apparatus, which had steadily grown, continued to interfere in both civil and political society with its legal and administrative force. Although this is arguable, depending on how the relationship between the civil society and the state is defined, under authoritarian political power headed by a military bureaucracy, the civil society was in fact subsumed so that its autonomous sphere was negligible or nearly non-existent in this period.

The struggles and self-sacrifice of the general public up to the Democratization Struggle expanded the sphere of civil society and introduced into South Korean politics procedural democracy. The natural course of social

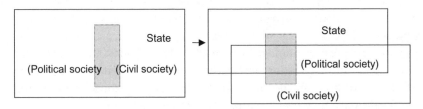

Figure 5.1: Changes in the status of the public sphere within the relationship between the state and the civic society

change then was the expansion of the sphere of both civil society and political society and the implementation of democratic if minimal social reform. From the standpoint of the ruling class, the situation was the greatest crisis since 1980. Faced with such a crisis, the ruling class succeeded in making a compromise with the pro-democracy forces through the democratization of election procedures and the partial relinquishment of power. Consequently, structural crisis in the ruling order was overcome. Through such a process, procedural democracy was introduced, while the actual democratization of society at large remained an incomplete task.

The civil society of South Korea, which had thus grown through the Democratization Struggle, was not only unable to dominate the corrupt conservative alliance but also saw the conservativization of the middle class, thereby bringing about a highly unstable relationship between the state and civil society in the 1990s. Moreover, following the foreign-exchange crisis of 1997, conglomerates and the conservative press were able successfully to establish a neoconservative hegemony that relegated democratic reform and social welfare to a secondary position, with market competitiveness as the primary goal. Civil society therefore came to be weakened by the conservative press and corrupt political power, and the conservative press in turn became the vanguard and producer of an ideology that criticized government policies protecting laborers, human rights, social welfare, and the reform of conglomerates as obstacles to market competitiveness.

As civil society thus changed, the South Korean press likewise underwent the following transformation. First, after the amalgamation of the press in 1980, the South Korean press grew as monopoly capital and closely linked itself with the nucleus of ruling power. While the ruling power guaranteed the press monopolistic profits (one newspaper per province; cartels; privileges in taxation; loans and finance; etc.), the press in turn established itself as a mouthpiece of the ruling bloc. In other words, the South Korean press came to serve not as a monitor of power but as an organ of power itself from the 1990s onward (Youn, 2002; Yim, 2001).

Second, the ruling power produced innumerable power-oriented journalists by mobilizing journalists and installing them in crucial positions of influence. This is proven by the fact that, since 1980, the profession to produce the greatest number of members of the National Assembly was none other but that of journalists (it is worth noting that, just as military officials have been all too prone in South Korea to consider becoming politicians once they have been promoted to generals, journalists have all too often entertained the thought of "naturally" becoming ministers once they have been promoted to chief editors) (Kang, 1993).

Third, the development of the media industry and the growth of political power have elevated journalists, as a group, to the status of a ruling class with high salaries, various privileges (studies abroad, education and training, support for children's educational expenses and scholarships, various accommodation privileges, all through public funds). According to relevant data, less than 30 percent of all South Korean journalists (those working for central dailies) received salaries above the minimum living costs up to the early 1970s. The salary average reached the level of that of university-educated employees of large private enterprises in the late 1970s; the situation was reversed in the 1980s. By the late 1980s, journalists were receiving salaries higher than those of any other profession. This high level of salary was possible because newspaper companies were able to make considerable profits from their collusion with the ruling power instead of struggling with competition in the market.

Fourth, a salary level far below minimum living costs up to the early 1970s drove journalists to depend on a distorted source of income: bribes. The generalization of such a structure of corruption through which journalists exchanged their ethics for money continues even to this date, when journalists' salaries have risen to the highest level. In a survey conducted by the Korean Press Foundation (KPF) in 2000, only approximately 30 percent of journalists nationwide replied that bribes should never be accepted. Others' replies differed, thus clearly revealing the corrupt ethical sense of journalists: "[Bribes are] acceptable as long as they do not affect news contents" (34 percent); "if possible, [bribes] should not be accepted" (34 percent); and "[Bribes] may be accepted" (2 percent).

Finally, in spite of all these problems, it must be pointed out that there was a movement for the democratization of the South Korean press that rejected power orientation, criticized the collusion of politicians and the press, and insisted on the democratization of both society and the press. By dismissing nearly 1,000 journalists in 1980, however, the new military regime silenced such journalistic resistance. Following the press labor union movement of 1987, the dismissal and arrest of journalists has increased considerably – the Korean Broadcasting System (KBS) strike in 1989, the dismissal of journalists from Munhwa Broadcasting Corporation (MBC) and Pyunghwa Broadcasting Corporation (PBC) in 1990, and the dismissal of journalists from the *Kyunghyang Daily News* are some of the noteworthy cases. As a result, the press's editorial independence and progress on its democratization have suffered a setback. When journalists enjoy the highest level of salary, opportunities for entry into politics, and generally comfortable and satisfying lives, it becomes difficult for them to ponder the oppressed and democratization.

The five above-mentioned structural conditions that form the basis of the values and behavior patterns of South Korean journalists as a profession also function as the foundation of the ideological orientation through which the conservative press views society at large. At the same time, the press has served as the greatest supporter of conservative ideology in South Korean society.

These structural conditions are the reason that the conservative press of South Korea, despite its considerable autonomy in editorial rights, has continued to play the role of a savior to the political system in times of crisis. Indeed, since the 1990s, the South Korean press has changed from the handmaiden of power to a power in its own right, something that may be called "unelected power." The source of such power is the conservative alliance newly formed in the 1990s, which consists of corrupt politics, conglomerates, and the conservativized press.

The Conservativization of the Civil Society and the Demand for an Alternative Public Sphere

In the early 1990s, theoretical and practical discussions on the civil society became extremely active. For the democratization of South Korean society, civil society began to be seen as an alternative to the state, which had grown excessively following the Liberation and in the course of the installation of military dictatorship. It was also true that civil activist organizations such as the Korean Women's Associations United (KWAU), the Korean Federation for Environmental Movement (KFEM), and People's Solidarity for Participatory Democracy (PSPD), though different from labor movement groups, had paved the way for a new sphere of praxis. Whether they emphasized their uniqueness from the traditional labor movement as a class movement or presupposed a complementary relationship with the latter, these civil activist organizations sought to provide a critique of and alternatives to existing laws and policies for economic reform, and aimed for the democratization of the political decision-making process within the context not of the state or capital but of the state and civil society. Despite the accomplishments of such civil movements, however, the reform policies of administrations headed by Presidents Kim Young Sam and Kim Dae Jung were fruitless except for a few cases, such as reform of the military and finance and the "Sunshine policy." At the same time, the general public began to ensconce themselves in an ideology that prioritized economics above politics.

This utter disappearance of reform in the past several years prompts us to ask the following questions again: Is democracy a possibility for South Korean society? Do we still want democracy? Despite the prevalent and varied use of the modifier "democratic" – e.g., "democratic government," "democratic participation," "democratization of society at large," and "economic democratization" – in South Korea today, do we truly believe that we *need* democracy? Perhaps South Koreans believe that the situation is improving in spite of some deficiencies, since they can now vote for their leaders, see candidates holding discussions on the television, make critical comments on the President, and watch television dramas depicting the Fourth Republic (1972–81). Now that South Korean society has experienced the Democratization Struggle, the establishment of the so-called civilian government in 1992, and the peaceful transfer of political power to the then opposition party in 1998, should we set politics aside and concern ourselves with economics?

Although everyone cries out for the reform of corrupt politics, once we get to the polling place, precisely *who* will we trust to reform the continuing regional factionalism that characterizes South Korean voters, and in what manner? Does the general public think that, in order to survive the merciless competition among nations today, to avoid becoming yet another Latin America, and to outpace the rapidly developing China and southeast Asian nations, all efforts must be devoted to economics? Do we believe that, in order to survive the expanding and increasingly international movement of capital and fierce competition, laborers only need to be more patient so as to increase national wealth, and that they must not be overly hasty and seek only to secure their own profits?

To all of the questions above, I must answer in the affirmative. Indeed, it is my belief that we have become self-contented all too soon. It would be wrong, however, to view such self-satisfaction as a reflection of the majority of the middle class's satisfaction with the social reforms that have been implemented to date. Instead, it is a result of the successful mobilization of the general public by the discourse of the "second modernization," which contends that "economic growth will save the nation," and "welfare, justice, and democracy will follow later" (Kang, 2000). The symbolic discourse of internationalization and globalization, which has formed the dominant discourse of South Korean society in the past several years through the efforts of the conservative alliance, successfully won over the middle class in civil society and was able thus to exclude the critical discourse of more fundamental institutional reform and the demands of the laboring class. In other words, political symbols such as "Let's leap again," "We popped our champagne too soon," and "southeast Asia is on our heels" have been able to conceal problems including the intensification of economic concentration, labor–management conflicts, and corruption among politicians; while at the same time seducing the general public with the theory of second modernization under the slogan "Let's prosper once again." Such success of the dominant discourse was empowered to a considerable degree by the mobilization of the public sphere, which otherwise should be an arena for the critical awareness and discussion of reality, in a politics of the populist mobilization of public opinion.

In this context, it is of the utmost importance for the various interest groups and the general public in South Korean civil society to secure a democratic public sphere where they can voice their interests and demands. Previously seen as the drivers and movers of democratization, the citizenry have come to be contented with reality and depoliticized. This is not because they are satisfied with reform, however. Instead, it is, to a considerable degree, due to the exclusion, by the ruling power and capital, of resistant discourse and critical demands regarding the distortion of the public sphere, from any form of decision-making process; and due to a reality where the middle class's desires and needs cannot be voiced through public institutions of communication.

Indeed, since 1987, the general public have been excluded from a chance to participate in socially important decision-making processes except elections, and the arena for the expression of their collective opinion has continued to be distorted. In such circumstances, neither the democratization of the state nor the institutionalization of civic power can be achieved. In order for them to express their opinions and to participate in decision-making processes, the general public above all need information and knowledge that will enable them to recognize the given social situation and provide them with a public sphere, an arena for the discussion of conflicting ideas and interests, that is operated openly and freely. In this respect, the deferral of democratization, the internal conservativization of civil society, and the exclusion of alternative demands and opinions, all require the reorganization of the public sphere and the creation of an alternative where such voices can be expressed and heard.

The Search for Alternative Plans for the Democratization of the Press

As has been pointed out above, the changes in the South Korean press since 1987 need to be examined anew from the perspective not only of politics but also of the press market. This section will therefore examine the nature of the press market and the process through which the press has come to be yet another political force; and this section will search for alternative plans. In the past 30 years, the government has not applied its principles with respect to regulations in general to those specifically regarding the press. For instance, policies such as the prohibition of cartels and of monopoly and oligopoly in the press market, all of which are *economic* regulations, have not been enforced on newspaper companies. Acts such as the collective prearrangement of advertising costs and newspaper prices and the nondisclosure of circulation have not at all been subject to government regulations. Instead, the government has distorted the market principle in the press market through the forcible amalgamation of newspaper companies and through privileges regarding finance and taxation. Of course, such distorted policies with respect to the press market were the "carrot" used by dictator regimes to "tame" the press. This may then be called the "failure of the government" in terms of policies on the press.

To put it crudely, the bulk of dailies nationwide were but small or medium private enterprises incapable of making profits from newspapers themselves up to the mid-1970s (Kim, 1994). With the full-fledged implementation of the system under the Revitalizing Reforms, the Park regime subsumed the press as a tool of dictatorship and, at the same time, provided the basis for newspaper companies' growth as conglomerates through the introduction of loans and tax privileges. This is proven by the fact that, under the system established through the Revitalizing Reforms, a number of central dailies rapidly increased their fixed investment, such as the construction of new company buildings and the introduction of high-speed rotary presses (Ju, 1993).

The amalgamation of the press in 1980 served as the opportunity for South Korean newspaper companies to transform themselves into huge monopoly capital. In other words, the restructuring of the newspaper industry came about not through competition in the market and along with the accumulation of capital in society at large but through the consolidation of an oligopolistic system based on newspaper cartels. That system in turn was established through regulations on newcomers' entry into the newspaper market (with the possession of facilities for the publication of periodicals as the standard), reduction in the total number of newspapers, the prearrangement of circulation and the number of pages, a collective forwarding system, collective adjustment of holidays, and the prearrangement of the number of orders for advertisements to be received.

Since the government's relaxation of its regulations on newcomer entry in 1987, the newspaper market has seen fierce competition. Excessive investment, inevitable due to heightened competition, drove numerous newspapers to encroach on their own capital. This happened to the *Kyunghyang Daily News*, the *Munhwa Ilbo*, and the *Segye Times* in the same year. Most other central dailies suffer from excessive debts. According to the Korea Press Institute (1999), it costs approximately 3,000 won to produce a 32-page daily and 1,500 won to distribute it, with the result that the publishing cost for 100,000 free copies amounted to 5.4 billion won per year as of the end of 1996. Although it is difficult to estimate the total number of free copies of central dailies at this moment, 1 million copies mean publishing costs of 54 billion won and 2 million copies mean over 100 billion won. In addition, the three major dailies, which boast the greatest circulation, have competed by providing "premiums" within the price range of 100,000 won, such as electric fans, refrigerators, and bicycles, to new subscribers so as to increase circulation. Due to such unfair practices in the newspaper market, the market share occupied by these three dailies has increased and small newspapers are barely surviving.

In this a situation, theoretical requirements of the press, such as customer service, the provision of quality information, and an arena for democratic discussion, are neither practicable nor possible. To win orders for advertisements, journalists cannot pen articles that may displease conglomerates and private enterprises but must write ones that are indistinguishable from advertisements. The problems of the South Korean press, which thus combines the failures of both the government and the market, can be summarized in three points.

1) The Expansion of Journalistic Power

The press is a link between civil society and the state (political society). South Korean newspapers and broadcasting, which were loyal mouthpieces of military dictatorship up to 1987, have, with the instatement of civilian government, styled themselves as partners of the ruling power and as the "populist opinion leaders" demanded by current administrations (Yang, 1995). Since the transfer of the government to the then opposition party in 1998, the press has posed as a supporter of a conservative alliance consisting of the bureaucracy, the Chaebuls, conservative intellectuals, and those with vested political and economic rights – notwithstanding a short period of identity crisis at the beginning (e.g., the argument on whether the *Chosun Ilbo* now was to be seen as the opposition-party organ and the *Hankyoreh* as the ruling-party organ). In the name of the market and of reform through autonomy of the civilian sector, the press continues to be the ideological channel for opinion that resists the overall reform demanded by the rest of society. The press uses journalistic power to mobilize public opinion in support of the conservative alliance.

2) The Distortion of the Press Market

Newspapers and broadcasting stations that survived the amalgamation of the press in 1980 have grown into newspaper conglomerates through various privileges and favors. Indeed, the nondisclosure of circulation, the collective prearrangement of the prices of advertisements and newspapers, and privileges in taxation have enabled the press to grow at a rate double that of manufacturing industry. Moreover, the relaxation of government regulations on newcomer entry into the market in 1987 has brought about competition among newspaper companies in terms of free copies and number of pages, thus intensifying overall competition in the market. Excessive investment and competition, which have characterized the South Korean newspaper and broadcast industries – in particular, regional commercial broadcasting and the cable industry – since 1987, are not signs of the restoration of the market principle but the inevitable consequences of the absence of management and a market that grew on political favors from dictatorship. As a result, all dailies except a few newspapers suffer from financial deficits, and regional newspapers, which are far too numerous in comparison with the size of the entire market, are searching for survival strategies in a distorted market. Likewise, regional commercial broadcasting stations and the cable industry are faced with a crisis of bankruptcy.

Despite and amid such distortion in the press market, the majority of newspapers and broadcasting stations are fighting desperately to survive instead of withdrawing from the market. This is risky because the situation in turn may lead the South Korean press to: (a) solicit the government for unreasonable support, and (b) depend on advertisers.

Indeed, the first of the two problems cited above has already surfaced in a variety of forms. The cable industry and regional commercial broadcasting stations have claimed through seminars and reports that the government is responsible for any excessive investment not based on their own judgment regarding the market. Likewise, the second risk has already emerged, so that not only central and regional newspapers but also all broadcasting stations, so as to continue receiving orders for advertisements, are criticizing government policies in the name of the "neoliberalist vision of market autonomy" which is the standpoint of conglomerates and enterprises.

3) The Absence of Orthodox Journalism and Journalists

In a situation where the relationships between political power and the press, and capital and the press, are structurally distorted, press coverage too has led public opinion so as to fulfill newspaper companies' interests as members of the conservative alliance, instead of the press being faithful to its proper role as the provider of information and an arena for public forums. In other words, rather than providing a variety of information and discussion on the mechanics and direction of social reform faced by South Korean society, the press has distorted and resisted reform from the viewpoint of capital and conservatives with vested political and economic interests. As a result, journalists and newspapers that endeavor to be true to their proper role are being criticized as opportunists and conspirators.

Arguably there are three ways of reforming such distortions in both the press and the press market, as follows:[1]

1) The Independence of Editorial Rights

The most crucial task for the democratization of the press is none other than the restoration of autonomy to journalists and producers in the process of information collection, news coverage, editing, and production. As has been mentioned above, a conservative alliance consisting of bureaucracy, private enterprises, intellectuals, and those with vested economic and political rights has reorganized the market thoroughly in its favor and is attempting to exclude the political and social rights of civil society. Despite its neoliberalist pretexts, such as small government and market autonomy, the conservative alliance actually means to realize a market principle from which consumers and laborers are absent, while government only plays a supporting role and does not impose any regulation. What is needed is the normalization of the press so that it can, independently from capital, the ruling power, and those with vested political and economic power, collect data and report events autonomously.

Independence in editing and production therefore signifies a role for the press and journalists that is independent from the conservative alliance. In the case of newspapers, this means the editorial board's independence from newspaper company owners; as for broadcasting stations, it means independence from political power and capital.

2) The Restoration of the Market Principle (Normalization of the Press Market)

South Korean newspapers and broadcasting did not have exposure to market forces before 1987. Activating the market principle in the media therefore will not only normalize corporate management but also have the political effect of breaking the collusion of politicians and the press. This is because, in the case of newspapers, the restoration of the market principle signifies the rationalization of the press market and the division of ownership and editing (more specifically, a decrease in company owners' influence). As for broadcasting, it means restructuring and the rationalization of management.

3) Independence

Finally, journalism that is independent from both political power and the market is crucial. A situation where large newspaper companies that have evaded tax resist government crackdown on tax evasion and call it oppression of the press, or support particular political parties or presidential candidates during elections (this is done not through the editorial but through news production and editing), is bringing Korean journalism to a serious crisis. In order to solve the problem, journalist organizations such as the Journalists' Association of Korea and newspaper-company labor unions must start an autonomous cleanup campaign so that they can distance themselves from political and market power.

Note

1   These ideas for press reformation have been proposed by many media-watch activists and media reform movements since the civilian government began (Yim, 1998; Sohn, 1998).

References

Chung, Jin-suk (1990). *A History of Korean Press.* Seoul: Nanam Publishing.

Ju, Dong-whang (1993). "Effect of Press Policy on the Changes of Korean Newspaper Industry." Ph.D. dissertation, Seoul National University.

Jung, Jin-suk (1985). *A Modern Media History of Korea.* Seoul: Junyeawon.

Kang, Myung-koo (1993). "The Journalists Moved to Political Power: Past and Present." *Journalism* 28: 125–47.

Kang, Myung-koo (2000). "Second Modernization Failed: Discourse Politics from 'New Korea' to 'Globalization.'" In A. MacRobbie and L. Grossberg, eds., *Without Guarantees: Anthology for Stuart Hall's Retirement.* London: Polity.

Kim, Min-Hwan (1999). *A Study on the Lag of Development of Modern Newspapers in East Asia.* Seoul: Nanam Publishing.

Kim, Kyu-Whan (1978). *Press and Propaganda Policy under Japanese Colonial Rule.* Seoul: Yee-U.

Kim, Nam-suk (1994). "A Political Economy of the Structural Change of the Korean Newspaper Industry." Ph.D. dissertation, Seoul National University.

Korean Press Institute (1999). *Crisis and Reform of Korean Newspaper Industry.* Seoul: Korea Press Institute.

Rim, Hyuk-bak (1994). *Market, State, Democracy: Democratization of Korea and Theories of Political Economy.* Seoul: Nanam Publishing.

Rim, Hyun-jin and Song, Ho-keun (1993). "Deferred Transformation and Market Fantasy." In Jang-jip Choi and Hyun-jin Rim, eds., *Challenges of Civil Society.* Seoul: Nanam Publishing.

Sohn, Ho-chul (1999). *Politics of Korea in the Age of Neo-liberalism.* Seoul: Puronsup.

Sohn, Suk-chun (1998). "Ten-year History of the Korean Media Labor Movement: An Evaluation." *Proceedings of the Ten-year History of the National Federation of Media Labor Union.* Seoul.

Yang, Seung-mok (1995). "Democratization and Change in the Korean Media." In Jae-chun Yu, ed., *Changes of Korean Society and the Media.* Seoul: Sowha.

Yim, Young-Ho (1998). "The Labor Union Movements and Politics of Production." *Journalism Criticism* 25: 25–39.

Yim, Young-Ho (2001). *The Newspaper Industry and Democracy in the Age of Transformation.* Seoul: Hannarae.

Youn, Young-chul (2002). *Democracy and Media in Korea.* Seoul: Yumin Cultural Fund.

6

"Forward-Looking" News?: Singapore's News 5 and the Marginalization of the Dissenting Voice

Sue Abel

This chapter is based on a study of a close reading of seven 7:00 p.m. *News 5* bulletins, recorded in September and October 1995 on Singapore television, and uses discourse analysis to show how ideological underpinnings work in practice. Each bulletin was videotaped on a different day of the week so as to get a more representative sample. I analyzed only those stories which were seen by *News 5* to have a direct relation to Singapore. This disqualified most, but not all, of the coverage of overseas events. Sports news was also excluded, leaving 75 separate news stories. The study shows that there are two dominant discourses: a discourse of nationalism and a discourse of looking to the future at work. These discourses mask present-day problems and divisions within Singapore, and work both separately and together to support the present political and economic status quo. The study also argues that at times the voice of television news and the voice of the government overlap, and uses the coverage of the Domestic Violence Bill to illustrate how the status quo position is naturalized and opposing views are marginalized. In such instances television news also serves to support the present political and economic status quo.

The Discourse of Looking into the Future

Several writers have suggested that the leadership of Singapore maintains a "discourse of crisis" or "discourse of survival" as a means of social control.

Birch, for example, suggested in 1993 that Singapore maintains "some major reality-myths which position Singapore as a society always in danger, always attempting by hard work and sacrifice to avert some *future* crisis, and always subject to external uncertainties and influences" (1993a: 3). He further argues that "Certainly within Singapore the very maintenance of a discourse of crisis is one of the main strategies adopted by the Singapore government to maintain its ideology of control, anchor its people to the nation and create a climate of domestic uncertainty about the fragility of the state and the economy" (1993b: 74).

Two years later the dominant discourse present in *News 5* is, like the discourse described above, a future-oriented discourse. Fully one-third of all local stories were concerned in some way or the other with the future. But rather than presenting the future as something to be continually on one's guard about and emphasizing the Total Defense necessary if Singapore is to survive (as one would in a discourse of crisis), *News 5* presents the future as something that the country's leaders have, as much as possible, under control because of the constant plans and improvements they are making in technology, business, research, housing, education, and health. *News 5* suggests (but never sets out in any detail) positive scenarios of what the future will be like when the particular plan being announced takes effect.

The constant emphasis on the future gives *News 5* a "good news" feel, as some examples from the presenter's introductions to stories demonstrate:

A one-stop women's clinic is slated to open to cater for gynecological needs of a woman from childhood to menopause. It will be headed by the man stepping into the shoes of Professor S. S. Ratanam, father of Asia's first test-tube baby. (Sat. 9/23/95)

More than 30,000 visitors have trekked through the Citytrans exhibition at the World Trade Center since Thursday. Many were there to catch a glimpse of how some futuristic models can lead to a smoother flow of traffic. (Sat. 9/23/95)

Setting common standards for health food could move the food industry forward, says the Minister of State for Trade and Industry at a conference, and they'll aim to do just that eventually. (Tues. 9/26/96)

The Singapore Tourist Promotion Board says it'll change the way it will market the Lau Pa Sat Festival Market. The Board says it will emphasize getting locals to frequent the old market which was sold yesterday. (Fri. 9/29/95)

Vaccines for peptic ulcers and gastritis can be available within three years. NUS has successfully studied the bacteria which is responsible for the disease. (Fri. 9/29/95)

Finding vaccines for gastritis is only one of the many research projects going on in NUS. Thanks to such research you can also look forward to more local, brand-new innovations. (Fri. 9/29/95)

Bringing residents and grassroots organizations closer together. Hong Kah North embarked on several projects last night to bring that about. (Sun. 10/15/95)

The Information Technology or IT industry is expected to grow about 30 percent a year within the next two years. Acting Prime Minister B.-G. Lee gave this bullish outlook at the opening of Comdex Asia '95, an IT exhibition. (Thurs. 10/26/95)

Future-Oriented News as the "Natural" Way to Report News

This discourse of looking to the future is so dominant that it replaces other ways of presenting the news and seems to be the "natural" way. One senior journalist I spoke to asked me, "How else would you present news?," when I commented on this emphasis on telling viewers what is going to happen. And it is true that several of the stories introduced above would have been presented in the same way by news organizations in other countries. Other news bulletins, however, do not have such an unrelenting diet of good news about what is going to happen, what plans have been put in place or will be put in place. This is not necessarily the "natural" or the only way to report daily news. Many news organizations report news when it happens, rather than when someone says something is going to happen, or even "could" happen. Galtung and Ruge's (1965) research on news values common to news media around the world shows that for daily news organizations news value is attached to that which happens within the previous 24 hours. *News 5* does, it is true, usually use the "peg" of a conference or the opening of a building or some public ceremony to "hang" the news story on. Several of the introductions above demonstrate this. But the aspect of the story which is highlighted is that which has not in fact yet happened.

There are other angles to take. For example, the story about the health-food industry could have been postponed until common standards had actually been established. Or another approach might have been taken –

that of investigating what the present standards actually are in traditional health foods.

"Problems" in the News

One of the consequences of this discourse of the future is that it detracts attention from present-day reality. Such a reality is hinted at right at the end of the health-food story discussed above, when the reporter tells us: "They say that much more needs to be done before standards can be achieved, but what they'll try to do is to set out some recommendations and more research."

This suggests that there is much more that could have been said (or asked). For example: Is the present state of the health-food industry a matter of concern? Are Singaporeans putting their health at risk by using these products? How widespread is the problem? Why has it not been regulated before? Are some companies more at fault than others? Are some companies making claims for their products that are not in fact true? Are there other views about this issue? The *News 5* story does not address any of these questions, concentrating instead on discussing the marketing potential for traditional health foods, and the possibilities of future scientific research into such foods.

This story is an example of how the future orientation of news stories erases or minimizes the existence of a problem in the present. Looking at plans for improvement and plans for the future replaces defining the nature and extent of a problem here and now in the present day.

The future orientation also ignores questions of causality and responsibility, and of consequences. Nobody is responsible for the present situation. A closer look at one of the introductions shows how this operates:

> More than 30,000 visitors have trekked through the Citytrans exhibition at the World Trade Center since Thursday. Many were there to catch a glimpse of how some futuristic models can lead to a smoother flow of traffic.

A *smoother* flow of traffic? It seems there might be a problem here. Again, what is the nature and extent of the problem? What currently impedes the flow of traffic? What are the consequences of this for Singapore? And above all, whose responsibility is this?

Fairclough argues that in instances like this the media have the power to disguise its power: "It is the power to constrain content: to favour certain interpretations and 'wordings' of events, while excluding others. It is a form of hidden power, for the favoured interpretations and wordings are those of the powerholders in . . . society" (1989: 52). This erasure or de-emphasizing of the presence of a problem is compounded by the depiction of present-day problems as "challenges." This is implicit in most of the stories, and spelled out in two:

> National Development Minister Lim Hong Kiang says Singapore is now faced with a greater *challenge* in preserving community ties as people become more affluent. (9/26/95)

> Singapore's labor *challenges* are real bread-and-butter issues, says Singapore Polytechnic's outgoing principal Khoo Kay Chai, who urges Polytechnic graduates to gear themselves up for the future or risk being left out. (9/26/95)

The choice of the word "challenge" in both of these examples naturalizes the problem. It is just there – it is not the result of any action or inaction on the part of the government or any other institution or body. Again, causality and responsibility disappear. It is a challenge to be met by "Singapore," by all of "us," or by the leaders on behalf of all Singaporeans.

The seriousness of any present-day problems or "challenges" is further mitigated because such "challenges" only seem to get on the news agenda when the government or some other institution has come up with plans to remedy the situation. So one story tells us of a report which documents teachers' stress levels, but the point of the story is that measures have been identified to help remedy this. Lau Pa Sat is at the moment a commercial disaster, but plans are afoot to change that. Traffic flow may (or may not) be an issue, but "futuristic models" at the Citytrans exhibition offer a potential solution. This pattern even extends to human-interest stories. Before the commercial break on 10/8/95 the presenters announce details of a story about a young Singaporean which will feature later in the program:

> *Christine Tan*: "Coming up: an 11-year-old boy diagnosed with congenital liver disease . . . "
> *Paul Tan*: "But – a successful liver transplant in London."

The Illusion of Participatory Politics

Birch argues that one new way of control being explored by the ruling party in Singapore is "the illusion of participatory politics in order to stem the flow of those who defect from the dominant discourse," and that "the maintenance of a continued sense of participation, within the postcolonial framework of survivalist politics and culture, is an essential communications strategy within contemporary Singapore" (1993a: 12). It can be argued that *News 5* contributes to such a sense of participation, and that the discourse of looking to the future contributes to an illusion of participatory politics. On one level *News 5* does an excellent job of delivering information to Singaporeans. It tells them what services are available to them. A story about a proposed new Multimedia Software Engineering Diploma course ends: "So if you think you're ready for the multimedia era, applications will be open after the release of O-level results" (10/9/95). And a report about a study on anorexia in Singapore tells viewers: "One place to get help is the Institute of Mental Health which has a clinic as well as a support group" (10/15/95).

News 5 also tells its audience ahead of time what the government plans in a range of areas, and gives the impression of Singapore as state of well-informed, up-to-date citizens. The dominance of news plans gives a semblance of consultation because viewers are learning about what is going to happen, rather than being told something has happened. This is especially so when future plans are expressed in a conditional way, suggesting that the plans are provisional:

> Residents of these flats flanking the multistory car park may soon look down on a nicer view. (10/26/95)

> And, as Business Desk finds out, if it all goes well, other banking transactions may soon be possible in the comfort of your home. (9/26/95)

> They [housing experts] suggest more facilities for the elderly and using rooftop space as other ways to strengthen community bonds. (9/26/95)

The second excerpt above is also an example of news which addresses the viewer as a participant in and someone who benefits from the currency of Singapore's technology, as does: "Thanks to such research you can also look forward to more local, brand-new innovations" (9/29/95). Further examples of citizen participation are spelled out in some stories. The quote from the housing report above is followed by: "And getting residents involved in the plans further binds them with one another." And on many occasions reporters have gone to "ordinary" Singaporeans for their (sometimes dissenting) reaction to an issue or an event. Ordinary Singaporeans in fact featured in 41 of the 113 soundbites during the sample week. This is a reasonably high proportion when compared with news bulletins from other countries. But what we have here is truly "an illusion of participatory democracy." The events and issues that citizens comment on or are involved in are not major political, economic, or social issues. Rather, visitors react to exhibitions, students express their admiration for retiring principals, spectators respond to a ballet performance in a park, and refuse collectors explain how tough their job is becoming now that they are getting older.

Discourse of Nationalism

Positioning the viewer

As demonstrated in the discussion of visual images above, discourse in news is conveyed in more than just the script spoken by the presenters and reporters. News discourse is also "spoken" by the presentation style of the news. The carefully established studio setting for the presenters is chosen to convey authoritativeness, as are the presenters themselves. Their clothing, their body language, the titles that are used to introduce them, their tone of voice and accent, along with what Root (1986) calls the "steady style of auto cue direct address," all work to make the news seem neutral, commonsense, and authoritative. At the same time, however, presenters often use language in a way which addresses the viewer as one of "us," part of a collective group which includes all the other viewers as well as the presenters themselves. In doing this, television news assumes naturally-given values in its mode of address. The use of personal pronouns is crucial to establishing a common identity between news presenter and audience. News exploits a vocabulary of "we" and "us" and "you" that invites the viewer not only to go along with the values of the program, but also to consider themselves as part of a larger unity of "the nation," a nation unified. For example, I discussed above two excerpts where the use of the personal pronoun "you" addresses the viewer as a "Singaporean," a participant in and someone who benefits from Singapore's advances in technology.

In *News 5* bulletins the use of words and phrases like "here," "local," and "this country" work to remind the audience that they are part of the same geographically situated and politically defined community as the news crew, but they can also serve as part of a larger discourse of nationalism. The presenter's statement, "Thanks to such research [at NUS] you can also look forward to more local, brand-new innovations," bursts with national pride (and enthusiastic tautology). This, along with the direct address to the viewer, can make it hard for viewers to resist the discourse of nationalism with its subject position of "proud and loyal Singaporean." In one story the role of the presenter in articulating assumed common values is particularly clear. The topic of the story is a controversy over the Long Service Award for civil servants[1] because some civil servants would apparently prefer cash to payments in kind like vouchers or home appliances. An assistant chief engineer who has given 17 years of service argues that payment in kind would be more meaningful. He tells us, "When they receive those at least they are very proud that their service with the company has been recognized." The reporter then adds, "Something that this country has always believed in," assuming consensus and invoking nationalism.

In other stories the position is not spelled out so specifically, but in order to make "sense" of them, viewers of *News 5* have to adopt the position of loyal and proud Singaporean citizen. Fairclough points out that "since all discourse producers must produce with *some* interpreters in mind, what media producers do is address an *ideal subject*, be it viewer, listener or reader. Media discourse has built into it a subject position for an ideal subject, and actual viewers or listeners or readers have to negotiate a relationship with the ideal subject" (1995: 49; emphasis in the original). Birch has argued that a "good" Singaporean citizen is constructed as one who shares the government's illusion of citizenry – constructed as compliance rather than opposition; one of joining with, rather than questioning, the government (1993a: 73). *News 5* presents an overwhelmingly positive view of Singapore in which it is difficult for the viewer to imagine being anything else.

Poulantzas's conception of ideology can also provide a useful insight into how television news in general, and *News 5* in particular, addresses its audience. He suggests that dominant discourses "mask" facts of class exploitation and class interests (or any other unequal power relations) "to the extent that all trace of class domination is systematically absent from its language" (1965: 214). Dominant discourses also "fragment" the audience, addressing them not as members of a class (or, by implication, gender, ethnic group, or religious group) but as individual citizens and consumers (what Poulantzas calls "individuals-persons"). The audience is then reconstituted as individuals into "imaginary unities" such as "consumers," "the consensus," "public opinion," and "the nation." So television news never addresses its audience as workers, or members of different classes, genders, and races. By focusing on categories that bind people together, television "displaces" or hides their differences and potential social antagonisms. In this the discourse of nationalism plays the same function as the discourse of looking to the future.

Singapore as a world player

A subcategory of the discourse of nationalism is that of "Singapore as a world player." This was present in 12 out of the 75 stories studied. For example, the verdict in the O. J. Simpson case (10/4/95) was used as evidence in the following story to "prove the wisdom of Singapore's decision to abandon the jury system some 25 years ago." There were numerous references to developments which are "first in Asia" or "first in the world," or of other countries wanting to share Singapore's expertise in specific areas. The only statement about Singapore's position in the world that could be construed as negative was a statement that "Singapore's R&D [Research and Development] expenditure ranks 23rd in the world"; but this was presented as a reason for the announcement by the Trade and Industries Minister that the government was injecting S$300 million into a research investment scheme. This story therefore also follows the pattern of announcing what might be seen as a negative element or a problem at the same time that a solution or improvement is being announced. *News 5* then not only assumes that of course the viewer is a proud and loyal Singaporean before all else, but also provides the viewer with evidence for this.

"Singapore" as an imaginary unity

Another mechanism that contributes to a discourse of nationalism is the conflation of "Singapore" and its constituent parts. Individual successes such as breakthroughs in research, or business successes overseas, are described and celebrated as "Singapore's" successes, "our" successes. A story about research success by an individual science professor becomes "another milestone in medical science" for the National University of Singapore (and by implication for "Singapore") and *News 5* takes pains to point out how "you," the individual Singaporean watching the news, will benefit. Individual companies are represented as "Singapore's industry" and their private nature is ex-nominated.[2] For example:

> A new packaging computer software that helps local companies cut distribution costs. Techtrends looks at the program developed for the first time here by SISIR, the Singapore Institute of Standards and Industrial research. (9/26/95)

This story has the self-congratulatory tone of several others in which success is claimed as "ours" by the use of "here" and "local." It is implied that the ability of local companies to cut costs will also benefit the wider society.

The story of a technological advance achieved by the DBS Bank which will enable banking transactions by internet is also presented as a wider advance. The viewer is told that other banks will soon follow suit, and that "If you're hooked up to the internet you can now check on housing loans just by surfing the net." The viewer is once again addressed as a Singaporean who benefits from "our" advances. When the private sector is specifically nominated as such, it is in a story about potential cooperation with the government, as in a story about housing projects on September 29, 1995. Here the private sector is represented as "good citizens who are working for the greater good." And above all this, the government is represented as a facilitator, enabling companies and institutions (and hence Singapore and Singaporeans) to progress. So on October 4, 1995: "Building up the automation industry, Mr. Lim said, would help Singapore better respond to the increasing complexities of manufacturing processes." Here the future may be a challenge in terms of economic competitiveness, but the government is helping companies/Singaporeans prepare for it. And on October 9, 1995, the Trade and Industry Minister is reported as saying in Shanghai: "The government will carry on with facilitating trade enquiries and identifying business opportunities for companies." This conflation of individuals, institutions, and companies into the greater ideological concept of "Singapore" masks what is "an economically and ethnically stratified population" (Chua 1995: 5), while the representation of all business successes as successes for "Singapore" and "Singaporeans" erases questions about, for example, emerging class differences and the distribution of wealth in Singapore.

Inscribing Dominant Discourses and Marginalizing Alternative Ones

The discourses outlined above are not the only discourses present in *News 5* – on occasion competing discourses are included. Writing about the British news media, Stuart Hall (1977) has argued that because the media contains a number of conflicting views, it appears to be very democratic, but that the views represented are drawn from within certain boundaries. In a similar vein, the Glasgow Media group has argued, "Information which contradicts the dominant view, if it appears at all, exists as fragments and is never explored by news personnel as a rational alternative explanation. It is not used by them as a way of organising what they cover, or selecting what they film, or structuring their interviews" (1976: 29). So the dominant discourse predominates, inscribed into the text on many levels, naturalized and often rendered invisible.

In Singapore's *News 5* the government voice is inscribed on three different levels. The first is in the form of soundbites, where we see politicians making statements either directly to the media, or at some public function. A strict headcount shows that politicians only feature in 14 of the 113 soundbites, a comparatively low figure when compared with Western news bulletins. This does not, however, take into account the prominence that politicians are given in the way stories are structured. It is a common pattern for a story to open with an announcement from a minister, and then for the reporter to speak to professionals or experts in the field for elaboration. Some stories also highlight government members in other ways. For example, a report from the World Housing Congress held in Singapore opens with two boxes on the screen behind the presenter, instead of the usual one. The first box is a photo of the National Development Minister, and the second is a visual representation of housing. The story opens with a reported statement from the Minister before it moves to suggestions for housing improvements from the Housing Congress. Here the Minister is in effect given a right of reply before the event.

It is a fact of life that those in positions of power have more access to the media, and are seen on television news in settings which both demonstrate and add to their authority and status. Research done by the Glasgow Media Group (1976) in the UK suggests that in labor disputes people from management who are filmed seated at a table in an ordered, quiet office are seen as more credible than union officials filmed in work clothes on a work site which is quite likely to be noisy and chaotic. So in *News 5* it can be argued that the status of the PAP leadership is enhanced because they are shown center-stage at a press conference with reporters waiting to take down their words, or cutting ribbons to open buildings, or giving speeches at other official functions. This tendency, inherent in television news everywhere, is more pronounced in *News 5* because of the dominance of future-oriented news. It is difficult to find visual images to illustrate the future, and so camera operators shoot more pictures of the relevant politician to accompany the reporter's voiceover.

At the second level are stories which feature reporters quoting politicians or government ministries in indirect speech. A story often opens with a soundbite from a politician, and then the rest of the story continues the report on his speech in indirect speech. Sometimes such indirect reporting fills the whole story. At the third level are stories where the government line is not reported directly or indirectly, but instead speaks through the editorial voice of the bulletin. In a story on October 4, 1995, a retiring unionist outlines some of the actions taken "protecting workers and fighting for their rights" in the earlier years of his involvement with the labor movement. The reporter tells us: "But the situation is different today." A story about a proposal to set up a Singapore International School in Indonesia ends with the reporter announcing "The Singapore International School will certainly help families to stay together."

One story in particular bears closer analysis because it was treated by *News 5* as the major domestic story of this period. Issues involved in the Family Violence Bill proposed by Nominated Member of Parliament Dr. Kanwaljit Soin, and the government's subsequent response with its proposed amendments to the Women's Charter, were the lead stories in two of the seven bulletins in the sample. The same topic was also the lead story on a night outside of the sample bulletins. It was clear that there was public debate about the best way to deal with family violence. The analysis below demonstrates some of the mechanisms by which, through script, visuals, and soundtrack, the *News 5* coverage supports the PAP leadership position and works to marginalize and discredit other views.

The Family Violence Bill was introduced into Parliament on September 27, 1996, by Nominated Member of Parliament Dr. Kanwaljit Soin. In an attempt to reduce the rate of domestic violence in Singapore,[3] the Bill sought to enable police to investigate any such reported cases without the need to wait for sanction from the courts. This would remove the often complicated burden of obtaining protection for the victim. It also offered voluntary counseling for a first offender as an alternative to prosecution, mandatory counseling for subsequent offenders, and set out a clear framework of penalties for offenders. During the following month Government MPs argued that, while they agreed with the sentiments behind the Bill, the situation could be dealt with by amending the existing Women's Charter rather than by introducing separate legislation. When he announced the proposed amendments to the Women's Charter on October 26, Acting Community Development Minister Abdullah Tarmugi said he did not think that the police should interfere in all cases of domestic violence, or intrude too early in a relationship. His arguments against the Family Violence Bill were that it suggested that domestic violence was a key social problem; it would exacerbate already fragile family relationships by putting police in the situation; and that it would lead to a more litigious society, undermining the emphasis on promoting and strengthening family values (*Straits Times* 10/27/96: p. 1). The Family Violence Bill was subsequently rejected at its second hearing in November 1996.

In the sample week *News 5* had two lead stories on the government's proposed amendments to the Women's Charter. Two reporters were assigned to produce the story screened on 10/26/95. This would seem to suggest that *News 5* took the challenge to the government's hegemony on family values very seriously. On Sunday October 15 the fact that there were to be amendments to the Women's Charter was announced for the first time on *News 5*. Acting Community Development Minister Tarmugi was reported as announcing this during a visit to Serangoon Gardens Estate where the question was raised during a question and answer session. The issue was presented at this stage as essentially noncontroversial. The script asked the question, "So is there still a need for a separate law with the strengthening of the Women's Charter?"; rather than (for example), "What areas does the Family Violence Bill cover that are not covered in the proposed amendments to the Women's Charter?"

The following Thursday, October 26, the proposed amendments were spelt out in *News 5*. The headline that opened the bulletin was:

"Why there's no need	1) *Camera pans around press conference in formal room*
for separate legislation to handle	2) *Mid-shot Minister seated at table, talking*
family violence."	3) *Over-the-shoulder shot of parent and child reading book together*

This was presented as a statement rather than as a question, and the statement was presented as fact, not as a statement of opinion by the Minister or his government. Many Singaporeans, including those who worked on the Family Violence Bill, would no doubt disagree with the statement as it is set out. Shot 3 supports the Minister's assertion, with its ideal depiction of family life that suggests all is well with Singapore's families.

The presenter's introduction reads:

"Good evening. The government has proposed amendments to the Women's Charter to give it more powers to deal with family violence. The changes will give greater protection to victims of	*Box on screen contains the words "Women's Charter" and shows a diagram of three women grouped around a computer.*

family abuse so there's no need for a
separate piece of legislation for family
violence. The proposals were spelt out
by Acting Community Development
Minister Abdullah Tarmugi."

The third sentence once again sets out what was only an assertion on the part of the government – that a separate piece of legislation is no longer needed – as if it were a fact. It does not make clear that this is actually a report of a statement made by the Acting Minister. The picture in the box on the screen behind the presenter highlights the fact that the focus of attention is the Women's Charter, and a shot of three women with a computer ignores the issue of family violence. Rather than seeing the government's proposed amendments as essentially a reaction to the Family Violence Bill, *News 5* privileges the Women's Charter and gives the government the position of taking the initiative. The following evening, NMP Dr. Soin is put in the position of responding to this initiative of the government. She is also only given 46 seconds to put the case for the Family Violence Bill, while the Minister receives a total of 3 minutes 47 seconds over the three stories, and other voices opposing the Bill get another 2 minutes 36 seconds. While such content analysis does not always give the true picture when considering questions of fairness in the news, the following analysis shows how the position represented by Dr. Soin was in fact discredited and marginalized. The story itself reads:

"Mr Abdullah Tarmugi says the government's
mission of strengthening families and keeping them intact remains unchanged.

1) *Long shot of press conference, with the Minister in center of shot*
2) *View of room from behind Minister, showing many reporters taking down his words*

He said the proposed amendments of the Women's Charter will protect all members of the family, male and female, young and old.

3) *Mid-shot Minister sitting at table, talking*

There will be a wider coverage on what constitutes violence such as causing physical injury, placing victims in fear of physical injury, confining or detaining victims against their will, destroying or damaging property with intention to cause distress and annoyance, and even continual

4) *Onscreen graphics: blue screen with words setting out the proposed amendments*

harassment with the aim of causing distress. With the amendments, victims can file for a Personal Protection Order even before the violence takes place. The Courts will also be given greater powers to issue more than protection orders, such as referring the abuser to a counseling body or issuing a Power of Arrest if the abuser is deemed likely to inflict injury.

Also those who disobey protection or expedited orders will be penalized. Another proposal – to allow guardians, relatives, or officers appointed by the Minister to file applications on behalf of the victims.

Briefing reporters, Mr. Abdullah called for a sensitive approach to the problem.

5) *Group of reporters seated at tables*

6) *Long shot with Minister in center*

7) *Long shot of reporters*

8) *Medium close up of Minister*

[Abdullah Tarmugi, Acting Community Development Minister:]
'You must understand the mechanics of the relationship, the complex mix of emotions when persons who purportedly love each other, a person tied by either blood or marriage, why do they hurt each other? So it's a very complex matter.'

He said there's no need for a Family Violence

9) *Reporters; pan to put Minister center-stage again*

Bill as the Women's Charter already takes into account all aspects of family violence.

Pushing for the Family Violence Bill will give the impression, the Minister said, that family violence is a key social problem.

10) *Long shot of parents and children in park*

11) *Long shot of beach, parents and children*

It will also criminalize family violence and set the tone for a more litigious society. Moreover, the Minister added,

12) *Long shot swimming pool, families relaxing*

13) *Long shot recreational area, person with balloons*

the emphasis on promoting and strengthening family ties and values will also be undermined. Mr. Abdullah said the amendments should be seen in the wider context of what the government's been doing, such as working with the police and	14) *Shot from child's height of 3 children whose parents pat them on head to show affection and approval*
	15) *Social worker with family*
	16) *Woman helping boy with homework*
other social organizations."	17) *Same shot from different angle*

In the first section of this story the visuals show us the Acting Minister center-stage at a press conference. The long shots give the viewer a good look at the size and formality of the room and the number of reporters gathered. In contrast, NMP Dr. Soin is shot the following night in a medium close-up which cuts out any background setting. While this is probably not a deliberate ploy on the part of the camera operators and editors, there is no doubt the contrast in shots and setting favors the Acting Minister.

In the script, the Acting Minister is reported to describe the government as having a "mission" to "strengthen families and keep them intact." He therefore implicitly casts the Family Violence Bill as antifamily. This theme is stated more specifically later in the item, when the script tells us that "pushing for the Family Violence Bill" will mean that "the emphasis on promoting and strengthening family ties and values will also be underlined." This is perfectly fair reporting in itself – it is reported as the minister's view and not necessarily as fact – but, as I argue below, the story is constructed and illustrated in a manner which supports the Acting Minister's view.

The script proceeds to list what the proposed amendments will cover. These are spoken at the same time as they are spelled out graphically on a blue background, adding impact and clarity to the proposals. The proposals in the Domestic Violence Bill did not receive this treatment. Further impact is added by the reporter's stress on the word "even," as in "and *even* continual harassment with the aim of causing distress" – the tone of voice suggests that these proposed amendments are truly comprehensive. This is repeated: "With the amendments victims can file for a Personal Protection Order *even* before the violence takes place."

In the last section of the story the Acting Minister argues that the Family Violence Bill will "set the tone for a more litigious society." Such a statement ignores the provisions in the Bill for compulsory counseling before police action is taken for first offenders, but as it is not a practice of *News 5* to question Ministers, the audience is denied this important piece of information. He also suggests that "Pushing for the Family Violence Bill will give the impression that family violence is a key social problem." The visuals support his view. The shots change to idyllic pictures of happy families. There are four different shots of families at play together, in East Coast Park, around a swimming pool, and at a public recreational area. The weather is sunny, we hear the sound of seagulls and children playing, and even see a child carrying brightly colored balloons. This peaceful and happy world being created for us is far removed from the one portrayed by NMP Soin in her promotion of the Family Violence Bill. The script continues: "Moreover, the minister added, the emphasis on promoting and strengthening family ties and values will also be undermined," and we see a child's-height shot of three laughing children with their parents, who seem to be expressing affection and pride. Next come two shots of what look like professional people talking, with a parent and child in one shot and parents helping a child to read in the other, to support the Minister's statement that the government is already "working with police and other social organizations" in this field. The visuals therefore support the minister's assertion that family violence is not the major issue that NMP Soin says it is. The item is followed by another piece to camera by the presenter about the results of a pilot project for police to take a greater role in spousal abuse cases – the majority do not want outside intervention. The counterargument to this is not presented – rather, the results of the project are presented as unproblematic. As well as being chosen as the first item, this story is given further prominence by the presenter's pieces to camera both before and after the item. The only other time this happened in the seven bulletins I analyzed was when the verdict in the O. J. Simpson trial was released. This was followed by a short piece on the dangers of juries, and therefore the superiority of the Singapore court system.

Here then is an example of considerable overlap between reporting the minister's statements and editorial comment. The script and the visuals support and add to the Minister's statements. Further support is given by the lack of coverage given to the Domestic Violence Bill. The government is given credibility by *News 5* for all the progress they are making in their proposed amendments, without acknowledging that the groundbreaking work was actually done by Dr. Soin and her associates in preparing the Family Violence Bill. Where sections of the Domestic Violence Bill are stronger than the proposed amendments to the Women's Charter, the Bill is misreported and charged with being antifamily in approach. The view the Dr. Soin's Bill represents is thus marginalized and misrepresented by *News 5*.

Sue Abel

Conclusion

Fairclough points out that "the effects of media power are cumulative, working through the repetition of particular ways of handling causality and responsibility, particular ways of positioning the reader, and so forth" (1995: 54). This chapter has demonstrated that there is indeed repetition of patterns of representation in *News 5*, and that such patterns have ideological implications. I discussed earlier Birch's (1993a) argument that the Singapore government utilizes a discourse of crisis in order to maintain control. Such a discourse was not apparent in the bulletins collected for analysis for this study, where a more positive notion of the government as fully prepared for the future prevailed. At the time of writing, however, a prominent issue in the news media was a concern that Singapore would face tough competition in the future as challenges to its economic position arose from neighboring countries. Clearly, these discourses are related, as they both address the individual as "Singaporean citizen" (through a discourse of nationalism as outlined above), they are both future-oriented, and they both position the government, and only the government, as having all the answers. It would appear that the government is able to draw on either discourse as seems appropriate, and that this discourse is then reproduced by news media, including *News 5*. The example of the news handling of the Domestic Violence Bill outlined above indicates what happens when other individuals or groups suggest that they might have an answer.

I have argued that the relentlessly positive nature of the news bulletins in the case study has ideological implications. It is not my intention to denigrate positive news *per se*. In some ways, *News 5* is producing the kind of news that many viewers in Western countries, for example, have been asking for – news which does more than concentrate on crime, disasters, and violence; news which reports successes instead of concentrating on negativity; news which gives time to areas such as health, education, and housing. But it is the unremittingly positive nature of *News 5* with its discourses of nationalism and looking to the future that makes questions about the distribution of social, economic, and political resources seem unthinkable. In this way, *News 5* supports the present structure of power relations in Singapore.

There is one key issue that I have not discussed, and that is the extent to which the messages of *News 5* are taken up by viewers and incorporated into their understanding of the nature of Singaporean society and government. Reception studies have demonstrated that any reading of a text "is a product of the interface between the properties of the text and the interpretative resources and practices that the interpreter brings to bear on the text" (Fairclough, 1995: 16). While the dominant discourses present in *News 5* can be seen as working to constrain and limit the range of interpretations, oppositional readings are always possible. In a society such as Singapore, however, where challenges to the government are not encouraged and other views of government actions and decisions are not widely available, it can be argued that the "interpretative resources and practices" that viewers bring to *News 5* are in themselves limited. In this way *News 5* can be seen as contributing to the present status quo in Singapore.

Some Afterthoughts on Cross-Cultural Research

This ideological analysis of Singapore's television news program *News 5* raises two interrelated issues which need to be discussed, and which in themselves raise further questions which may be seen as rendering my conclusions provisional. These are:

a) My reading position as a Pakeha (white) New Zealander watching Singaporean news. To what extent do cultural misunderstandings and misinterpretations of the overt content come into play? Is it possible that, like Liebes and Katz's Arabic focus group (1990), I may actually "misread" information in a way which makes it more compatible with my own cultural horizon? Rather than having an "imperialist text," am I an "imperialist reader"?

b) My subsequent application to the news content of an ideological analysis based on a British cultural studies model is an issue. How relevant is such a "Western" approach to what might be assumed to be a "non-Western" media text? Is such an approach merely another form of colonialism which, by assuming Western theory can be "understood as a kind of universal template or a form of global cartography" (Perry: 1998), compares a Singaporean media text against a Western model?

Reading news cross-culturally

Because the majority of cross-cultural readings of media texts occur in a situation where programming has been exported from the West to the rest of the world, research on cross-cultural readings has focused on non-American and non-Western audiences reading American or Western programming. The classic examples of this deal with audience reception of American soap operas (Ang, Liebes & Katz, Miller) and conclude that, rather than being overwhelmed by the Western values that underlie such programs, local audiences make their own readings and uses of global media. There appears to be no research about Western reception of non-Western programming.

In terms of levels of cross-cultural comprehensibility and literacy, Messaris argues that Hollywood entertainment and US primetime television cross cultural boundaries, and that cross-cultural problems in visual communications seem more likely to arise from informed resistance and attitudinal barriers than from incomprehension of any cultural allusions. Again, there is no research that looks at Western comprehension of non-Western media.

Studies of news audiences are comparatively rare, especially cross-cultural studies. One that does purport to deal with the globalization of news from an audience-driven perspective takes as its case study audiences in Britain, Germany, France, and the United States (Kavoori, 1999) – a situation where the cultural values and news values in the text(s) are likely to be more aligned with those of the audience than they may be with, as in this case, a white New Zealander reading an Asian text. None of this gets me anywhere in understanding my own position and, in the absence of doing specific research, I am forced to fall back on "commonsense" assumptions. Singapore as a nation-state has an ambivalent cultural status. Ang and Stratton (1997) usefully describe Singapore as being positioned as a country which is both non-Western and always-already Westernized, and as an empowered East which has appropriated and reconstituted Western modernity. Certainly the English news media in Singapore have adopted the formatting and reporting techniques of the dominant Western media, and many of the same news values. The issue of how Asian values such as the importance of an orderly society, respect for authority, and consensus inform both the selection and representation of news is an issue that is too large and complex to be addressed here, but I refer to it again below. Given these factors, and my own position as a resident of Singapore for seven years who, as a media academic, maintained a watchful eye on the English-language media while at the same time trying to be aware of cultural differences and quasi-political restrictions, I would position myself as a "reader" somewhere between an "insider" and an "outsider." Such a position can be seen as having advantages for an ideological analysis of Singapore's television news. The ability to create an oppositional decoding depends on access to alternative or oppositional discourses, access to which someone educated in the Singaporean system may not have to the same degree.

Applying Western media theories to Asian media

Stuart Hall has already raised one of the issues involved here. Discussing cultural studies and the politics of internationalization, he has said, "It was always a question for many of us, me included, whether cultural studies wasn't in some way so deeply embedded, even in an unconscious way which we can't understand, in the problematics of Western modernity, that it was untranslatable to other cultures; that there couldn't be an African or Asian cultural studies" (Chen, 1996). However, the conclusions he comes to assume a local rather than outsider approach to cultural studies research: "Clearly . . . globalisation itself makes it possible for us all to address [cultural studies] issues from within the 'local' specificities of our own cultural situation" (ibid.: 407). David Birch (2000) argues for more interest in the rest of the world by Western cultural studies. This would seem to implicitly argue for a cross-cultural, transnational scholarship which at the same time recognizes what Stuart Hall argues: "One always has to remember that cultural studies is not an island on its own. It takes its coloration from social and cultural forces, especially if you are interested in the political articulation of cultural studies. One has to have in mind the cultural and political space in which cultural studies is obliged to operate" (Chen, 1996: 397).

In the Singaporean situation I would include as part of the "cultural and political space" the concept of Asian values, some of which I outlined above. The intent of my argument has not been to denigrate the inclusion of such values in news selection and presentation. As I have suggested above, news bulletins which do not focus primarily on conflict, crime, and disasters, which give time to topics such as health and education that get much less coverage in television news in (for example) New Zealand, and which highlight the positive rather than the negative, are, in my personal opinion, to be encouraged. My aim is to consider their implications in one particular news program in terms of the maintenance of power by the current elite.

A question arises, however. Both Birch and Hall, in discussing the internationalization of cultural studies, argue for the return of a more politically engaged cultural studies that examines cultural practices from the point of view of their relationship with, and within, relations of power. Birch, for example, argues that "Cultural studies began with public intellectuals prepared to speak out, prepared to push for change. We limit cultural studies and what it can achieve if we limit its role to what we do as academics only, rather than what we do as public intellectuals. Asia has a long tradition of the public intellectual, gagged or otherwise; dissent is not simply an academic nicety in some situations there, it is often a life-or-death struggle. Cultural studies has a significant part to play in that struggle" (2000: 151). There are issues here of, first, the extent to which such an approach conflicts with Asian values, and secondly, how practicable such a position is in an authoritarian neoliberal state like Singapore.

The concept of Asian values is no longer as sacrosanct as it used to be. One of Singapore's leading figures, Professor Tommy Koh, has argued that some of east Asia's political leaders have given Asian values a bad name by seeking to justify their abuses of power and the inequities of their societies in the name of those values (1999: 10). Zaharom Nain (2000) makes a similar point in his discussion of the Malaysian media, and I quote him at length because of his relevance to this chapter:

> There have been numerous attempts – more often than not with dubious results – among media academics and practitioners in Asia to "redefine" media studies for the region and assert the need for "Asian" theories of communication and the media. Not surprisingly, these attempts have been buoyed in recent years . . . by declarations made by heads of government, such as Malaysia's Mahathir and Singapore's Lee Kuan Yew and Goh Chuk Tong, about the need for Asian societies to seriously consider "Asian values," Confucianism, and Islam as viable alternatives to so-called "Western values and Western civilisation." . . . In arguing for the need to discover "new" theories and research strategies, often they end up helping to legitimize repressive regimes, undemocratic practices and tightly controlled media systems whose *raison d'être* is to uphold and help perpetuate these regimes. (Nain, 2000: 149)

Nain goes on to argue that the role of media studies in Asia is threefold:

> First, to analyse critically how [the ideological] apparatus operates and how the power of the state and/or market is translated in the media and possibly reinforced by the media. Second, to argue in turn, and in a convincing fashion, how this would be detrimental to the development of ideas and, invariably, detrimental to different segments of society. Third, to strategically locate ways in which alternative policies and structures could be realised to make the media – systems, organizations, practices – more representative, more egalitarian, more liberating. (Nain 2000: 150)

Such an analysis and call to action sounds very similar indeed to what Hall and Birch see cultural studies as being about.

Asian reception of this chapter

This piece of work was originally commissioned in 1996 by Phyllis Chew, one of the editors of a then forthcoming book *Textual Practice in Singapore Culture*, at that stage to be published by Routledge in England as part of their "Language, Media and Culture" series. However, this series was discontinued, and the editors instead finalized a contract with Times in Asia Academic Publishing (Singapore). The final draft of the chapter was approved by both editors, and submitted to the publishers along with the other chapters. To Chew's surprise, the publishers asked that my chapter either be substantially rewritten, or withdrawn. Their concern was not with the inappropriateness of my approach, but with what they saw as the potentially "libelous nature" of the chapter. Two other chapters, both written by Chinese Singaporeans, suffered the same fate.

I subsequently presented a chapter based on my research at a sociology conference in Kuala Lumpur. The reaction there was not that my arguments were invalid, but that I was "brave" to make them. I argue therefore that the main issue in doing cultural studies research as a Westerner in Singapore was not in this instance one of cultural dissonance, but rather one of trying to present what was perceived to be a dissident voice in a society of limited democracy, where the boundaries of critical public discourse are not clearly set out, but where narrow and unilateral application of laws of libel may be imposed if a boundary is seen to be crossed. In the end I am happy to let my analysis stand as a case study which may or may not be taken up and debated by Asian scholars.

Notes

1   This is one of the few stories where any suggestion of controversy is admitted. The controversy, however, is within limits which do not threaten the existing distribution of economic resources and political power.
2   A term coined by Barthes (1973) to show how the economic determinants of a society are absent from representations of that society – they are literally unnamed.
3   Soin quoted statistics which showed that every day 6 women in Singapore reported beatings by their husbands to the police. Professionals in the field have suggested that the true figure for domestic violence incidents is probably 3 or 4 times higher than this reported rate.

References

Abel, Sue (1997). *Shaping the News: Waitangi Day on Television.* Auckland: Auckland University Press.

Ang, Ien (1985). *Watching Dallas: Soap Opera and the Melodramatic Imagination.* London: Methuen.

Ang, Ien and Stratton, Jon (1997). "The Singapore Way of Multiculturalism: Western Concepts/Asian Cultures." *New Formations* 31 (Spring/Summer).

Barthes, Roland (1973). *Mythologies.* London: Paladin.

Bell, Alan (1991). *The Language of News Media.* Oxford: Blackwell.

Birch, David (1993a). *Singapore Media: Communication Strategies and Practices.* Melbourne: Longman Cheshire.

Birch, David (1993b). "Staging Crises: Media and Citizenship." In Gary Rodan, ed., *Singapore Changes Guard: Social, Political and Economic Directions in the 1990s.* New York: Longman Cheshire.

Birch, David (2000). "Transnational Cultural Studies: What Price Globalisation?" *Social Semiotics* 10(2).

Chen, Kuan-Hsing (1996). "Cultural Studies and the Politics of Internationalization: An Interview with Stuart Hall." In D. Morley and Kuan-Hsing Chen, eds., *Stuart Hall: Critical Dialogues in Cultural Studies.* London: Routledge.

Chua, Beng-Huat (1995). *Communitarian Ideology and Democracy in Singapore.* London: Routledge.

Clammer, John (1993). "Deconstructing Values: The Establishment of a National Ideology and its Implications for Singapore's Political Future." In Gary Rodan, ed., *Singapore Changes Guard: Social, Political and Economic Directions in the 1990s.* New York: Longman Cheshire.

Fairclough, Norman (1989). *Language and Power.* London: Longman.

Fairclough, Norman (1995). *Media Discourse.* London: Edward Arnold.

Fowler, Roger (1991). *Language in the News: Discourse and Ideology in the Press.* London: Routledge.

Galtung, Johan and Ruge, M. (1965). "Structuring and Selecting News." In Stanley Cohen and Jock Young, eds., *The Manufacture of News: Deviance, Social Problems and the Media.* London: Constable, 1973.

George, Cherian (1989). "The State and the Press in Singapore: In the National Interest?" Unpublished BA honors dissertation, University of Cambridge, UK.

Glasgow University Media Group (1976). *Bad News.* London: Routledge & Kegan Paul.

Hall, Stuart (1977). "Culture, the Media and the Ideological Effect." In J. Curran et al., eds., *Mass Communication and Society.* London: Edward Arnold.

Hall, S., Critcher, C., Jefferson, T., Clarke, J., and Roberts, B. (1978). *Policing the Crisis.* London: Macmillan.

Kavoori, A. P. (1999). "Discursive Texts, Reflexive Audiences: Global Trends in Television News Texts and Audience Reception." *Journal of Broadcasting and Electronic Media* 43(3): 386–98.

Koh, Tommy (1999). "Differences in Asian and European Values." *Asian Mass Communication Bulletin* 29(5).

Liebes, T. and Katz, E. (1990). *The Export of Meaning: Cross Cultural Readings of Dallas.* New York: Oxford University Press.

Messaris, Paul (1997). "Visual 'Literacy' in Cross-Cultural Perspective." In Robert Kubey, ed., *Media Literacy in the Information Age.* New Jersey: Transaction Publishers.

Miller, Daniel (1992). "The Young and the Restless in Trinidad: A Case Study of the Local and Global in Mass Consumption." In R. Silverstone and E. Hirsch, eds., *Consuming Technologies: Media and Information in Domestic Spaces.* London and New York: Routledge.

Nain, Zaharom (2000). "Globalised Theories and National Controls: The State, Market and the Malaysian Media." In James Curran and Myung-In Park, eds., *De-Westernising Media Studies.* London and New York: Routledge.

Perry, Nick (1998). "Travelling Theory, Nomadic Theorizing." In *Hyperreality and Global Culture.* New York: Routledge.

Poulantzas, N. (1965). *Political Power and Social Classes.* London: New Left Books.

Rampal, Roy (1995). "Media Credibility: A Case Study of RTM2 and TCS5 English-Language News Broadcasts." *Media Asia* 22(3).

Rodan, Gary (1993). "The Growth of Singapore's Middle Class and its Political Significance." In G. Rodan, ed., *Singapore Changes Guard: Social, Political and Economic Directions in the 1990s.* New York: Longman Cheshire.

Root, Jane (1986). *Open the Box: About Television.* London: Comedia.

Van Dijk, Tuen A. (1983). "Discourse Analysis: Its Development and Application to the Structure of News." *Journal of Communication* 32(2): 20–43.

7

Beyond the Fragments: Reflecting on "Communicational" Cultural Studies in South Korea

Keehyeung Lee

"The problem of interpreting any cultural text, social practice, or historical event must always involve constituting a context around it . . . but contexts are not entirely empirically available because they are not already completed, stable configurations, passively waiting to receive another element. They are not guaranteed in advance, but are rather the site of contradictions, conflicts, and struggles . . . in Gramscian terms, any interpretation . . . [or] historical practice is an articulation, an active insertion of a practice into a set of contextual relations that determine the identity and effects of both the text and the context . . . these articulated connections are sometimes fought over, consciously or unconsciously, but in any case, an articulation is always accomplished . . . and will always have political consequences."

– Lawrence Grossberg

"There is no way out of the game of culture."

– Pierre Bourdieu [cited in Robbins]

Introduction

The purpose of this chapter is to present a critical yet sympathetic reading of the "communicational" cultural studies which has emerged in South Korea (hereafter Korea) in the mid-1990s onwards. By communicational cultural studies, after Grossberg (1997), I refer to a subfield in cultural studies that deals predominantly with the construction and reception of a range of popular media forms and practice – television programs, film, ads, photography – using various qualitative methods. Communicational cultural studies has adopted textual analysis – e.g., Hall's "encoding/decoding" model – that seeks to interpret the polysemic meanings in media texts, as well as qualitative audience reception analysis that maps out the audience's negotiated interaction with various televisual texts. The chapter is divided into two parts. First, I will introduce and reflect on several different and yet loosely connected analytic and methodological concerns in local communicational cultural studies. Second, I will provide a series of assessments and critiques of communicational cultural studies work. In particular, I shall focus on the work of Munhwa Yonku Bunkwa (Cultural Studies Division; hereafter MYB), which has been a main cultural studies group in the area of media and popular culture.

MYB, a branch of the Korean Association of Broadcasting Studies, is mostly composed of US- and British-trained media scholars who work under the formative influence of the "Birmingham school" (strongly associated with Stuart Hall) and Anglo-American cultural studies. Most of the MYB group members were trained in the metropolitan institutional settings where CS-centered curricula were readily or at least partially available. In terms of its members' disciplinary affiliations, MYB is composed of scholars in media and communications programs who, for years, have selectively introduced, applied, and reworked the ideas of Raymond Williams, Stuart Hall, David Morley, and other scholars who have been active in the tradition of Anglo-American cultural studies. As a loosely connected group, so far, MYB have produced three books: *Cultural Studies of Television* [*television munhwa yonku*, 1999], which brought together a diverse range of textual and reception analysis of television programs, as well as critical reading of the changing media culture; *The Themes and Thematics of Cultural Studies* [*munhwa yonku iron*, 1998], which introduced various methodologies in Anglo-American cultural studies; and *The Lover: Television Drama and Society* [*Aein: television dramawa sahoe*, 1997] which analyzed a highly popular local television melodrama by using genre, content, textual, discursive, and reception analysis.

Munhwa Yonku Bunkwa and the Emergence of Communicational Cultural Studies

As Yongjin Won (2000; 2001) points out, from its inception, MYB has taken issue with, if not confronted, two dominant approaches in local media studies. First, they criticized the deeply entrenched positivistic tendencies in the dominant communication paradigm that have been preoccupied with causal effects and have been at the same time politically conservative. Rather than pursuing narrowly defined "effects" of various media programs on *passive* audiences, MYB has looked into the multifaceted workings of textual codes and strategies adopted in various media genres and texts. It also has examined a range of social discourses and "intertexts" in the public arena that are generated and mediated by various media texts and events. In this strand of research, MYB has examined the complex interaction between tele-visual texts, social discourses, and audiences as heterogeneous communities.

Second, against the political-economic approach which more often than not deals with the macro-question of media power, industries, and own-ership, MYB has brought in a series of diverse and "micro-scale" researches that illuminate the *relative autonomy* of media practices, the constructive power of media texts as key representational vehicles of social meaning, as well as the *active* role of audiences as the symbolic negotiators of social meaning (Jeon, 1999; Yoon, 1999). MYB has also researched how audiences as differentially positioned subjects in the social arena who have different economic and cultural capital consume and utilize various media and cul-tural texts, thereby utilizing particular sets of symbolic resources in their media reception as well as forming particular forms of moral and emo-tional economy. As Youngho Im (1998) and others have suggested, against the dominance of mainstream media research, communicational cultural studies in Korea has manifested "revisionism" [*sujungjuui*] in the field of communication and media studies by introducing alternative theoretical frameworks and methodologies that tend to emphasize the "ritualistic" side of communication and cultural processes. MYB's research marked the beginning of a new phase in media studies and popular cultural studies in the local arena: their work has ushered in various experiments in text-centered media analysis and new ways of thinking about viewer activities as "cultural production." Though MYB's work has predominantly revolved around the problematics of media culture and the activities of audiences in everyday settings, it has also worked on others areas of interest. They have introduced various qualitative methodologies and explored broader cultural-studies problematics, which include the globalization of culture and the politics of youth culture, by selectively adopting Anglo-American cultural-studies frameworks (Jung, 1998). Put differently, MYB's work can be located at an intersection where hitherto underrepresented cultural and sociological analysis of the media and the varied reception of cultural forms meet. In the following, let me introduce and assess MYB's representative work on media practices, in particular television programs and discourses.

To begin, MYB has collectively explored the, power, place, and use of television texts in everyday life from various methodological angles and analytic gazes. First of all, they have adopted *textual and semiotic analysis,* and provided a number of studies that shed light on the workings of various ideologies and connotative codes in televisual texts. Several methodological and interpretive trends are found in this strand of research: first, MYB has located the ways dominant patriarchal/gender ideologies and myths structure various media texts using semiotic-interpretive analysis. Second, MYB has criticized the "monovocal" and reductionist aspects of "old" ideological analysis of media texts and has brought in a more detailed and supple understanding of media texts and its power to hail and situate viewers within particular narrative and semiotic chain of meaning. It has introduced such new concepts as the "structured polysemy" of text and "preferred/negotiated/oppositional readings" performed by media audiences. Under the influence of Eco, Iser, Jauss, Fiske, Hall, and Radway – whose "encoding and decoding" model was highly influential on MYB scholars – the group has adopted narrative, semiotic, and genre analysis and provided sophisticated understandings of social meaning triggered by audiences' negotiation with television texts. MYB has looked into the operation of particular textual devices – character, plot structure, representative codes, visual and lingustic syntagm, the implied author and readers – as well as the workings and "naturalization" of various ideological signs in television texts. By selectively borrowing some versions of film theories – "suture" theory and theory of the "cinematic apparatus," some MYB members have also examined the ways media texts as powerful signifying practices construct spectatorship and viewer position (Lee, 1999).

Third, some MYB members have adopted a psychoanalytic method and explored the ways the oedipal narratives hail and position male and female viewers differentially. In doing so, they have symptomatically read-off the patriarchal norms embedded in popular television drama and examined the gendered representation of television characters and personas (Park & Kim, 1997). In a related vein, other members in the group who have adopted a feminist approach have examined how popular television genres, such as melodramas, television serials, situation comedies, and talk shows, create the gendered pleasures, "emotional realism," "tragic structure of feeling," and fantasies that are enacted by female viewers. They have noticed that television viewing requires "feminine" competences and a rich knowledge of the genre that are as sophisticated and detailed as that of the experts. They have also found that female viewers tend to create the "negotiated space" between the fictional texts and their real life (Park, 1999; Kim

& Park, 1999). In doing so, some MYB members have attempted to fore-ground what is often called "the politics of the living room," and associated television viewing with the ritualized and active negotiation of cultural meanings and realities in the domestic sphere.

The second research method MYB has deployed is *discourse analysis* that examines the articulation among media and other cultural discourses. Whereas the aforementioned textual analysis has concentrated on the inter-nal workings of various ideological codes, and textual and narrative devices in media texts, discourse analysis has extended the notion of text and at the same time has engaged with larger sociohistorical and moral issues mediated and produced by media texts and institutions. By using discourse analysis, MYB has looked into the social and power relations in which a particular media text is situated. To take an example, Insung Hwang, Yongjin Won, and others, in the 1997 study mentioned above, analyzed a tremendously successful television melodrama, "The Lover" [*aein*], which dealt with adultery and mid-life crisis. Their research collectively demon-strated that the received moral consensus once surrounding the theme of adultery in the local arena was being eroded, and the theme itself became a point of social contention. They investigated three dominant discourses that were generated by the reception of the melodrama in the local public arena: conservative discourse attacked the drama for its representation of adultery as an "acceptable" feature of life. Moralistic "opinion leaders" in journalistic institutions and academia wrote articles that warned the moral crisis and problems that were reflected in, and partially triggered by, the drama. Some of them even attempted to pressure the media professionals to modify the theme while the program was still aired. MYB documented the varying social commentaries on the drama and revealed the ways such moralistic and paternalistic views defended the traditional notion of marriage and gender roles. "Reflectionist" discourse treated the drama as a "barometer" and an "index" of rapid sociocultural change underway, through which marriage as an institution was under increasing challenge as Korean society experienced rapid *detraditionalization* and the received definition of marriage was increasingly contested (Lee, 2000). Feminist dis-course focused on the agency and choices of female characters in the drama who were portrayed not as the victims of patriarchal power, but as self-conscious social subjects who could make their own decisions regarding marriage, romance, and work. Feminist discourse drew attention to the gendered representations and subject positions that were formed in media texts that could invite potentially subversive readings. Jeon and others in MYB found out that the reception of the drama was significantly influenced by the competing sets of social discourses and intertexts that involved acute social and moral dilemmas, and thereby the production of meaning mediated by the drama was always necessarily "overdetermined" (Hwang & Won, 1997; Jeon, 1999). Thus, though MYB has not clearly elaborated its position on the effectivity of media texts, it has adopted a process-oriented, more dynamic, and yet modest model in which the effectivity of media text is located at a particular site and in a specific context where the power of such a text is not assumed in advance and the "audiencing" has become a key contextual factor. Through detailed discourse and sociological analyses that track down the uneven articulation and transfer of social meanings among media discourses and social discourses, MYB has explored the question of cultural hegemony in the media representation of the family, gender roles, work, and personal choices. In MYB's research, television has often been considered as a narrator that represents rapid social-historical transformation rather than as an agency of dominant ideologies and class interests which had been a main object of analysis in the critical media studies tradition in the 1980s (Cho et al., 2000; Hwang, 1999).

The third method MYB has adopted is *reception and ethnographically influenced analysis*. This has gradually became its favorite research method. Having realized the gaps and shortcomings in text-oriented media research, MYB has brought in several nuanced methodological strategies and concerns in locating the activities and roles of media audiences as concrete meaning-making social subjects who are differentially situated across the social field. First, under the influence of scholars in the tradition of ethnographic audience research, represented by Ang, Radway, Modelsky, Van Zoonen, Morley, and Brunsdon, MYB has brought in the possibilities of "negotiated" readings performed by media viewers, and more importantly their insertion of such readings into their life as daily rituals. They have moved from a text-oriented and relatively abstract model of polysemy and multi-accentuaity to a more diverse and differentiated model of context that surrounds, constantly makes inroads into, and reshapes the particular text under analysis. MYB's use of "media ethnography" has been influenced by Anglo-American reception analysis in which ethnography "makes a concerted effort to note the range of daily practices and to understand how historical subjects articulate their cultural universe" (Radway, 1988: 36). By adopting ethnographic methods, MYB has moved into a more context-oriented analysis of media texts in which multilayered interrelations among texts, the flows of social meanings, and audience activities are located on a larger intellectual and analytic canvas. By doing so, MYB has started to look into more fluid and extended cultural and emotional economy of media viewers in particular social settings and their "micropolitics" [*misijungchi-hak*] at everyday level, which is in part mobilized through their engagement with various media forms and the use of accumulated media knowledge. By adopting various qualitative methods, at one level, MYB has endeavored to present nuanced understanding of audience activities and the "bottom-up" view of the culture of particular groups of media viewers. Such an attempt has been strategically made to legitimize emerging reception studies and the ethnographically inclined work in the local media field which has long been dominated by functionalist and supposedly "value-neutral" mass communications research.

At another level, MYB has pursued subtle realism, gendered and trans-gressive pleasures, other emotional and affective engagements formed between the media text and "actual" media viewers. In doing so, MYB has started to perceive the media from the viewpoint of *everyday life and poetics*. Through detailed empirical research that uses in-depth and semi-structured interviews, group discussions, participant observation, and ethnographic analysis of particular groups of viewers, MYB has endeavored to capture the voices, lived experiences, and symbolic activities of media viewers in its analysis. Thus the fixed correspondence between the media text and audiences once unproblematically assumed in dominant research models has been replaced with more pluralistic, relativistic, dialogical, and less instrumentalized aspects of media use and consumption. In particular, MYB has found out that media audiences have their own interpretive frames and strategies and that they continuously negotiated with media texts through the production of social meaning. In a related vein, MYB has explored the ways media audiences create their own particular identities, fandoms, and subcultures by utilizing symbolic and cultural repertoires, cultural themes, and styles provided by various media forms and events. One notable study was done by Sunhee Yoon (1999), who selectively adopted a Deleuzian notion of the "nomadic subject," postmodern theories on the production of sign economy, and a psychosemiotic framework. Through the participant-observation of the production of popular music programs in the television studio and in-depth interviews with young people, Yoon researched how teenagers actively embraced the images and styles of popular stars as their "idealistic self" and utilized their passions, emotions, and investment on popular music, images, and cultural styles as key resources for constructing their own "space of cultural resistance that is not permitted in reality." At the same time, she zoomed in on the very context in which local youth was situated. In particular, she explored the ways youths who were caught in a highly oppressive educational system and with little parental or social recognition of their desires watched popular programs – entertainment programs and music videos – and constructed and enacted their fantasy as a source of pleasure, affective investment, and bonding. Put in different terms, she provided an exploratory study of the emerging "nomadism of desire" enacted by youth as an effort to carve out their own space – a "smooth space" – for maneuver against the interventions of various disciplinary agents – the school and parents – and the boredom in their lives. She argued that such a shared desire among youth could be articulated with youth's ways of finding an escape route from the suffocating life. In a way, by not fully endorsing a flawed model of "semiotic democracy," but presenting a more dynamic reception model based on the symbolic transgression and the production of social differences by youth, Yoon attempted to provide a new angle in reception studies that took seriously the ongoing tug of war between reterritorializing and deterritorializing forces in the field of media and subculture.

From a different angle, some members of MYB have focused on the shaping of social and gender differences in media texts through what might be called an "ethnography of television professionals." Hunsoon Kim and Dongsook Park (1999) interviewed the female authors who wrote popular television melodramas. They explored how female writers dealt with and were shaped by the dominant genre conventions, production values, and male-centered institutional norms in the media industry. Through detailed interviews and methods of naturalistic inquiry, they found out that though not all female writers embraced politicized feminist causes, nonetheless the majority of them worked on varying topics centered on women's conditions and predicaments in Korean society, and would insert women's perspectives and concerns into their rhetorical and narrative strategies. Put differently, their research explored the potential of "écriture feminine" (a phrase associated with French feminists such as Hélène Cixous and Luce Irigaray) in the domain of television dramas. Taken together, *though in large measure its research has remained exploratory*, MYB has focused on the group differences in consuming media texts. Second, MYB has worked on the link between media and other social texts by utilizing both discursive and audience research.

A Critique of MYB Group: The "Birmingham in Korea"?

For years, MYB has been one of the active groups that have endeavored to form various modes of cultural studies in Korea. The group has translated some of the main theoretical frameworks and methodological tools that are originated from the "Birmingham school." It has also provided culturally nuanced analysis of a diverse range of cultural texts and people's use of these texts in their natural settings.

Nonetheless, their work contains several significant drawbacks, shortcomings, and still uncharted territories. First, as is exemplified above, the combined scholarly objective of MYB has been to come to terms with the questions surrounding the power of media texts, audience formation, and popular cultural analyses. As Changyoon Ju (1997) points out, the members of MYB have demonstrated, above all, a narrowly confined "mediacentric" tendency: rather than tackling the mediation between and across a diverse range of televisual and social discourses and settings. MYB's key research area of interests have been devoted to text- and audience-centered analyses that rarely ventured outside of the received perimeters of media studies. In doing so, as Youngjin Won (2000) acutely points out, MYB has taken the route to "revisionism" in media studies: it put the analytic spotlight on the often neglected activities of media audiences in mainstream communication research and the efficacy of various media and cultural texts in producing and mediating social meaning (see Curran et al., 1996). At the same time the group has brought into the local media studies field a range of communicational cultural-studies concepts – text, polysemy, audiencing, intertextuality, cultural hegemony, ideological state apparatus, etc. – as well as a number of qualitative research methods that can engage with various forms of media and cultural forms from alternative angles. Certainly MYB has provided more nuanced and differentiated notions of culture, signifying processes, the active role of media viewers and cultural consumers, and played a productive role in the midst of the boom in discourses on culture, media, ideology, and knowledge in the local arena. Though some members of the group called for an extended and more politically active role for "cultural politics," which necessarily entails engaging with larger critical and sociopolitical issues and concerns in the local arena – to name a few, cultural and economic globalization; the alliance between cultural studies and social movements; cultural studies and policy concerns; the legacy and the presence of (neo)colonial modernity; etc. – the majority of MYB members have shied away from such charged issues and thorny problematics that necessarily require nonmediacentric and more politicized forms of analysis. *Put bluntly, they have played their intellectual-disciplinary game too safely.* In Korea, the local division of labor in universities runs deep, and even with the occasional calls for "crossdisciplinarity" as an ideal, there has been little dialogue and critical engagement between cultural studies and other disciplines in the human sciences. To a degree, by selectively adopting the Birmingham approaches and residing within the relatively comfortable disciplinary boundary of media studies, MYB's "cultural politics" was manifested predominantly through the textual and discursive analysis of the complex textual characteristics, use, and the potential of media and popular cultural practices. It can be argued that MYB has exemplified an instance of [Edward] Saidean "traveling theories" in local media studies field by forming a "communicational" cultural studies that is strategically gleaned from and constantly under the influence of the Birmingham approaches.

Yet it should be accentuated that certainly the Birmingham approaches included more than media and popular cultural analysis and an unfailingly mediacentric trend in MYB's work invites a legitimate critique as to the political nature of communicational cultural studies. British cultural studies attempted to produce the more complex and rigorous forms of cultural marxism and Gramscianism in order to challenge the new and messy social realities as well as the recomposition of social forces in postwar Britain (Won, 2000; Dworkin, 1997). Put simply, the Birmingham school provided new and powerful ways of articulating culture and social power. To the extent that the Birmingham school's work has consistently been a formative influence and source of intellectual inspiration, such a limited adoption of critical methodologies in MYB's work invites a series of thorny questions regarding MYB's inability to intervene in the wider social arena and materialize its commitment to "radical contextualism." Though MYB has "successfully" emulated the approaches of British cultural studies in the area of media and popular culture, it has lacked a political spirit through which it can map out and actively intervene in the popular struggles and negotiations with the dominant social forces in postauthoritarian Korea. MYB has paid a scant attention to the popular struggles and the role of disciplinary power in everyday life. Put differently, except for a few occasions (see Kang, 2001; Jeon, 1998), MYB has not fully engaged with the formative influence of Gramscianism and its political potential. To take an example, MYB's use and construction of the politics of popular culture has not been properly articulated with the politics of social formation and counterhegemony. Unlike other cultural-studies groups in the local arena – such as Munhwa Kwahak (Cultural Science) or Ttohanauimunhwa (Alternative Culture) – MYB has rarely engaged with (post)marxism and other critical intellectual practices that have significant bearings on the Korean intellectual *cum* social fields. In short, rather than wrestling with the macro-analysis of the structure of domination and the changing relationships between cultural and other practices, MYB has often worked on the problematics that are associated with the consumption and reception of media and popular cultural texts (Ma, 1997).

What is at stake here is that, though often it has been self-consciously claimed that MYB engaged in cultural studies, its version of cultural studies lacks both clearly articulated political insights and methodological rigor. Put differently, though the group *at a theoretical level* embraced an articulation theory and radical contextualism as two intricately interlinked methodological and political practices, MYB's actual work has often skirted the thorny question of how cultural studies practitioners should construct developed theories of context and proper political strategies to re-articulate the given context. Its work, except in a few cases, has rarely drawn due attention to the particular conjunctures and contexts in which its research and intellectual pursuit are situated. In a way, MYB has wrestled with the deceptively simple yet nagging question, "where does the text end and context begin?" Yet the group has rarely been able to provide convincing methodological and political answers. In addition, MYB has not shown much interest in linking its intellectual project to or collaborating with other progressive scholars in the social sciences and humanities. The group has translated and attempted to localize various Anglo-American cultural-studies frameworks as useful and powerful explanatory tools. Yet the group's deployment of such theories is, on many occasions, not tested empirically. Instead, MYB has occasionally been preoccupied with a high theoreticism that has uneven and weak relevance to the local context and cultural struggles.

Second, MYB has brought in and established its specific subdisciplinary methodologies against the long-reigning orthodoxy of quantitative research in local media and communication studies. In doing so, the group has helped bring in a so-called revisionism in media studies (Won, 2001). To take an example of one of the main methodologies adopted by MYB, it has utilized "ethnographic" analysis that was often based on small-scale audience studies in which researchers did not literally spend much time "in the field." Ethnography as it has been adopted by MYB members should have rigorously been narrowed down and defined in specific fashion. I would argue that their ethnographic work does not deserve to be labeled as "ethnographic." In addition, in the work of MYB, there has been an implicit divide between "structural" and "cultural" analysis. MYB has focused on the latter by working mainly on the specific groups of audiences as cultural producers and *bricoleurs*. Hence, MYB's work has contained some degrees of "cultural populism" and romanticizing tendencies that do not interrogate the placement and distribution of culture and media in particular sites by powerful culture industries and social power. Perhaps "reflexivity" should have been a crucial element of MYB's use of ethnographic analysis. But the group has not utilized reflexivity that can interrogate the politics of its intellectual work and the distance between the researcher and his or her object of inquiry, whether it is fandom, the popular reception of televisual texts, or the symbolic resistance of particular subcultural groups (see Alasuutari, 1999). From a slightly different angle, as for the nature of reception analysis, MYB's use of the "audience" as a key discursive construct and organizing category contains some methodological problems. As Grossberg (1997) aptly puts its, "media audiences are shifting constellations, located within varying multiple discourses which are never entirely outside of the media discourse themselves." Though MYB has provided a series of detailed small-scale audience studies, the group has not fully elaborated on its use of audience. Considering that perhaps there isn't really such a thing as audience "out there," and the audience has been a powerful marketing term (see Allor, 1988), MYB should have interrogated its use of the term in principled fashion and acknowledged its methodological complexity, murkiness, and limits. In addition, it could have adopted other measures of "triangulation"; methods that can complement the methodological weakness in small-scale research carried out through reception analysis (Denzin, 1999).

Third, a similar critique can be made of the MYB's use of textual and semiotic analysis: it can certainly illuminate the power of media texts in detailed and new ways which gives the group's work intellectual potency. Having said this, MYB's efforts have largely been devoted to its interrogation of text as a basic unit of analysis. What was less pursued is the mediation between different media texts, sites of production, distribution, and reception of such texts in the larger sociohistorical terrain (see Martin-Barbero, 2000). Considering that local culture industries have grown rapidly and cultural/media globalization has become a powerful social force and part of the lived process in contemporary Korea, research analysis that is centered on a single text has an inbuilt limit. Put differently, MYB has lacked conceptual frameworks that can situate the dizzying flows of media *cum* cultural forms, images, and meanings circulating in the social field. Though some MYB members have suggested more dynamic and spatial concepts that can situate the media and cultural practices in the era of highly flexible and predatory globalization – to name a few, "mediascapes," "cognitive mapping," "satellite modernities," more refined models on media "flows" in a multichannel environment, "power geometry" between people and places – there has only been a small number of exploratory studies that have attempted to situate the uneven articulation between "local" and "nonlocal" forms of cultural production and hybridization (Ma, 1997; Won, 2000; Jeon, 1998). The group has only sparsely engaged with the ongoing "space–time compression" and "distanciation" at work in and beyond the local arena. Taken together, MYB's work does not always successfully break out of the dominant textualist tendencies, though it often criticized such reductionist tendencies and emphasized radical contextualism.

Fourth, any media practice necessarily entails the production and articulation of popular emotions, desires, pleasures, and fantasies that are generated and performed by the socially positioned subjects in everyday settings. Though there have been certain MYB "pilot" studies that have zoomed in on, say, the political economy of desires, their research as a whole has been limiting and predominantly exploratory. Often Deleuzian nomadism of desires or Ang's notion of fantasy as powerful, imagined social force have been extrapolated into the small-scale analysis of popular cultural reception or fandom without closely examining the multiple channels and routes through which such desires and fantasies are produced and anchored at particular sites and moments. At the same time, the local adoption of the "rhizomatics of desire, pleasures, and fantasies" tends to undervalue the power of media institutions which continuously attempt to commercialize – or "reterritorialize" – the emerging fandom and rearticulate its potential.

Fifth, though some MYB members have started to discuss the "policy" turn in cultural and media studies as an active attempt to go beyond the bipolar model of cultural "resistance" and "co-optation," the questions regarding the limits of communicational cultural studies and the potential role of cultural studies as an actor in the interventions into media and cultural institutions have rarely been addressed. Since the late 1990s, Korean government has implemented a number of aggressive cultural policies and invested to develop various forms of media and culture industries as a key export sector. In such an environment, local cultural-studies practitioners could have seized the opportunities by using their sophisticated intellectual resources (see Bennett, 1998). It seems understandable that MYB is somewhat wary of the consequences that can result from their potential "collaboration with" the state and private sector in the name of "local turn to policy." Perhaps no serious local scholars in cultural studies want to be identified yet with the label "cultural technicians." In a local context in which the cooperation between the state and the intellectual communities in the area of the arts, media, film, and culture has already begun, local cultural studies scholars, including MYB members, may consider using the opportunities for different forms of cultural intervention other than the usual counterhegemonic struggles. In this respect, though indeed there is a danger of transforming cultural studies into a new management wing of the state, MYB, I believe, may consider providing detailed and progressive cultural programs to complement carefully selected government policies and private groups of cultural producers. The following comment of Tony Bennett (1998: 192) is highly suggestive at this point:

> The "policy debate" was itself a symptom of what was already a clearly emerging division between revisionist tendencies within cultural studies – tendencies, that is, wishing to embrace reformist rhetorics and programs – and tendencies still committed to the earlier rhetorics of revolution or resistance. The "policy debate" viewed in this light, served a catalysing function in serving as a means of clarifying options which were already evident as emerging tensions within cultural studies . . . It is clear that the references to policy serve to flag a more general set of issues concerning the kinds of political stances, programs, styles of intellectual work and relations of intellectual production that can now cogently be claimed for cultural studies work.

As Kyunchan Jeon (1999: 82) and others suggest, television in the post-authoritarian and rapidly globalizing Korea can be "an institution of communication, polyphony, and openness rather than an institution of repression." Though he also calls for a more "reformist" and interventionist policies that should be provided by local cultural-studies practitioners, so far such a new thinking that links cultural studies and media/cultural policies has only occasionally materialized. It is fair to argue that the policy turn has enormous intellectual as well as social implications for cultural-studies practitioners in the local arena who want to explore new forms of cultural coordination and intervention. Yet it is still a project to be launched and explored cautiously.

On the Border of Media and Cultural Studies: Crossing the Boundaries, Moving Beyond the Fragments

Communicational and more socially inclined cultural studies in Korea have collectively provided the scholars and postgraduate students in academia as well as cultural critics in the popular-cultural field with much-desired new tools for nuanced social and discursive analysis that could come to terms with new and messy realities to a significant degree. I want to argue that, from its inception, cultural studies in the local arena has engaged with two interrelated "fronts": for one, it has explored the various theoretical and methodological frameworks on culture and ideology which were borrowed from Anglo-American cultural studies. For another, it has attempted to locate the emerging everyday practices and cultural formations that had not been seriously tackled by mainstream disciplines. In doing so, cultural studies gained almost immediate popularity and wide acceptance. Cultural studies contributed significantly to put the more fluid, complicated, constructive, and transgressive role of cultural practices and the significance of "micropolitical" issues – the politics of difference, subcultures, consumption, and identity politics – on the local intellectual map. Employing a variety of semiotic, (post)structuralist, psychoanalytic, and discursive analysis, cultural studies has introduced and worked on culturally and linguistically nuanced problematics that include the following: the political significance of language and sign, the "relative autonomy" and radical diversity of a range of cultural practices through the work of the "Birmingham school," Gramscian hegemonic politics and the historical sedimentation of "common sense" in the sociopolitical arena, the rearticulation of Althusserian ideology and decentered formation of subjectivity, the Foucauldian notion of discursive and genealogical analysis and the "microanalysis of power," etc. In doing so, cultural studies in Korea *at least theoretically and methodologically* has provided sophisticated and cross-disciplinary intellectual tools that can come to terms with the workings of various cultural/media forms, strategies, and practices. It has also brought in a new understanding of "cultural politics" and "the politics of the everyday" that has been vastly underestimated in the dominant left discourses.

Having said this, at the empirical level and in the wider social field, I believe, cultural studies, including communication cultural studies, has not produced rigorous and historicized studies of the dominant social discourses and the historically specific forms of domination and opposition (Lee, 2002). To generalize, cultural studies in Korea, especially the "communicational" or popular cultural-studies strand, has been under the formative influence of the Birmingham school and, though local cultural-studies practitioners have produced detailed culturalist methods and critiques in the form of refined reception and textual analyses, they nonetheless stop short of actively and rigorously engaging with vexed social and political questions in contemporary Korea. I argue that communicational cultural studies tends to "play it safe." Put in different terms, I believe cultural studies in the local arena needs to expand its problematics and rigorously engage with vexed sociohistorical issues and concerns beyond the narrow confines of mass-media and cultural texts.

References

Alasuutari, Pertti, ed. (1999). *Rethinking the Media Audience.* London: Sage.

Allor, Martin (1988). "Relocating the Site of the Audience." *Critical Studies in Mass Communication* 5: 217–33.

Avery, Robert and Eason, David, eds. (1991). *Critical Perspectives on Media and Society.* New York: Guilford Press.

Bennett, Tony (1998). *Culture: A Reformer's Science.* London: Sage.

Blundell, Valda, et al., eds. (1993). *Relocating Cultural Studies: Developments in Theory and Research.* New York: Routledge.

Chen, Kuan-Hsing, ed. (1998). *Trajectories: Inter-Asia Cultural Studies.* London: Routledge.

Cho, Haejoang (1994). *The Postcolonial Era Intellectual's Reading Strategy and Reading Life* [in Korean]. Seoul: Ttohanaui munhwa.

Cho, Haejoang (1995). "A Boom in Finding Us." Unpublished manuscript, Dept. of Sociology, Yonsei University, Seoul, Korea.

Cho, Haejoang (1998). "Deconstructing and Constructing 'Koreanness' in the 1990s." In Cru C. Gladney, ed., *Making Majorities: Constituting the Nation in Japan, Korea, China, Malaysia, Fiji, Turkey, and the United States.* Stanford: Stanford University Press.

Cho, Haejoang (1999). *Reflexive Modernity and Feminism* [in Korean]. Seoul: Ttohanaui munhwa.

Cho, Hangjai, et al., eds. (2000). *Paradigms for Twenty-first Century Media Studies* [in Korean]. Seoul: Hannarae.

Contemporary Cultural Studies Editorial Committee, ed. (1992). *Apgujung-dong, Utopia Dystopia* [in Korean]. Seoul: Hyunsil munhwa yonku.

Contemporary Cultural Studies Editorial Committee, ed. (1993). *How to do Cultural Studies* [in Korean]. Seoul: Hyunsil munhwa yonku.

Contemporary Cultural Studies Editorial Committee, ed. (1994). *Discourse on the New Generation: Chaos and Order* [in Korean]. Seoul: Hyunsil munhwa yonku.

Contemporary Cultural Studies Editorial Committee (2000). *Reading Culture: From Pamphlet to Cyberculture* [in Korean]. Seoul: Hyunsil munhwa yonku.

Curran, James and Gurevitch, M., eds. (1991). *Mass Media and Society.* London: Edward Arnold.

de Certeau, Michel (1998). *The Practice of Everyday Life.* Berkeley: University of California Press.

Curran, James, Morley, D., and Walkerdine, V., eds. (1996). *Cultural Studies and Communications.* London: Edward Arnold.

Denzin, Norman K. (1989). *The Research Act: A Theoretical Introduction to Sociological Methods*. NJ: Prentice Hall.

Denzin, Norman K. (1999). "From American Sociology to Cultural Studies." *European Journal of Cultural Studies* 2(1): 117–36.

Dworkin, Dennis (1997). *Cultural Marxism in Postwar Britain*. Durham, NC: Duke University Press.

Editorial Committee for Munhwa kwahak, eds. (1997). Special issue on Cultural Policy, vol. 12 [in Korean]. Seoul: Munhwa kwahak-sa.

Frow, John and Morris, M., eds. (1993). *Australian Cultural Studies: A Reader*. Champaign, IL: University of Illinois Press.

Giroux, Henry and McLaren, P. (1994). *Between Borders: Pedagogy and the Politics of Cultural Studies*. New York: Routledge.

Gray, Ann and McGuigan, J., eds. (1993). *Studying Culture: An Introduction*. London: Edward Arnold.

Grossberg, Lawrence (1992a). *We Gotta Get Out of This Place: Popular Conservatism and Postmodern Culture*. New York: Routledge.

Grossberg, Lawrence (1992b). "Is There a Fan in the House?: The Affective Sensibility of Fandom." In Lisa Lewis, ed., *The Adoring Audience*. New York: Routledge.

Grossberg, Lawrence (1997). *Bringing It All Back Home: Essays on Cultural Studies*. Durham, NC: Duke University Press.

Hagen, Ingunn and Wasko, J., eds. (2000). *Consuming Audiences? Production and Reception in Media Research*. Cresskill, NJ: Hampton Press.

Hall, Stuart (1988). *The Hard Road to Renewal: Thatcherism and the Crisis of the Left*. London: Verso.

Hall, Stuart (1992). "Cultural Studies and its Theoretical Legacies." In L. Grossberg, C. Nelson, and P. Treichler, eds., *Cultural Studies*. New York: Routledge.

Hall, Stuart and du Gay, Paul, eds. (1996). *Questions of Cultural Identity*. London: Sage.

Hall, Stuart and Gieben, B., eds. (1992). *Formations of Modernity*. Cambridge: Polity.

Hall, Stuart, Hobson, D., Lowe, D., and Willis, P., eds. (1980). *Culture, Media, Language: Working Papers in Cultural Studies, 1972–9*. London: Hutchinson.

Hall, Stuart and Jefferson, Tony (1976). *Resistance through Rituals: Youth Subcultures in Post-war Britain*. London: Unwin Hyman.

Hebdige, Dick (1982). "Towards a Cartography of Taste 1935–1962." In B. Waites, T. Bennett, and G. Martin, eds., *Popular Culture: Past and Present*. London: Croom Helm.

Heelas, Paul, Lash, S., and Morris, P., eds. (1996). *Detraditionalization: Critical Reflections on Authority and Identity*. Oxford: Blackwell.

Hills, Matt (2002). *Fan Cultures*. New York: Routledge.

Hong, Sukkyung (1997). "Television Drama and the Modality of Social Communication" [in Korean]. In Hwang Insung and Won Yongjin, eds., *The Lover: Television Drama, Culture, and Society*. Seoul: Hannarae.

Horak, Roman (1999). "Cultural Studies in Germany (and Austria) and Why There is No Such Thing." *European Journal of Cultural Studies* 2(1): 109–15.

Hwang, Insung, ed. (1999). *Cultural Studies of Television*. Seoul: Hannarae.

Jameson, Fredric and Miyoshi, M., eds. (1998). *The Cultures of Globalization*. Durham, NC: Duke University Press.

Im, Dongeun (1999). *Nomadic Living in Seoul* [in Korean]. Seoul: Munhwa kwahak-sa.

Im, Youngho (1998). "The Compartmentalization in Korean Journalism Studies and the Crisis of Its Identity." *Korean Journal of Journalism and Information* 11: 3–31.

Jeon, Kyunchan (1998). *Cultural Studies in the "Post" Era* [in Korean]. Seoul: Communication Books.

Jeon, Kyunchan (1999). "Media, Cultural Studies and Cultural Policy in the Age of Cultural Openness." *Korean Journal of Journalism and Communication* 43(3): 270–300.

Ju, Changyun (1997). "Cultural Studies: Where is it Heading?" [in Korean]. *Contemporary Thought* 4: 68–84.

Ju, Enwoo (1995). "The New Generation and their Consumer Culture in 1990s Korea." *Economy and Society* 21: 70–91.

Jung, Jaechul, ed. (1998). *Themes and Theories of Cultural Studies* [in Korean]. Seoul: Hannarae.

Kang, Myung-koo (1994). *Consumer Culture and Postmodernism* [in Korean]. Seoul: Minem-sa.

Kang, Myung-koo (1999). "Postmodern Consumer Culture Without Postmodernity: Copying the Crisis of Signification." *Cultural Studies* 13(1).

Kang, Myung-koo (2001). "There is No Korea in Korean Cultural Studies." Keynote speech, May 2001, University of Iowa.

Kang, Naehee (1996). *The Problematics of Cultural Studies* [in Korean]. Seoul: Munhwa kwahak-sa.

Kang, Naehee (1997). *Space, Body, and Power* [in Korean]. Seoul: Munhwa kwahak-sa.

Kang, Naehee (1999). "Living in Korea in the 1990s." On-line paper, http://moonkwa.jinbo.net/naehee.

Kang, Younghee, et al. (1993). *Television: Looking Closely, Reading from a Distance* [in Korean]. Seoul: Hyunsil munwha yonku.

Kim, Eungsook (1998). "Cultural Studies and the World of Experience: Walter Benjamin/Media and Modernity." *Korean Journal of Journalism and Communication* 42(3): 66–99.

Kim, Hunsoon and Park, Dongsook (1999). "A Study of the Women Writers of Television Dramas" [in Korean]. In Hwang Insung, ed., *Cultural Studies of Television*. Seoul: Hannarae.

Kim, Jinsong (1999). *Permit the Dance Halls in Seoul* [in Korean]. Seoul: Hyunsil munhwa yonku.

Kim, Jungki and Park, Dongsook (1999). *Mass Media and Audiences* [in Korean]. Seoul: Communication Books.

Kim, Sungki (1996). *Cultural Critique Contained within the Fastfood Restaurant* [in Korean]. Seoul: Minemsa.

Lee, Dongyeon (1997). *New Topics in Cultural Studies* [in Korean]. Seoul: Munhwa kwahak-sa.

Lee, Dongyeon (2002). *Popular Cultural Studies and Cultural Critique* [in Korean]. Seoul: Munhwa kwahak-sa.

Lee, Haeyoung, ed. (1999). *The 1980s: The Age of Revolution* [in Korea]. Seoul: Sarounsaesang.

Lee, Kangsoo (2001). *Audience Analysis* [in Korean]. Seoul: Hanul.

Lee, Keehyeung (2000). "Detraditionalization of Society and the Rise of Cultural Studies in South Korea." *Inter-Asia Cultural Studies* 1(3): 477–90.

Lee, Keehyeung (2002). "Toward a Cultural History in the Korean Present: Locating the Cultural Politics of the Everyday." Unpublished dissertation, Institute of Communications Research, University of Illinois at Urbana-Champaign.

Lee, Sooyeon (1999). "An Understanding of Television Discourse" [in Korean]. In Hwang Insung, ed., *Cultural Studies of Television*. Seoul: Hannarae.

Ma, Donghoon (1997). "Cultural Theory, Cultural Studies, and Media Studies." *Media and Society* [in Koean] 18: 180–92.

Martin-Barbero, Jesus (2000). "The Cultural Mediations of Television Consumption." In I. Hagen and J. Wasko, eds., *Consuming Audiences?: Production and Reception in Media Research*. Cresskill, NJ: Hampton Press.

McGuigan, Jim, ed. (1998). *Cultural Methodologies*. London: Sage.

Morley, David and Chen, Kuan-Hsing, eds. (1996). *Stuart Hall: Critical Dialogues in Cultural Studies*. New York: Routledge.

Morris, Meaghan (1995). "A Question of Cultural Studies." Unpublished paper.

Morris, Meaghan (1998). *Too Soon Too Late: History in Popular Culture*. Bloomington: Indiana University.

O'Connor, Alan (1993). "What is Transnational Cultural Studies?" *Border/Lines* 29: 46–9.

Park, Dongsook (1999). "The Power of Audience Interpretation." In Jungki Kim and Dongsook Park, eds., *Mass Media and Audiences* [in Korean]. Seoul: Communication Books.

Park, Dongsook and Kim, Hunsoon (1997). *Mass Media and the Symbolic Order of Gender*. Seoul: Nanam Publications.

Radway, Janice (1988). "Reception Study: Ethnography and the Problem of Dispersed Audiences and Nomadic Subjects." *Cultural Studies* 3.

Robbins, Derek (2000). *Bourdieu and Culture*. London: Sage.

Shim, Kwanghyeon (1998). *Postmodern Cultural Studies and Cultural Politics* [in Korean]. Seoul: Munhwa kwahak-sa.

Shim, Kwanghyeon (1999). "The Task of New Cultural Movement Towards the 'Society of Culture'" [in Korean]. In Youngjin Won, ed., *Munhwa Kwahak*, vol. 17.

Ward, Graham, ed. (2000). *The Certeau Reader*. Oxford: Blackwell.

Williams, Raymond (1989). *Resources of Hope*. London: Verso.

Williams, Raymond (1993). *The Politics of Modernism*. London: Verso.

Won, Youngjin (2000). "Reflecting and Assessing Media Studies" [in Korean]. *Korean Journal of Broadcasting* 14(3): 180–230.

Won, Youngjin (2001). "The Present and the Future of Cultural Studies in Communication Studies." *Korean Journal of Journalism and Communication* 45: 157–89.

Yoo, Sunyoung (1998). "A History of Identity Formation through the Gaze of the Ocelli." *Korean Journal of Journalism and Communication Studies* 43(2): 427–67.

Yoon, Sunhee (1999). "Popular and Youth Culture on Television" [in Korean]. In Hwang Insung, ed., *Cultural Studies of Television*. Seoul: Hannarae.

8

Re-advertising Hong Kong: Nostalgia Industry and Popular History

Eric Kit-wai Ma*

This chapter tries to map the nostalgic practices in Hong Kong at a key moment of political transition. It explores the discursive energies that activate and articulate social desire through the production and consumption of a 60-second nostalgic TV commercial for a major bank in Hong Kong. Recent media studies have moved away from textual determinism and have increasingly been privileging the moments of textual reception. The new emphasis on popular culture "from below" fosters a notion of idiosyncratic cultural consumption which, at times, leads to populist claims that media consumers can find their way out of the hegemonic control "from above." Taking a revisionist approach, this chapter articulates textual ideologies at both the production and consumption ends. It tries to give a big picture of how self-proclaimed "authentic" coding and encoding of popular meanings can be, in Anthony Giddens's term, structurated within the ideological formation of the political economy at large. And within these signifying processes, there are gaps from which individuals can find nostalgic pleasure through their idiosyncratic reading of ideological texts. Moving beyond the binary of seeing popular texts as sites of control or resistance, this case study will show the interlocking connections of ideological discipline and interpretative pleasure in a politically unofficial popular history and an ideologically "official" narrative of transnational capitalism.

Despite their idiosyncrasy, the particular nostalgic practices of Hong Kong people are deeply embedded in the sociohistorical context of sovereignty reversion. Within restrictive discursive spaces, the history retold in the TV commercial under discussion is shaped by the advertiser, the

Hong Kong and Shanghai Bank (hereafter Hong Kong Bank), which was a quasi-central bank privileged by the colonial government and is still one of the dominant players in the Hong Kong capitalist economy. Although the history of Hong Kong represented in the TV commercial is highly selective, the text is produced and consumed with a strong commitment to modernist ideas of progress and factual historicity. On a microlevel, these nostalgic practices of textual production and consumption are also regulated by the strong social desire for continuity at a time of extraordinary change. Combining analyses of contextual control from above and reading from below, this article tries to attend to the political economy of nostalgia as well as to the fine-grained negotiations of cultural politics.

I will begin with the questions of how historical meanings are orchestrated in the televisual text, how nostalgia is produced and consumed, and how these nostalgic practices are embedded in and complicated by the political economy of capitalist culture. By posing these questions through the particular case of a Hong Kong TV commercial, I want to touch on issues of general theoretical concern. The first set of questions is about historicity in an age of image processing. Recent scholarship has significantly problematized the past, deconstructing all of its forms into discursive imprints of the present.[1] This project could easily slide into yet another attempt to problematize memory and history and repeat the cliché of "history as invention." The case at hand could not sustain a full-blown epistemological reexamination of various forms of history. Instead, I will explore the discursive effects of the persistent belief in modernist historicism. My questions are: How does a belief in historicity render the consumption of historical realism so gratifying? How does a covert commitment to factual history heighten the academic pleasure of cultural elites in deconstructing popular history? How can modernist historicism be related to industrial capitalism?

The second set of questions concerns the nexus of social anxiety and nostalgic desire under a weak nationalism and a strong globalized capitalist economy. Hong Kong is located at the political periphery and lacks a strong and distinct nationalism.[2] Not until very recently has there been a powerful discourse on historical origins and cultural heritage after the sovereignty change in 1997.[3] If there is no strong nationalism to activate an identity-conferring history, where does the nostalgic desire for a historical rootedness evolve from? Does the urge derive from within the community, which has been granted a sociocultural space under noninterventive politics by both Britain and China? Can transnational capitalism be a source of discursive energy for constructing a highly localized historical narrative for very contextualized consumption?

The last set of questions is related to the conflicting articulation of capitalism and re-sinicized nationalism in the popular culture of Hong Kong. Since the open-door policy, Hong Kong popular culture has been quite influential in mainland China through the cultural and commercial processes of demonstration, modeling, overspilling of televisual signals, joint media ventures, and direct and indirect networking.[4] However, influences have increasingly been reciprocal. Whereas in mainland China, capitalism and the state are negotiating control and a position at center stage, Hong Kong's popular culture, until now running wild, is navigating a return to the orbit of China. How does Hong Kong's popular culture renarrate a history that is compatible with both China's brand of nationalism and Hong Kong's brand of free capitalism? How does Hong Kong negotiate its identity by repositioning its past and future connection with the globalized economy? Does Hong Kong's globalized position trigger or dilute the desire to consume a local past?

The first three sections of this chapter will pay attention, respectively, to the nostalgic text, its production, and its consumption. The last section will conclude by addressing the above-mentioned issues through an examination of the nostalgic connection of modernist historicism, nationalism, and transnational capitalism.

The Nostalgic Text

In the year before the Sino–British sovereignty transfer, Hong Kong Bank produced a "fisherman commercial" and released it on all major television channels. Shot in black and white, the commercial recapitulates the history of Hong Kong through the eyes of a fisherman. It attracted widespread attention and won an award for best TV commercial of 1995.[5]

The aesthetic style resembles a sober documentary, with contemplative narration over gracefully crafted images. In the story, a determined and calm fisherman struggles against the hardships of the sea. Clusters of icons such as a fisherman's hat, a fishing boat, and sails are deployed to tap the powerful discourse about Hong Kong's humble origins as a small fishing village. The story begins with this voiceover: "My grandfather said when you earn a living from the sea, you depend on the sky. I said you can only depend on yourself." The visual story then mixes the personal life history of the protagonist with three historical events in postwar Hong Kong.

The first event is a typhoon that hit Hong Kong in 1962 and caused heavy casualties.[6] Newsreel footage of typhoon signals, roaring waves, and broken ships are seen from the point of view of the fisherman standing on the waterfront: "After Typhoon Wanda visited Hong Kong, I was left with nothing. It was no big deal. I started with nothing. So I rented a boat and started again." The second event is the widely remembered period of water shortages in 1963. On the screen we see sails in strong winds and women and children lining up for water. "Then came the water shortage," the narration continues. "While people complained about their misfortune, I delivered water and made a small fortune. Enough to buy a new boat."

The third historical event is the rainstorm and floods in 1972.[7] The commercial uses the news footage of massive landslides that submerge a skyscraper by a hillside. The image of the devastated building with its top flats ruins is instantly recognizable by old-time Hong Kongers.[8] The fisherman sighs, "Eventually it did rain and it never stopped, resulting in the floods of 18 June. Water, all my life, water." We see the whole family gathered for dinner under a dim light. Then we see the wedding of the fisherman's son. The bride emerges from the fishing boat and goes ashore. After all these hardships, the fisherman's family is able to move away from the sea. "Today I live in a flat, and my son is grown up." Now the family has started their own business, selling fishball noodles in a bustling shop. "He doesn't want to catch fish. I say it's no big deal. I also say if you want the sun to shine, don't depend on the sky. In Hong Kong, whether you make a living all depends on you." This last line of voiceover runs over a close-up of the old fisherman and his bamboo hat hanging on the wall. A slow fade-out ends the story, followed by the logo of Hong Kong Bank with the slogan "Your Future Is Our Future."

The documentary aesthetic

In the discourse of postmodernism, a nostalgic aesthetics is said to have contributed to the disappearance of historicity by its hybridization of styles of different historical periods and its destabilizing use of parody and creative intertextual references. However, this argument should be applied to the Hong Kong case with extra care.[9] In the years before and after the handover, the upsurge of nostalgic media in Hong Kong has been characterized by a strong commitment to modernity. Behind the trend of nostalgia is a collective urge to rediscover the "authentic" and factual history of Hong Kong. Yet this commitment, as will be illustrated below, does not prevent nostalgic texts from being ideological. The irony is that the currency of historicity is actually enhancing the ideological power of nostalgic practices.

The use of black-and-white images, the attention to details and dressing props, and the allusion to newsreel footage in the fisherman commercial, all cast an authentic aura. The style resembles the documentaries produced by the Hong Kong Film Unit in the 1960s. The unit, a publicity arm of the colonial government, was headed by expatriates who explicitly brought in the tradition of British documentary filmmaker John Grierson.[10] Some of the footage used in the fisherman commercial was taken directly from the documentaries produced by the unit. In fact, the discursive outputs of this colonial unit have frequently been used by the local media as authentic self-representations of Hong Kong's past. Far from being devoid of ideology, the Griersonian aesthetic, it is argued, is a sustained and skillfully crafted statement about progress, modernity, and history. The representation of Hong Kong history in the commercial has a strong intertextual link with a popular historical narrative in the documentaries of the film unit, in travel guides, in colonial history books, and in popular media. It goes like this: when the British came, Hong Kong was just a small fishing village on barren rocks, and now it has developed into a world financial center under British rule. This version of Hong Kong history is highly ideological and oversimplified. Hong Kong had a vibrant trade culture before the British came, but this part of Hong Kong history has been suppressed and marginalized by both the British and the Chinese literati.[11] The documentary aesthetic not only enhances the historicity of the TV commercial; it constitutes the ideology of actuality by naturalizing its strong ideological treatment of Hong Kong's past.

The nostalgic reassurance

The lesson drawn from this piece of history is clear: past experiences demonstrated that the people of Hong Kong were able to survive crises. This is similar to the general pattern of collective nostalgia in other parts of the world. Nostalgia contributes to the maintenance of solidarity in societies undergoing "untoward historic events."[12] The strains produced by these situations typically elicit historical image repertoires that highlight the collective fortitude exhibited by citizens during previous crises. In the case of Hong Kong, the unprecedented sovereignty transfer triggered widespread anxiety. The rise of nostalgic media,[13] of which the fisherman commercial is an illustrative instance, can be seen as a collective psychological response to the crisis at hand. The kind of retrospective nostalgia expressed in the fisherman commercial is not found in the TV commercials of Hong Kong Bank in the 1970s and 1980s. Most of these previous commercials were forward looking and explicit in building the image of Hong Kong men in the immediate present. In a commercial produced in the 1970s, a Hong Kong man walks past a Hong Kong Bank in London, Paris, and Los Angeles, valorizing Hong Kong's connection with the globalized economy. In contrast, the fisherman commercial looks back to history for reassurance in the face of the sociopolitical changes and discontinuity of the 1990s.

The narrative exhibits tremendous faith in the upward mobility of an open society. The fisherman believes that if one tries hard enough, one can survive and earn a living in Hong Kong. Ironically, this social optimism is a discourse of the early 1980s rather than a reflection of the public senti-ment of the 1950s and 1960s, the time periods in which the story is located. In the 1950s, two-thirds of the Hong Kong population were newcomers from the mainland after the Communist takeover of China in 1949. These sojourners treated Hong Kong as a temporary refuge, and their primary concerns were daily survival. In this hostile territory, where everybody had to compete for a living, the public mood was less than optimistic. The kind of faith and confidence expressed in the commercial was a later develop-ment, after the economy had taken off in the 1970s. Since the 1970s, the increase in educational opportunities, combined with the structural expan-sion of the job market, has created a new generation of affluent middle class. In several social indicator projects, an overwhelming percentage of the respondents agree or strongly agree that Hong Kong is a place full of opportunities, and that it is individual efforts that count in one's success or failure.[14] This social optimism carried on into the 1990s and became the underlying ethos of the fisherman commercial. Like other nostalgic prac-tices, the commercial actually frames past events in the popular mindset of the present.

I would not dismiss this belief in upward mobility as merely ideologi-cal. There was actually a structural expansion in the Hong Kong economy in the 1970s and 1980s. However, social mobility studies have found that Hong Kong society is not as open as its residents perceive it to be. Members of the working class find it more difficult to move into other classes than persons in the upper and middle classes; there are visible structural con-straints along class lines.[15] The success stories of a portion of the popula-tion have constructed the dominant and powerful discourse of upward mobility for the whole society. There has been a continued economic downturn in Hong Kong since 1997, the myth of upward mobility has become tarnished, and success stories like the fisherman TV commercial have no longer been popular in the media. Yet the ideological logic demonstrated in this case is still applicable to other cases of mediated political transition.

Decontextualized individualism

The fisherman commercial is also embedded in a very radical form of individualism. It sets an atomized man against the hostile world of natural disasters. The man depends on faith in himself. Natural disasters like typhoons, landslides, and droughts could have inspired collective action, demands for better welfare and social protection, and even a political critique of colonial practices. But the story as told in the commercial has omitted the many social and political issues that had been raised in these historical events. For instance, during periods of water shortage, the colonial government used public money to ship fresh water to the expatriate community; however, the general public could only have a few hours of water supply once every four days. In the rainstorm of 1972, grassroots communities organized remedial support for victims.[16] The fisherman story is decontextualized from the thorny disputes between local fishing communities and the government on issues such as pollution, reclamation, and resettlement. Collective action, including social protests and demonstrations, is not included in the story.[17] Hong Kong's past is represented in such a way that the individual and his family become the primary unit of social action. The protagonist protects his family against the strong winds of fate. This kind of atomized individualism is highly compatible with Hong Kong's capitalist system, which is hailed by economists as the haven of the purest form of capitalism, where cash and commodities are pursued by individuals in a jungle of free competition. The fisherman story looks historical. Yet it is a statement of capitalist ideology in nostalgic disguise.

The Production of Nostalgia

The commercial was produced by a local advertising firm from the brief proposed by Hong Kong Bank. Its major motif is that "nothing can get in the way of the success of the people of Hong Kong, and that Hong Kong Bank backed up the people of Hong Kong in the past and will continue to do so in the future." The brief was jointly drafted by executives from Hong Kong Bank and the advertising firm. It was then passed on to a creative team, which was given a free hand to make up stories for the campaign.

Team members recalled that when they first presented their idea, the bankers "had strong feelings and identified strongly with the story." The submission and production of the commercial was one of the rare occasions in which the management, the client, and the creative team supported one another. "We all wanted to contribute something to the society in times of trouble," said one team member. They did not have visible ideological differences in perceiving the history of Hong Kong. However, on further discussion, the creators mentioned that they clearly knew beforehand that their client did not want anything political. The selective frame had already been in place during the earliest stage of the creative process. When asked about revisions, they said that there were many, but all were only very minor changes. Yet when I asked about details, three revisions seem significant to me.

The first revision concerned a big fire on the nearly completed Jumbo floating restaurant in Aberdeen harbor in 1971.[18] The idea was proposed in the initial storyboard but rejected in the production meeting. Although the incident was not a very important historical event, the team thought it tied in nicely with the fisherman story, since the Jumbo restaurant symbolized how the fishing industry in Hong Kong moved into restaurant-related businesses. After the fire, the floating restaurant was rebuilt and has become a famous tourist site and landmark. The blaze of the large, luxurious, floating restaurant, with an architectural design mimicking a Chinese palace, was visually dramatic and could have reinforced the theme of crisis and survival. However, Hong Kong Bank has a strong policy that its promotion activities "cannot play with fire." This is because in 1992 there was a fire in one of its branches that killed 13 staff members.[19] It was the full-page, headline story for several days, and the bank does not want any reference to fire in its commercials, which could trigger this public memory. After the interview, I searched for the newspaper clippings of the events, which amounted to more than a hundred pages. I was quite surprised at how poor my own memory was. The story was, in fact, very alarming. A man troubled by marital problems set the bank lobby on fire by lighting two small bottles of paint thinner. It was a small fire, but the staff members were choked to death by the heavy smoke. For security reasons, the bank did not have any exit except for the front door, and the office was protected by an electric double door, which meant that one door had to be locked before the other could be opened. The office became a deathtrap with no escape. After the fire, the bank was accused of placing security above safety. The media carried very dramatic stories about the victims, which left vivid impressions on the public. However, Hong Kong Bank has been quite successful in suppressing this collective memory. The interviewees in the audience study (see below) did not recall the incident at all when we talked extensively about Hong Kong Bank. I do not want to overdramatize the censorship process, since there was no great moral reason for the creators to insist on including the Jumbo fire incident. Yet the outcome of this deletion is that we now have a more decontextualized story of a lone fisherman struggling against natural disasters. The sanitized history is more apolitical, atomized, and individualistic.

In the second revision, the bankers wanted a large seafood restaurant operated by the fisherman's son to be downsized to a small family noodle shop. This change, in fact, was a rehabilitation of the myth of excessive commercial success, which has been for a long time a powerful and very popular discourse perpetuated by the mainstream media in Hong Kong. Of course this minor change proposed by the bankers is not a cultural critique of the myth of success; rather, it is an adjustment reflecting the commercial repositioning of the bank. In the past, bankers did business with major investors and big companies and factories. In recent years, banking services have been reconfigured to include personal financing for the general public. The reason behind this minor revision of the storyline was Hong Kong Bank's desire to build an image of care and support at the grassroots, thus bringing the bank closer to its customers. The discursive spaces are thus a function of commercial positioning.

The third revision was also considered minor by the creative directors but in fact has theoretical significance. The success of the commercial owes much to the contemplative voiceover narration, which expresses strong feelings of sincerity, maturity, and dignity. To create an authentic touch, the producer and art directors went to fishing harbors and waited there for several hours. They asked every passing fisherman to speak to them and finally found the voice they needed. However, the voiceover as it is now was not the version that the producers liked most. The best one was done by a fisherman with a strong Hohklou accent.[20] The dialect is authentic because many fishermen in Hong Kong use it in their everyday conversation. The producers proposed keeping that dialect and using Chinese subtitles. The bankers rejected this idea on the ground that TV audiences do not bother to read subtitles; the commercial was for a mass audience, and Cantonese would be more direct and understandable. They were probably correct, because the Hohklou accent would have given a stronger sense of locality and specificity at the expense of general accessibility. Despite the fact that the protagonist belongs to a restricted group of Hong Kong people, the commercial was decontextualized and domesticated to make it accessible to the general public. The people of Hong Kong now see the story as their own story, the history as their own history. Without this domestication, the story would not have invited its audience so readily to engage in collective nostalgia.

The fisherman commercial invites the audience to relive the past and fosters a sense of continuity and belonging. This invitation was perhaps intended to counterbalance the bad publicity when Hong Kong Bank announced, in 1990, that a new holding company having direct ownership of the bank was to be set up in the United Kingdom.[21] The bank was accused by its critics of turning its back on Hong Kong in times of trouble. Hong Kong Bank was the territory's biggest financial institution privileged by the colonial government. It was started by British interests in 1865, and its history was intertwined with the history of imperialist expansion.[22] Since Hong Kong does not have a central bank, Hong Kong Bank was given that role. It is still responsible for issuing most of the currency and providing for check-clearing facilities, and it has also been acting as lender of last resort for the banking system.[23] But due to the sovereignty transfer in 1997, the bank has internationalized its operations and shifted its holding company to the United Kingdom. The move was heavily criticized by the public. The bank stated that Hong Kong remains an important and profitable market and that the bank's operations would continue to be managed from there. However, as analysts have pointed out, actions speak louder than words. In the early 1990s there was even a rumor that inside the headquarters of the bank in Central, an important landmark of the territory, things had already been packed up in secret containers and the offices could leave the territory within days. In response the bank started a series of campaigns to repair its image. Partnership and commitment have been the themes of the bank's recent projects. Hong Kong Bank exploits its very special position in Hong Kong financial history and narrates Hong Kong history in an authoritative and official manner. From a privileged vantage point, the bank is able to promote the image of a longtime partner with the place and the people, thus contributing to the selective forgetting of its structural move away from Hong Kong. Hong Kong Bank, a local capital manager originating from colonial privilege, was transnationalizing its operation to fend off possible attack from new nationalistic imperatives. But this transnationalizing in the structural dimension is accompanied by an image-building campaign of localization. The bank is localizing its image as a tactic to facilitate and legitimize its transnational operations.

The previous production analysis has brought to light the articulation between corporate interests and the nostalgic texts. But it is not my intention to override the analysis with the theoretical discourse of political censorship and leave the impression of conspiracy and manipulation on the part of the production team. During the interviews, I sensed a strong commitment on the part of the producers to express in the text their own genuine feeling and love for the territory. They kept repeating that they found the assignment gratifying because they thought that the commercial could help Hong Kong regain confidence. They believed the commercial was a true representation of Hong Kong people despite the minor revisions mentioned above. The capitalist logic does not impose an ideology from without but incorporates beliefs, desires, and practices through a history of ideological formation of a full-blown capitalism. Capitalism becomes part of the personal histories and "authentic" experiences of individuals making a living in Hong Kong. As I shall discuss in the next section, this empathy and sense of collectivity was carried over to the audience. Nostalgia practice, despite its ideological nature, is able to foster cultural solidarity. It is both ideological and cultural.

Reading Nostalgic Texts

Besides production and textual analyses, I conducted in-depth interviews to explore the nostalgic practices of strategically selected informants. Although textual studies have increasingly been attuned to reception politics, textual reception is notoriously difficult to pinpoint and interpret. To avoid uncritical realism or solipsistic reflexivity in dealing with interview data, a few tactics have been deployed to modulate between the extremes of liberal interpretation and restrictive agnosticism. These tactics include interviewing in domestic settings, selecting sensitized informants, and anchoring readings within memorable experiences.

Hong Kong is primarily a Chinese immigrant society where waves of mainland Chinese have arrived and assimilated into the mainstream in different historical periods. In the 1970s and 1980s, mainlanders were stigmatized as the significant others in relation to which Hong Kongers strengthened their own identity by drawing a line between "them" and "us." As Hong Kong has now become part of China, the identity border has been undergoing complicated restructuring. To exploit this shifting identity border, ethnographic interviews with different immigrant groups and local-born Hong Kongers were conducted to provide grounded cases for exploring the interplay between mediated history, personal experiences, nostalgic practices, and identity formation. The readings of nostalgic texts are located within the informants' experiences of "crossing" the identity border when they first arrived in Hong Kong. Structurally, the set-up of the interviews privileges meanings embodied in sensitive experiences rather than the enunciated ideologies of speaking subjects.

The interview data analyzed in this chapter is part of a larger project that includes interviews on the lifestyles and consumption histories of various groups of Hong Kong people.[24] Included in this chapter are 9 interviews and 15 informants; some are family members and were interviewed in groups. In order not to detach the informants from their families, I asked the interviewees to allow me, if possible, to interview them in their homes in the presence of other family members. Six of the 9 interviews were conducted in domestic settings. These interviews were conducted in March and April 1998, one year after the fisherman commercial ceased to be aired on television. Most interviewees recalled having watched the commercial before I showed the clip to them. Unlike many other TV commercials that are buried in massive televisual flows, the fisherman commercial is widely remembered and has left a lasting impression on the audience.

Nostalgia and ideology

The fisherman commercial, as indicated in the textual analysis, is a discourse of upward mobility and individualism in nostalgic disguise. The ideological operation of the nostalgic text is quite discernible in the reception analysis. Most of the informants expressed strong identification with the story and agreed strongly with the last line of the voiceover: "Whether you make a living in Hong Kong all depends on yourself." They said the story of individual survival expressed their own attitude about life in Hong Kong. A few informants said in a matter-of-fact manner, "It is the history of Hong Kong." Six informants were born in Hong Kong or had come to Hong Kong long enough ago to be considered Hong Kongers. They by and large subscribed to the ideology of the commercial. More revealing were the accounts of those who did not have direct experience with the drought, rainstorm, and typhoon described in the commercial. They were conscious of this and said, "I don't know about the drought, but I identify with the survival spirit of the story." They could, with ease, recontextualize their own personal stories and intertwine them with the story of the nostalgic text.

Miss Chau, a social worker who came to Hong Kong in the early 1980s, related details of her teenage years in Hong Kong, telling me how she managed her father's noodle stall. "Yes, in Hong Kong, you can only count on yourself. I stood all day in the street selling noodles. At that time I was only 15. I had to carry large packs of noodles up and down a five-story building . . . We had to overcome lots of hardship in order to achieve the prosperity we now enjoy. My story is different from the commercial, but the feeling is the same."

The commercial relates the story of a particular group of fishermen in a very particular historical situation. Yet it demonstrates extraordinary power, in that people who do not share the same history can identify with it. Two things are clear: First, the history in the TV commercial has been decontextualized to fit the taste of the general audience. Not only have esoteric elements (such as the Hohklou accent) been sanitized, but the specificity of historical events is embodied in the appealing themes of man-against-nature and endurance-in-time-of-crisis. Second, the nostalgic text is operating at the ideological level for mainland immigrants. These informants only arrived in Hong Kong after the 1970s; they had different life histories. But they were eager to cross the identity border and be assimilated into the collective lifeworld of Hong Kong. Their easy identification with the fishermen reflects their desire to subscribe to Hong Kong's way of life; they were embracing Hong Kong capitalist ideology rather than the historical specificity of the fisherman commercial. This shows an ideological compatibility rather than a nostalgic sharing of collective history.

Ideology and practice

By elaborating on the ideological nature of the nostalgic text, I am not suggesting another thesis of dominant ideology that confers extraordinary powers on the media.[25] The fisherman commercial does not exercise its power on its own. There are strong intertextual links with the mainstream media that show similar discourses of individualism and upward mobility.[26] The commercial reinforces something that already exists. Besides intertextual links, the life stories of my informants suggest that ideology and social practice are mutually constitutive; one does not have a linear effect on the other. The informants had learned and been practicing the ideology of the fisherman commercial for a long time. The ideology is constituted by, and re-reinforces, social practices.

When the interviewees were asked what they thought of Hong Kong before they came, two recurrent themes emerged. First, Hong Kong was a place where they could earn a living. No matter how vague a picture they had of Hong Kong, they had a clear idea that Hong Kong was full of opportunities. The second recurrent image was of Hong Kong as a place of material affluence. They recalled their first perception of Hong Kong came via a radio, a TV set, or a bottle of Coca-Cola their relatives brought to China from Hong Kong. Miss Chau talked about the smell of the plastic bag when her father unpacked a new TV set in her home in China.

When they arrived in Hong Kong, they had to work very hard to earn a living. Material affluence did not come easily. Since they were somewhat marginalized by established Hong Kongers, most of them had very few friends. They worked on their own. In Hong Kong, they believed, there was a way to move upward. They aspired to do so even if it meant a very dehumanizing way of life. In fact, upward mobility is not merely a myth in Hong Kong. All of my informants, although some are still confined to a low social class, managed to get some form of material reward for their hard work. Mrs. Mok arrived in the late 1990s. She was a physician in Beijing but was not recognized as a doctor in Hong Kong. She managed to save enough money to open a private home for the elderly by herself. Her daughter is a university graduate who came to Hong Kong just two years earlier. She could not find a job in Hong Kong because her academic qualification is not recognized here. But she was still a true believer in the fisherman commercial. "I'll work twice as hard. Like my mother, I believe I can finally succeed in Hong Kong." Their border-crossing experiences illustrated that Hong Kong's capitalist system is not perpetuated by "soft" ideology alone but is also sustained by social practices. Ideology and social practice are mutually constitutive within the lifeworld of a capitalist society. Their identification with the fisherman commercial is actually a reaffirmation of their own ideological practices in Hong Kong.

Atomized individualism

The textual analysis indicated that the fisherman commercial is a strong statement of individualism. Two interviewees were selected as border cases to dramatize this ideological statement. Mr. Tze is a composer and vocalist who came to Hong Kong in the late 1970s. He has been working as a private music tutor, a conductor, and a freelance critic for 20 years. He is a Malaysian-born Chinese who received his musical training in Beijing. There he worked as a vocalist in several leading choirs. He arrived in Hong Kong with a strong determination to develop a career in classical music, which is marginal at best in this commercialized city. He stressed that he seldom went to shopping malls, he lived a very simple life, and he did not need expensive clothing, watches, and other fancy stuff. "I stay home most of the time," he said. "I am very satisfied with my music." His small apartment was filled with thousands of CDs. He showed me piles of clippings of music commentaries he had written for newspapers and magazines. "Hong Kong is a city without a culture," said Tze. "People here are only concerned about making money. There are no serious musicians, no innovative inventors, no great artists." He was very critical of Hong Kong culture.

Contrary to my expectation, when I showed him the fisherman commercial, he said he liked the story very much and strongly agreed with the fisherman. "Yes, you should depend on yourself. Like me. I am fine, because I have professional skills." Although Tze was very critical of commercialism, he could identity with the fisherman and subscribed to the ideology of individual survival. His strong attachment to his music became a survival tactic for him to work against marginalization. Here we see the appeal of atomized individualism. The capitalist culture of Hong Kong can "contain" critics like Tze by marginalizing him in his atomized habitat, and at the same time interpellate him with the ideology of atomized individualism.

Another informant was strategically selected as another border case for comparative analysis. Mr. Lam, the managing director of a local bank, moved to Hong Kong at age 10 and has been living there for 40 years. He has a very successful career in banking. I selected him because he is at the heart of Hong Kong's financial establishment. Unlike Mr. Tze, Lam was in favor of the capitalist system. He said that banking was one of the two major forces that made Hong Kong's economic miracle. The first was the production industry, which could expand and flourish because the banks took the risk of lending money to entrepreneurs. At first I expected that the ideological aspect of the fisherman commercial would not be visible to him, since he has been very successful in playing according to the rules of mainstream society. To my surprise, he was the only informant who disagreed directly with the atomized individualism of the commercial. He provided us with a panoramic view of Hong Kong's success at great length. "I admire the fisherman very much; he catches fish and then opens a noodle shop. He is a successful man. And Hong Kong Bank, as presented in the commercial, is behind his success . . . Yes, the commercial talks about the hardship behind Hong Kong success, typhoon, drought, and all that . . . But I think Hong Kong history is not that simple."

He said that in the past 30 years Hong Kong society has experienced a structural expansion. This expansion pushed you forward, giving you education and job opportunities and the possibility of improving your standard of living. "You cannot succeed on your own. You just can't make it if you only depend on your personal effort. There are many people helping you out directly or indirectly." It was the particular social conditions of Hong Kong in the past decades that contributed to individual success.

Compared with other informants – especially Mr. Tze, the vocalist – Mr. Lam was more supportive of Hong Kong's established system; he was not critical of material success and affluence. However, because he knew about the concrete mechanisms of the financial world, he was in a better position to discern the structural interconnectedness between the collective and the individual. He was able to point out that individual determination alone cannot guarantee upward mobility. In contrast, my other informants uncritically embraced atomized individualism as a key of success and resolution in time of crisis. Since they were situated in a social location relatively more remote from the establishment, they did not have the discursive capital to discern the problematic relation between individual struggle and upward mobility.

In line with this argument, I differentiate the degree of affirmation of the ideology of the fisherman commercial along the vector of the "closeness" with the establishment. All informants, except Tze, were affirmative toward material affluence. Tze stood in a remote social location from the establishment, disapproved of the pursuit of material affluence, but subscribed to and practiced an atomized individualism as a survival tactic. Mrs. Mok and her daughter, who had arrived in Hong Kong only a few years before, embraced the mediated discourse of upward mobility and individual struggle and held onto a genuine hope that one can finally make it if one tries hard enough. Several local Hong Kongers, who were in the lower or lower-middle class, aspired to material affluence and subscribed to the discourse of individualistic competition and survival, but they did not have the level of optimism expressed by the Moks. Since the locals had been here long enough, they were able to discern the limited chances of upward mobility, especially in light of the recent economic recession. At the opposite end was Mr. Lam, the banker, who had been in the financial establishment for 30 years; he affirmed the pursuit of material affluence but was able to discern the inadequacy of atomized individualism. Here we see a contradictory ideological articulation of subjects with differential discursive capitals, which I think is a significant concept for understanding oppositional reading. The complexity of ideological articulations in this study cannot easily be fitted into Stuart Hall's model of preferred, negotiated, and oppositional readings.[27] Preferred and oppositional readings could be working within the same individual along different ideological planes. Nevertheless, the ethnographic interviews have suggested that atomized individualism is a powerful ideology for maintaining a capitalist system.

The Nostalgic Articulation

Nostalgic desire and modernist historicism

In this concluding section, I shall address the general theoretical issues raised at the beginning of this article. First is the question of historicity. The case at hand could not sustain a discussion of the historicity of all forms of history. However, as a concluding note, I would like to discuss the paradoxical relation between nostalgic desire and the persistent belief in modernist historicism. The case suggests that in times of discontinuity and change, a documentary aesthetic is intensely gratifying for the general public, who share an epistemological commitment to factual history. It is this commitment that fuels the production and consumption of nostalgic texts with a powerful sense of authenticity. It also plugs into my endeavor to deconstruct popular history. In the course of narrating this case study, I have become more aware of my own unspoken desire for an "authentic" picture of Hong Kong's past. This is shared by Hong Kong elites who have been persistently calling for the preservation of Hong Kong histories in response to the sovereignty change. The dominant belief in factual history, among both the general public and the cultural elites, can be related to the ideological formation of Hong Kong's untamed industrial capitalism, in which time is disciplined into a homogenous, abstract, linear, and pro-gressive notion of historical development.[28] In the fisherman commercial, the fisherman's notion of time, which is characterized by cycles of idleness and intense labor, is reconfigured into a linear progressive development from the sea to the land, and from toiling at "primitive" fishing activities to running a small family business. The taming of natural disasters is accompanied by the building of the time regime of linear progression that has a symbiotic relation with nostalgic desire. In heterogeneous time, past experiences can be reincarnated in the present.[29] While in homogenous and progressive time, the past is forever lost. This sense of loss is structural to the yearning for an invented past that is natural, simple, and authentic. The time regime of capitalism can flatten the varied rhythms of work and life into a linear progressive development. This discursive formation expresses itself in the fisherman commercial; it also reinforces the belief in modernist historicism, which further renders the production and consumption of nostalgia, and sometimes the deconstruction of it, intensely gratifying.

Capitalism as official history

The second question concerns the creative nexus of nostalgic desire. Seen from the above analyses, the most obvious is the media–banker nexus, which seems to fit into dominant critical political-economy theories on media ideology. Through connections between political, economic, and media powers, an ideology in nostalgic disguise is produced and consumed to sustain the capitalist economy. Hong Kong Bank, as a financial institution, can assume the position to summarize local history, which is seen by the public as authoritative. Privileged by the colonial government, Hong Kong Bank had been participating in public projects and backing up other local banks; its senior executives were mandatory members of the Executive Council of the colonial government. Armed with these political privileges, Hong Kong Bank was one of the most powerful propellers of the colony's capitalist economy. Because of this "material base" of a privileged political and economic position, Hong Kong Bank can take up the discursive space of articulating, in the fisherman commercial, a version of local history that is highly compatible with the capitalist logics of individualism, competition, and the aspiration of upward mobility. In the reception analysis, the consumption of nostalgic text satisfies both the desire for communality and continuity and the desire for preserving an individualistic and competitive lifestyle. As I have argued, the intensity of desire/satisfaction is related to how far from or near the center of the ideological apparatus one is. The further one is from knowledge of how the media–banker nexus works, the easier it is to satisfy one's desire. This points to the classic notion of ideology as illusion that sustains asymmetrical relations. Yet the case also suggests that dominant ideologies are not all encompassing, and their power can be checked against the deferential discursive capital of audiences in different social locations.

Weak nationalism and strong nostalgic desire

Nevertheless, classic critical media theories cannot fully explain the strongly expressed desire for communality among both the producers and the consumers of the nostalgic text. These nostalgic practices reveal a deeply felt deficiency in a historical narrative of origin. Before 1997 the Hong Kong colony was one of the few places in the modern world that fostered a strong local culture without a nationalistic discourse. Most modern histories are constituted by the master narrative of a unified nation; cultural and social differences are given a certain fixity by the articulating principle of "the nation."[30] However, the colonial government of Hong Kong adopted a non-interventionist policy and refrained from instilling political commitment in its colonial subjects, while political movements in China were prevented from influencing the colony. Neither China nor Britain, before the sovereignty transfer, imposed any strong nationalistic or political identity on the territory. Local history was deliberately ignored in formal education to prevent the development of collective political efforts independent from the Sino–British dualistic political structure. Indeed, the Sino–British Joint Declaration describes the people of Hong Kong in neutral and neutralizing terms such as "inhabitants" or "residents," and local culture is rendered merely as "life-style." History was not deployed to describe a nation for political identification. Politics and history are absorbed in administrative terms. To the general public, local history does not have strong discursive expressions.

This discursive context of weak nationalism provides a space for, or a strongly felt lack of, historical positioning. As in other immigrant societies, family memories are difficult to sustain; a sense of collectivity is not derived from a common past but evolves from the opportunities of the present and a vision of the future.[31] However, in the years before 1997, a sense of disappearance and discontinuity triggered a sudden awareness of Hong Kong's lack of historical narrative. The upsurge of nostalgic media can thus be seen as a sudden urge to fill an empty cultural space. Popular media became the symbolic resource of fostering a sense of continuity and history. In this context the fisherman commercial easily takes up the discursive position to narrate the history of Hong Kong. This is also part of the reason why this popular history, constructed in the unorthodox media of commercial advertising, has been embraced so readily by the general public as an authentic history of Hong Kong. In the discursive context of weak nationalism and full-blown capitalism, Hong Kong Bank took up the position of the government to renarrate a decontextualized Hong Kong history by a capitalist logic of individual survival. Not only is the desire for nostalgia mediated by corporate interest; it is also derived from within the community, which has been granted a sociocultural space under the non-intervention politics of both Britain and China.

Local history, global capitalism, and re-sinicized nationalism

The last question concerns the connection between nostalgia and the discourse of the state and the market. In the fisherman commercial, the articulation between the political economy from above and the social desire from below produced an extremely popular discourse with a neat and seamless visual narrative. However, this narrative is steering through dangerous waters with undercurrents. Because of the sovereignty issue, Hong Kong's popular culture has to maneuver a soft landing by relocating local history to a safe ground where global capitalism can coexist with a re-sinicized nationalism. In the 1970s and 1980s, Hong Kong started to have a strong local identity and a vibrant popular culture. This Hong Kong identity was characterized by a sociocultural differentiation between Hong Kong and mainland China. Rephrasing this de-sinicized local culture to make it compatible with a re-sinicized nationalism is a hazardous endeavor. Crafting a discursive space for legitimizing globalized capitalism without triggering an association with treachery and betrayal is an even more challenging task. The fisherman commercial successfully constructs a version of history that satisfies these conflicting demands. First, seen as a localized nostalgic text, it can compensate for the lack of a grand historical narrative for local Hong Kongers. Second, this localized history is sanitized and individualized so as to dilute the once-popular and now politically incorrect discourse of Sino–Hong Kong differentiation. Third, this narrative of an atomized and upwardly mobile individual renews Hong Kong's connection with the globalized economy. This version of Hong Kong history leaves a legitimate space for Hong Kong Bank to internationalize its operations and maintain a localized tie at the same time. It allows the bank to compensate for the diminishing colonial privilege by claiming a share in Hong Kong's past success and providing a new transnational platform for its continued survival within and outside the region. The discursive strategy is to localize by decontextualizing and individualizing, so as to accommodate China's proposal for a re-sinicized nationalism, on one hand, and to renew Hong Kong's connection in transnational capitalism, on the other. In fact, this discursive strategy of Hong Kong Bank is also deployed by local Hong Kongers to maintain the territory's distinctive identity as a special zone differentiable from the mainland.

Thus the fisherman commercial actually reconciles the conflicts between nationalism, local identity, and transnational capitalism by exploiting an existing social desire for nostalgic communality in a time of extraordinary change. The discursive dissonance created by seemingly irresolvable conflicts and undercurrents of the larger political economy in fact heightens the desire for ideological closure and renders the production and consumption of a seamless nostalgic text more satisfying.[32] The case can be explained by neither top-down theories of media political economy nor bottom-up theories of populism. The unofficial popular history welcomed by the people from below is in fact the official ideology of a dominant agent of transnational capitalism. This transnational agent was acting with the autonomy licensed by the "State *in absentia*" at a key moment of political transition. This suggests that the popular nostalgic text is a discursive synergy that satisfies social desire as well as disciplining social behavior. The regulatory discourse generated from these cultural practices is both constraining and enabling, disciplinary and satisfying. The nostalgic commercial perpetuates a capitalist ideology but, at the same time, fosters cultural solidarity for Hong Kongers during discontinuity and change.

Notes

* This chapter is a case study of a nostalgic text achieving multiple ideological articulations in 1997. (It has previously appeared in *Positions* 9(1): 131–59. © 2001 by Duke University Press. All rights reserved. Used by permission of the publisher.) It describes how a TV commercial mobilized the faith in upward mobility at the moment of great political transition by reinforcing the myth of unfailing capitalism. Since 1997, the prolonged economic downturn in Hong Kong has almost demystified the Hong Kong success story. However, the general theoretical concerns of the article are surprisingly relevant to the post-1997 ideological struggle. The media in general and the TV commercials in particular are still serving as the prime sites for the synthesis of new discourses of nationalism and economic restructuring in multiple layers.

1   See John R. Gills, ed., *Commemorations: The Politics of National Identity* (Princeton, NJ: Princeton University Press, 1994); Eric Hobsbawm and Terence Ranger, eds., *The Invention of Tradition* (Cambridge: Cambridge University Press, 1983); Kevin Walsh, *The Representation of the Past: Museums and Heritage in the Postmodern World* (London: Routledge, 1992); Philip West, Steven I. Levine, and Jackie Hiltz, eds., *America's War in Asia: A Cultural Approach to History and Memory* (New York: M. E. Sharpe, 1998).

2   Fred Chiu, "Politics and the Body Social in Colonial Hong Kong," *Positions* 4 (fall 1996): 187–215.

3   Hong Kong has been undergoing a renationalization process since the mid-1990s. See Eric Ma, "Re-nationalization and Me: My Hong Kong Story after 1997," *Inter-Asia Cultural Studies* 1(1) (April 2000): 173–9.

4   See Joseph Chan, "Television in Greater China: Structure, Exports, and Market Formation," in J. Sinclair et al., eds., *New Patterns in Global Television: Peripheral Vision* (New York: Oxford University Press, 1996).

5   The fisherman commercial was elected by audience vote as one of the 10 best TV commercials of 1995.

6   There were 175 dead or missing. See *Wah Kiu Yat Pao* (a Chinese newspaper in Hong Kong), Sept. 3–4, 1962.

7   About 60 missing, 50 dead. See *Wah Kiu Yat Pao*, June 19–20, 1972, and a review in the *South China Morning Post*, April 12, 1973.

8   A Building was demolished on Conduit Road, killing 67 people.

9   Natalie Chan, "Nostalgic Films in Hong Kong," *Today Literary Magazine* 28(1) (spring 1995): 161–71.

10 philip Robertson, "Of Mimicry and Mermaids: Hong Kong and the Documentary Film Legacy," in G. Evans and M. Tam, eds., *Hong Kong: The Anthropology of a Chinese Metropolis* (Richmond, Surrey: Curzon Press, 1997), 77–101.

11 Wong Wang-chi, Li Siu-leung, and Chan Ching-kiu, *Hong Kong Un-Imagined: History, Culture, and the Future* (Taiwan: Rye Field, 1997).

12 Fred Davis, *Yearning for Yesterday: Sociology of Nostalgia* (New York: Free Press, 1979).

13 For example, on film see Natalie Chan, "Nostalgic Films," and on chain stores see Cheung See Ling, "Back to the Future: Herbal Tea Shops in Hong Kong," in Evans and Tam, eds., *Hong Kong*, 51–76.

14 Lau Siu-kai and Kuan Hsin-chi, *The Ethos of Hong Kong Chinese* (Hong Kong: City University of Hong Kong Press, 1988).

15 Tsang Wing-kwong, "Consolidation of a Class Structure: Changes in the Class Structure of Hong Kong," in Lau Siu-kai et al., eds., *Inequalities and Development: Social Stratification in Chinese Societies* (Hong Kong: Hong Kong Institute of Asia Pacific Studies, City University of Hong Kong, 1994); Thomas W. P. Wong and Lui Tai-lok, *Morality, Class, and the Hong Kong Way of Life* (Hong Kong: Hong Kong Institute of Asia Pacific Studies, City University of Hong Kong, 1993).

16 See *Wah Kiu Yat Pao*, June 10, 1972.

17 For the prolonged demonstrations and arrests related to the request of the fishing community in Yau Ma Tei, see *Ming Pao*, Dec. 18, 1978. For other political and social disputes see *Men Wei Pao*, June 17, 1967; *Wah Kiu Yat Pao*, Nov. 16, 1973, Aug. 4, 1989.

18 Thirty-seven people were dead or missing; see *Wah Kiu Yat Pao*, Oct. 31, 1971.

19 Four were killed instantly, and nine died later. The story was carried in all Hong Kong newspapers in the second week of January 1994.

20 See Gregory E. Guldin, "Hong Kong Ethnicity: Of Folk Models and Change," in Evans and Tam, eds., *Hong Kong*, 25–50, for a discussion of the complex issue of ethnicity in Hong Kong.

21 See *South China Morning Post*, Dec. 18, 1990.

22 Maurice Collis, *Wayfoong: The Hong Kong and Shanghai Bank Corporation* (London: Faber and Faber, 1978).

23 Eric F. K. Chiu and T. Y. Choi, *Hong Kong Banking System and Practice* (Hong Kong: Chartered Institute of Bankers, 1994).

24 More than 80 interviews have been conducted in the "Advertising the Hong Kong Identity" Project. One of the publications generated for this project is relevant to the present article: Eric Ma, "Consuming Satellite Modernities," in *Cultural Studies* 15(3/4): 444–63.

25 N. Abercrombie, S. Hill, and B. Turner, *Dominant Ideologies* (London: Allen and Unwin, 1990).

26 There was an upsurge of nostalgic television programs, publications, and exhibitions in the mid-1990s. See Eric Ma, " Reinventing Hong Kong: Memory, Identity, and Television," *International Journal of Cultural Studies* 1(3) (Dec. 1998): 329–49.

27 Stuart Hall, *Encoding and Decoding in TV Discourse* (Birmingham: Centre for Contemporary Cultural Studies, 1973).

28 paul Glennie and Nigel Thrift, "Reworking E. P. Thompson's Time, Work-Discipline, and Industrial Capitalism,'" *Time and Society* 5(3) (Oct. 1996): 275–99.

29 Akhil Gupta, "The Reincarnation of Souls and the Rebirth of Commodities: Representations of Time in 'East' and 'West,'" in J. Boyarin, ed., *Remapping Memory: The Politics of Time Space* (Minneapolis: University of Minnesota Press, 1994), 161–84.

30 Daniel A. Segal, "Living Ancestors: Nationalism and the Past in Postcolonial Trinidad and Tobago," in Boyarin, ed., *Remapping Memory*, 221–40.

31 Micheal Kammen, *In the Past Lane* (New York: Oxford University Press, 1997).

32 Charles W. Nuckolls, *The Cultural Dialectics of Knowledge and Desire* (Madison, WI: University of Wisconsin Press, 1996).

Part III

Moving Between: Formations of Audiences and Subjectivities

9

The Whole World is Watching Us: Music Television Audiences in India

Vamsee Juluri

Introduction

In an essay on the possibilities for media studies as a public intellectual practice in India, Dipankar Sinha (2000) notes with some irony that the critical discourse on media and cultural imperialism has become less visible precisely at the time that it is perhaps most needed. During the 1990s, the Indian mediascape went through a remarkable set of transformations as a powerful set of transnational and national forces under the twin labels of globalization and liberalization transplanted people in India from a single-network television environment to one of multichannel, 24-hour satellite broadcasting. If the rapidity and intensity of the social and cultural fluxes generated by the advent of satellite television in India seemed breathtaking, a greater surprise – especially for media scholars – would be the seeming normalcy into which these fluxes and transformations apparently disappeared. In other words, even as "cultural imperialism" was a rather commonplace concern in the Indian public sphere until the 1990s, by the end of the decade it seemed to have hardly the kind of currency one would expect it to have in the face of all the new challenges.

For example, in the early 1990s, a frequent question in graduate and postgraduate competitive examinations used to be about "cultural imperialism" in the context of the rise of satellite television in India (the other popular question as I recall pertained to the role of India and Non-Alignment in the post-Cold War world). Among my colleagues and fellow journalism trainees at that time, opinion used to be intelligently divided on this issue. Some of us appreciated the seriousness of what was happening, although we felt compelled to distance our critique from what seemed like an ancient and paternalistic critique coming from traditional quarters (retired public officials, ministers, sinecured public commentators). Some of us simply scorned the notion of a critique altogether, arguing that satellite television would be merely another harmless play-thing for Indian elites, who were all "Westernized" in some form anyway. In either case, we had been taught all about NWICO, and the tradition, and knew what "cultural imperialism" referred to. In 1997, as I conducted my interviews for my dissertation research, I was surprised to find that most of the participants – many of whom were well-informed and articulate students – said that they had never heard of the notion of "cultural imperialism." They all had heard of "globalization," though.

In this chapter, I discuss the state of Indian media studies at a moment when the inexorability of globalization confronts the inadequacies of prior critique as exemplified in the notion of cultural imperialism, and evaluate the growing importance of audience studies as a response to this moment. I argue that audience studies are important not only as a way of broadening the terms of analysis of media in India, but also as a way for Indian media studies to politicize its own international location in relation to the subdisciplinary tensions and polarities of media studies which in the Western academy have long been manifested as a needless opposition between the "cultural imperialism" tradition on the one hand and the "audience studies" projects on the other. In both these intellectual contexts, my aim is to show that attention to audience research in the postsatellite-television era in India can serve to strengthen a critical approach to media globalization that is rooted in what Ashis Nandy (1998) characterizes as simultaneously a "critical cosmopolitanism" as well as a "critical traditionalism."

Such a move is warranted not only by the particular intellectual and institutional politics of Indian media studies, but more importantly by the fact that the dominant feature of the postliberalization national social imaginary in India seems to be one of the complete opposite. One of the most pervasive television genres that has emerged in India since 1991 is music television, and its dominant theme may be summarized as one of an uncritical global-nationalism. While international music-television giants such as MTV and Channel V entered the Indian market with localization as their entry ticket, the rise of numerous Indian music-television channels and programs as well have all served to create a popular television discourse about being "Indian" in the age of globalization. For instance, one of the most popular music videos of the 1990s in India was Alisha Chinai's "Made in India," which shows a princess turning down suitors from different nations and finally choosing a man who is "made in India." Later in the decade, the self-deprecating slogan "world famous . . . in India" became well known on music-television promos. Music television, in short, promised a renewed sense of national identity in a rapidly globalizing context. But as I show in this chapter, on the basis of my own reception studies of music television in India, the global-national that is emerging among the middle-class Indian television audience is more a case of appropriation rather than a cause for celebration. Using the readings made by young middle-class music television viewers of "Made in India," I argue that the perception among these viewers of globalization as a process of international empowerment and recognition for India must be seen as neither simple audience victimization nor resistance, but instead as a site of epistemic struggle, and indeed domination, that media studies in India must confront.

It is my contention that these questions about Indian media and Indian media studies warrant closer attention to the notion of the audience – not only as a methodological step towards other analysis, but as a valid object of study in itself. It is useful, in other words, to conceive of the audience – in this case the satellite television audience in India – not merely as the end-point of media transmission, but more accurately along three dimensions: (a) the role it occupies in the constitutive "imagination" and measurement of desired audiences by media institutions (the first instance of political economy in which the audience is constituted in terms of purchasing power), or, in other words, how MTV (and others) built their audience in India; (b) the audience as it emerges from the textual implications of programming (what sort of demands do these new genres and programs place on audiences in order for them to "get" the meaning?); and (c) under what constraints, with what expectations, and with what possible consequences do people "become" audiences (the ethnographic moment)? It is my contention that Indian media studies have usefully engaged with the first and second moments described above (even if not always explicitly with the audience as a problematic), while the contours of actual reception – particularly in the context of satellite television – are only beginning to be addressed. The reasons for this particular configuration of research priorities, and the growing need for audience research, as I argue, are not incidental, but central to how the projects and formations of "Indian media studies" are implicated in a politics of epistemologies and institutions that seem well described by Arjun Appadurai's (2000) characterization as the "knowledge of globalization" and the "globalization of knowledge."

Indian Media Studies

Despite the characterization for analytical and polemical purposes of the kind of work I address in this chapter as "Indian," it is useful to note the transnational continuities (and tensions) that mark the development of the study of media in the broadest sense in the (ex)colonies and the metropolitan Western academy. It is important not to think of media studies in postcolonial contexts as merely an import; a mere benediction sent around to help those who have already been plunged into saturated media conditions lead better lives (or worse, figure out more efficient ways of making the media more pervasive and commercially successful). However, the institutional history of media studies in India may be usefully located in a global context that in a sense precedes the present-day context of advanced (and media-rich) globalization. Vasudeva and Chakravarty (1989) show that the institution of "mass-communication research" in India in the 1960s was implicated in the tensions of what was then the dominant tendency in international mass-communication research – the development communication and modernization paradigm. In other words, rather than dismiss this institution as a unidirectional imposition of Western thinking on the postcolonial context, it is also useful to see how the "Nehruvian" era that was so fundamental in its impact on mass-communication research was itself both national and international in its outlook.

While it is true that "national development" was often the unquestioned goal for the institution of mass-communication research (and training – the vocational thrust was, to be fair, perhaps what was considered most important), the assumption of modern/Western goals of modernization at the social and epistemological levels was articulated to the desire for national sovereignty; in addition, the nationalist position was also evident not in any kind of an isolationist, insular, thinking, but also situated in the context of a growing feeling of third-world anti-imperialist solidarity. So even if Wilbur Schramm went around setting up national institutes of mass communication in various countries (my own experience of this was curiously surprising, when I met in the US someone from Kenya who had been through exactly the same kind of journalism program I had been through in India), this was also an opportunity for actual interaction between postcolonial nations. The Indian Institute of Mass Communication in New Delhi, for instance, offered in addition to its various training programs for communication officers in the government, an advanced program for professional news reporters from Non-Aligned nations.

By the time of the rise of satellite television and liberalization, mass-communication research in India was taking on a number of challenges, not only from the urgency of the questions at hand (ranging from policy issues to curricular responses to meet a growing demand for professionals, particularly in the private-sector media), but also from the scholarship of nonresident Indian scholars, foreign-trained scholars, and local scholars with a critical orientation that was bringing in – in some form – the concerns of a critical cultural-studies approach to contemporary media studies. In the 1990s, as Sinha (2000) writes, there was a general increase in concern and visibility for media studies in India, ranging from curricular recognition (although, as he notes, the study of the "information age" needs to be included not only in mass-communication and journalism curricula but broader social science subjects as well) and policy recommendations to the growing presence of public commentary on media and culture in the press, and to some extent, television as well.[1] However, as Sinha points out, there still remains some unproductive divergence between the "traditional" or "mainstream" mass-communication research approach and the more nuanced but not always politically engaged "media-studies" approaches.

In particular, Sinha says that while the mainstream studies of mass communication in India (which, he laments, have not been too many in the first place) may have been somewhat "factual" and "technocratic," the cultural-studies oriented media studies have been "inward looking" and unable to engage with the connections between "textuality and subjectivity" on the one hand, and the broader politics of these on the other (2000: 4190). Sinha qualifies his critique by saying that it is not necessarily the fault of the nonresident Indian scholar that cultural studies of media in India have been unable to grapple with the politics as effectively as they do with the nuances of meaning and everyday life, especially in the shadow of Indian popular culture. Following Sinha's critique, one may usefully turn to the broader "politics of location" in communication studies in general, and how this has a bearing on what sort of studies do get conducted. More importantly, the question of whether media studies in India has the force and potential to do justice to the severity of its object of study needs to be addressed in this context. As Sinha points out, the possibilities for Indian media studies lie not only in terms of making the right methodological decisions, but more importantly by responding and remaking media studies with a suitable "local" epistemological focus that is appropriate to the global scope of its analysis. In other words, what would make for an "Indian" media studies in an age of "global" media? In this chapter, I examine how audience studies could respond to such a challenge, particularly by engaging with epistemic issues in reception in both "local" (or national) and "global" ways.

Globalization and Audience Studies

The tensions between the global and the national are as relevant in media studies as they are in media institutions. If the national was taken as the unit of development quite literally in traditional international mass-communication research (national integration, national development), the role of the national in the new globalizing project of media studies raises new questions, particularly in terms of the question of the audience. Has the rise of audience studies in the West found a response in the Indian context? What are the problems and constraints facing engagement with Indian audiences because of the institutional politics of audience studies in terms of its Western location and nascent Indian institutional parallels? Most importantly, why is the audience important to Indian media studies, and what are the possibilities for an "Indian" epistemological thrust to such a project?

The importance of audience studies to the Indian and global contexts comes from a number of factors. Within India, even the spate of scholarship that has emerged since the rise of satellite television in the 1990s has taken mostly a political-economy, institutional, policy-oriented, or at best, textual-analysis approach.[2] All the while, the most remarkable transformation was taking place on the ground in terms of the experience of hundreds of millions of people *as* television audiences, and global audiences, in some ways. The need for audience studies, however, comes not only from the urgency of this transformation, but also from the enduring significance of the "audience" as an object of study in media studies, and particularly the demands for attention for audience studies raised by recent developments in the globalization of media and media studies. As I have argued elsewhere (Juluri, 1998; 2003) the rise of interest in audiences since the spread of critical cultural-studies mandated work on media in metropolitan nations since the 1970s has been met by a new set of impasses in dealing with non-metropolitan contexts. Briefly, my contention *vis-à-vis* the politics of global media/cultural studies is that the postmodernist turn in audience theories and what Nightingale (1996) calls "cultural studies audience research" has been disenfranchising for audience studies and media studies in, on, and from nonmetropolitan contexts. While the rise of audience studies in cultural studies has clearly drawn due attention to the need to engage with the experiences of people in relation to media (rather than assume effects either from institutional analyses or from textual studies), a more recent tendency, as I have argued, has been to emphasize the unknowability of audiences as a rigorous global condition. In other words, an otherwise welcome critique of the presumptuousness and power implications of knowledge-claims embedded in institutional discourses about audiences has translated into a sense of defeat for the whole purpose of audience studies (see Ang, 1996).

Such a tendency becomes especially problematic when scholars from and working on nonmetropolitan contexts seek to address the experiences of audiences within media studies as a global and anti-imperialistic project. Thus, even if postmodern critiques of Western audiences rightly emphasize the limited nature of their ability to "know" audiences, the tendency to conflate this criticism with an overarching positing of unknowability of audiences and, by extension, lack of necessity for audience studies wipes out precisely those calls for marginal and nonmetropolitan voices that such critiques have sought to highlight. As R. Radhakrishnan (1994) has argued in his influential essay, "Postmodernism and the Rest of the World," the emphasis on relativism and openness that the postmodern critique of the Western episteme has sought to raise has itself become an absolute and totalizing condition, thanks to continuing dominance of the institutional structures of the Western academy on a global scale. The place of non-Western audience studies, in other words, is condemned to a mere afterthought to the canon of cultural-studies audience research, always having to apologize for its limitedness and supposed epistemic faults at worst; or having to qualify itself as a "marked" project: in other words, such audience studies tend to become sorted into categories such as "Asian" or "Indian" projects, while the very "British" or "American" audience studies are seldom marked that way, and enjoy the career of universal, unnamed normativity even if their specific authors do not make such claims.

These tendencies have been rightfully criticized within audience studies from a number of quarters. While postcolonialist media ethnographers like Natrajan and Parameswaran (1997) have argued that an actual engagement by researchers with non-Western audiences in their everyday contexts is necessary and cannot be done away with merely by recourse to more self-reflexive writing strategies by ethnographers, some audience researchers have also been assertive about the need for actual empirical audience research to supplement if not supplant both textually derived media analyses (Stromer-Galley & Schiappa, 1998) and the broader politics of "populism" in media ethnographies (Gibson, 2000). In addition to these critiques, the need to restore and claim a place for audience studies in non-Western contexts also arises from what is perhaps a foundational justification for audience studies in general: the paramount importance of engaging with issues of determination and power in media studies. The metatheoretical, self-reflexive critique of issues of power in the institutional practices of media studies set two goals for global audience studies: (1) that the "global" be taken seriously, with all its attendant implications for universalist ambitions that are driven by a critique of Eurocentric universalism while not losing sight of the possibility of alternative universalisms (Chen, 1998); and (2) that there is equally the need to forward theories of media determination based on engagement outside the academy with what is actually happening in the lives of people in relation to the media. Although the mandate and constraints of cultural-studies audience research imply that its conception of determination is not a simple unilinear one of either behavioral lines of effect from media to audiences (or functionalistic forces from audiences to media), the core concern for these studies, and I believe for audience studies in India, as I will show below, is the question of how "unnatural" power relations in the social formation come to be "normalized" through the process of reception. In other words, the central importance of audience studies comes not only from a need to include "other" voices in the debate, but to map out the ways in which how people become audiences – particularly in non-Western contexts – embodies the workings of cultural power in the broadest social and historical sense. In other words, what role do the media play in bringing audiences into a condition of hegemony – especially since "hegemony" needs to be thought of increasingly at the subnational and transnational levels as well? What would a sufficiently globalist critical approach to audience studies need to do in order to engage theoretically and politically with such a project? Finally, what role can be found for non-Western and nonmodern epistemologies in reception in such a project?

Audience Studies in India

Audience studies "in" and "on" India that have engaged with issues of power in this sense have not been numerous, but are nonetheless important and useful in engaging with the broad transformatory sweeps that have brought large populations via their construction and interpellation as audiences into various levels and forms of hegemony. In this section, I outline some of these projects, and then go on to address some of the questions raised by the rise of satellite television, and particularly music television in India, about the transnational and transgenerational aspects of hegemony that I have addressed in my own work.

The possibilities of audience studies in India have been demonstrated perhaps most notably in the ethnographic study conducted by Purnima Mankekar (1999) into the lives of women television viewers of Indian state television in the late 1980s. Mankekar's study engages with an important moment in Indian cultural politics and media that has both preceded and enabled the present-day problems of globalization that I address later in this chapter. The rise of a pro-capitalist Hindu right-wing political movement in India in the 1980s has been widely related to the popular success of two "religious" serials broadcast nationally on Doordarshan, the state-owned television network, during that time (see Rajagopal, 2000). These epic serials, the Ramayana and Mahabharatha, not only "centralized" what had earlier been a fairly regional and pluralistic set of popular sensibilities, but also did these within the shadow of increasing commercialization of state television on the one hand and the broader rise of a politically assertive and culturally fundamentalist middle class on the other. Mankekar's work, however, takes these issues "home" quite literally, not only in terms of the gendered nature of the reception of these programs and their translation into the emerging relations of power in the Indian context, but also outlines some epistemic possibilities in reception that some may say are distinctly "Indian" in their difference from Western/ modern epistemes – but which could equally usefully be interpreted as the core of an alternative universalistic episteme as I will show later in this chapter.

Such possibilities are also evident in the ethnographic study of poor, urban South Indian viewers of Tamil cinema by Sara Dickey (1996). Dickey's engagement with what has for long been the core audience in class terms of Indian cinema shows that the pervasive importance of cinema in their lives must be seen neither as their victimization by middle-class producers of escapist fantasies nor as a valiant reappropriation by resistive consumers. Instead, Dickey points out that the borderline of these two opposite forces is what constitutes the hegemonic moment of Indian cinema in the lives of its poor audiences – and this borderline is cast, importantly, in terms of the identification of viewers with the familial, relational, and emotional aspects of the narratives of Tamil films. In other words, even if Indian cinema with all its melodramatic grandeur and escapist fantasies perpetrates and perpetuates an interclass hegemony (poor viewers identifying

[handwritten margin note: importance of cinema in poor urban S. India]

with the lives of rich characters and sometimes even richer film stars), it is important that this identification takes place within the lines of familial identities and relationships. On the basis of my study, I will show later in this chapter how this particular tendency to foreground familial identifications in Indian media reception also constitutes a set of possibilities for an alternative epistemic sensibility and universalism in understanding audiences.

More recently, since the rise of satellite television and the broader media boom entailed by economic liberalization in India, media research and media research institutions have also sought to engage critically with the present moment. The work of Melissa Butcher on youth audiences and images of beauty and the body in Indian television (1999) has skillfully highlighted how the particularly visual aspect of television may be theorized in terms of reception. In other words, Butcher has shown how television audiences are becoming implicated not only in emerging forms of "looking" Indian, for instance, but also in how these visual forms constitute a new way of "knowing" one's self, as an "Indian," among other things. While Butcher's work has enriched traditional audience research issues such as comprehension, recognition, and pleasure with questions about the body, a more direct engagement with a quite literal bodily disciplinarity and power is evident in the ethnographic work being conducted by members of the Center for the Study of Culture and Society on Dalit (formerly "untouchable") viewers of South Indian cinema.[3] Their study addresses how cinema viewing rituals surrounding first-day shows of new releases and their negotiation by young, male, working-class fanclub members is marked by literal struggles over their bodies and activities by theater management and various disciplinary apparatuses.

As these four examples illustrate, audience studies in India are beginning to engage with a previously neglected area in media studies, but are also pointing out new and important lines of theorizing in audience studies that do not have to be perforce limited in their usefulness to "Indian" or "local" contexts. In the following sections, I outline how such lines of theorizing may emerge on the basis of one issue that has not yet been addressed – the epistemic politics surrounding audience identification with notions of the national and the global in the reception of Indian music television. In particular, I discuss how the experience of becoming a global audience through the reception of music television in India may point out not only the complexities of hegemony under the present moment of globalization, but also highlight some of the epistemic possibilities that may be claimed counterhegemonically not only as "Indian," but as "global" as well.

Global Audiences: Indian Music Television

The rise of satellite television in India has been dominated by one kind of programming perhaps more than any other – music television. In addition to the international music television channels such as Channel V and MTV, music television is widely watched in India through Indian music television channels such as Music Asia, as well as on a plethora of family/entertainment-oriented national and regional language channels. My study of music television audiences (Juluri, 2003) seeks to answer how and why music television (which may be summarily described here as consisting largely of Indian film songs and pop-music videos in a Western- or MTV-style format) has come to dominate postliberalization television in India, and some of its implications for audiences, particularly in terms of their negotiation of the meanings of nationality and globality pervasive in many music television programs. My concern has been not so much with the globality (or worldwideness) of music television or MTV itself, but more so with the globality of audiences in relation to music television; in other words, what meanings do audiences construct about themselves and their place in the world (as national subjects among other things) particularly in terms of how they read certain popular music-video texts that explicitly address "global" themes? As I argue in the following sections, what emerges from the reception of music videos in India is neither a case of simple cultural imperialism nor one of audience resistance, but instead a set of possibilities for understanding an alternative epistemic world that is being increasingly appropriated by the discourses of music television.

At the outset, it is useful to spell out why audience research was needed particularly in the context of this study. Theoretically speaking, in addition to the arguments with the literature described earlier in this chapter, there has been another fallacious tendency among cultural-imperialism theories to posit audience studies as somehow antithetical to the critique of media imperialism (see Roach, 1997). Despite the claims of even sophisticated theorists of media globalization like Tomlinson (1991) that audience studies can do little but confirm audience activity against assumptions of media imperialism, it is worth reiterating that it is perhaps through audience studies that media power can be best appreciated. In addition, the empirical reality of media globalization in India also complicates a simple assumption of cultural imperialism as the influx of Western media and culture. After a brief period of largely American programming, most satellite television channels have localized extensively in India. Both MTV and Channel V, for instance, frequently claim to be more "Indian" than the

other.[4] Thus, even if satellite television is "Western" at the level of ownership, it is clear as Chadha and Kavoori (2000) argue, that the bulk of
popular programming in India, and much of Asia, has been localized.

From the audience perspective, the localization strategy of music television has emerged as a widespread celebration of national identity in a
global context. One of the first music videos in India was Alisha Chinai's
"Made in India," which promoted what would become one of the first
commercially successful nonfilm music albums in India.[5] The popular
resonance of "Made in India" continued in Indian pop and film songs all
through the 1990s, culminating in a sense in a spate of releases to com-
memorate the fiftieth anniversary of India's independence in 1997. The
celebration of Indian identity by the Indian music and music television
industry, however, may be attributed to a more careful cultivation of youth
markets in India. Market researchers have sought to position a youth
market that is clearly defined in generational terms mainly in terms of its
particular experience of Indian national identity – a consuming, postliberalization generation as it were, "rebelling in" to the middle class world that
its parents had earlier avoided with their values of "Nehruvian austerity."[6]

For music television channels like Channel V and MTV, the cultivation
of the youth audience took place along two important axes, both of which
warrant the necessity of audience studies: one, following the dictum that
"Indian inside/Western outside" had strong appeal to Indian audiences,
these channels positioned themselves as global-Indian in a range of ways;
two, given the absence of two-TV-set households and the attendant lack of
a clearly demarcated presence of independent youth viewers, Channel V
sought to construct a broadly transgenerational audience, calling itself a
"youth channel in attitude but a family channel in demographics."[7] In other
words, the youth culture of music television in India was positioned to be
both global and Indian, and cool enough for youth but not offensive
enough for parents to vociferously object. It is also worth noting on this
point that despite the incidents of intolerance and violence directed against
artists and intellectuals by portions of the Hindu right wing, MTV and
Channel V have hardly been the object of any anger from fundamentalist
groups in India. On the contrary, Michael Jackson's concert in Mumbai a
few years ago was organized at the behest of the leader of the right-wing
Shiv Sena party.

My study of the reception of music television addressed a number of
themes, but what is perhaps more relevant to this essay is the negotiation of
meanings around music videos with explicitly nationalistic themes. The following excerpts are drawn from participant readings of "Made in India," as

well as some broader observations made by participants about their experience and understanding of globalization and satellite television in general. The interviews from which the following excerpts are culled took place in the south Indian city of Hyderabad in 1997. Participants were mostly middle-class high school and college students, and young professionals or postgraduate researchers. The interviews were structured around the viewing of a number of video clips, and were conducted in a mixture of English, Hindi, and Telugu (the regional language). Although most participants were largely viewers of national and regional language channels (MTV and Channel V were closely watched only by a small number of them), what was striking was the extent to which themes of globalization emerged from even exclusive viewers of regional language channels like Gemini and ETV. As the following section shows, the experience of globalization and national identity for these participants reveals contours of reception that not only surprise easy assumptions about globalization, but also highlight the need to address epistemic issues in the everyday construction of globality.

Made in India

The narrative of "Made in India" perhaps best summarizes what has emerged as the popular story about the experience of globalization in India. While the experience of globalization in everyday life in India may include such phenomena as friends and relatives going abroad to study or work, an increasing presence of consumer commodities (such as Kellogg's Basmati Flakes), and, of course, the internet and satellite television, the popular resonance of "Made in India" since its release in 1994 perhaps best summarizes the way a set of myths have caught hold of the emerging Indian global imagination. The story of the song, briefly, revolves around the languid wait of a fairytale princess called Alisha who turns down a series of "global" suitors while the lyrics of the song describe her desire for a "heart made in India." In the end, her dream suitor appears, carried into her court in a box marked "Made in India." In addition to the obvious importance accorded to the national and the global in this song, it is also worth noting at the outset the visual character of the video, and the particularly orientalistic images used to suggest a combination of exotic Indianness and generic fairytale-ness (elephants, snake charmers, yoga practitioners, magicians, tigers).

The popular appeal of this song arguably represents what many Indians would like to think of themselves in terms of their place in an increasingly globalizing world. While the song may appear to be an example of jingo-istic nationalism right at the outset, it is interesting that, at least in the course of my study, audience readings of this video showed a more complex engagement with the meanings of this song, and the meanings of global-ity and nationality in general (although this complexity is no sign of audi-ence resistance, as I argue later). At the outset, "Made in India" was clearly familiar and well-liked by most participants in my study, and its appeal was certainly not confined to Hindi speakers or MTV viewers, as the following statement by an older, professional, middle-class person shows:

> I thought that from the song, it talks about culture, our Indian culture. Something, saying that "Made in India," "Made in India." At the same time they are showing clippings of Kathakali [classical dance] arts which are famous in India. At the same time, they are comparing with Western also, with Japan, Russia, like that. Actually, I can't understand the full meaning of the song. I am very poor in Hindi. But I like this song. Why? Because the music was good, the visual was also very good.

The association of "Made in India" with a sense of Indian culture, however, was not merely a recollection of some stockpile of "Indian" imagery for participants, but seemed to represent a somewhat deeply felt sense of being Indian. Specifically, as the following statements show, at least two participants sought to convey the observation that "Made in India" was a representation of who they really were – as Indians – rather than a slo-ganistic injunction to "love the country" (as they thought state television often told them to do).

> ["Made in India" is] not a "patriotic" song, but has a lot of meaning in it.

> ... they [state TV] tell us about worshipping the nation, but not about the feeling, the Indian feeling. [*translated from Telugu*]

The notion of the "Indian feeling" was also expressed by a number of par-ticipants through the Hindi word "*dil*" or the Telugu word "*manassu*" (both of which could be translated as "heart" without implying a "head/heart" dis-tinction). Despite the rather simplistic use of *dil* in the lyrics of the song, it is interesting that participants engaged with this notion in various ways, most notably, in terms of relational values. For instance, when asked to clarify what being Indian or having an Indian "heart" meant to them, some participants said that it meant having a "good character," or being a "good husband," or being "respectful to elders." In other words, despite the broader media construction of Indian greatness in a global context in terms of commercial and military success,[8] it is useful to note that there is a sense of national identity expressed in everyday interpersonal terms as well, at least in relation to this video. While it may be easy to criticize these statements as being nothing more than a more nuanced interpretation of the sloganeering of the music video, it is perhaps more accurate to think of audience readings as going beyond such textual parameters as well (although this does mitigate a critique of media culpability in this context, as I show in the following section). Simply put, it appears that participants do not merely accept the notion of Indian greatness in this song and express it in relational terms, but actually get into the nuances of the narrative, which imply at the outset a setting up of Indianness in a competitive global market of "husbands" and "hearts," as it were. As the following comment by a female middle-class high-school student shows, Alisha is seen as choosing an Indian man not necessarily because he is Indian, but because he happens to have the "qualities" that she is looking for:

She wants a person from anywhere in the world, any corner in the world, but that person should possess the qualities she wants.

In other words, "Made in India" is not seen as directly exhorting Indian superiority, but merely pointing out that it in a fair and competitive marketplace an Indian may come out the winner. From this example, it would appear that despite the many critiques that could be raised at the institutional (a foreign-owned media corporation now provides national identification for Indians) and textual (India signified through orientalistic images) levels, audience readings are reassuring to the extent that participants combine what could be considered a nonmodern sense of community values with a modern and self-reflexive openness about their place in the world to express their feelings in this regard. However, on closer examination, especially in relation to broader media discourses about globalization and national identity in India as well as participants' perceptions of their national location in a global context in relation to media, a strong critique of media and cultural imperialism would seem well in order. As I show in the following section, the success of "Made in India" and numerous other film songs and music videos celebrating India in the global context (for example, the Hindi film songs, "East or West, India is the Best"; "I love my India"; and the pop song, "I'm an Indian") all may be related to an emerging but inaccurate perception of what exactly becoming global entails for Indians and Indian audiences. Furthermore, this perception is troubling not only because of its mythic quality and its embeddedness in a social context of globalization that is far from favorable to India in the way participants may like to think it is, but also because it represents, at an epistemic level, an appropriation of all that may be valued and commendable in everyday common sense by the discursive regime of the new music-television world.

Conclusion: The Whole World is Watching Us

In relation to "Made in India," and satellite television in general, there seems to be a perception among some participants that "globalization" represents not so much an influx of Western culture into India, but instead an outward spread – and a growing recognition of such a spread – of India and Indians into the global sphere. This perception is inflected at various levels. For instance, in the following example, the participant, a postdoctoral researcher, rightly notes that "Made in India" was made for the Non-Resident Indian market, and that (what was perceived to be) the successful presence of Indians in other countries shows how "Indian culture" is being recognized for its greatness all over the world:

> Basically this song, when it was thought of and made, it was aimed towards NRIs [Non-Resident Indians] . . . I don't think I'm 100% correct but they wanted to show this video, this video was specifically made for NRIs and in US it made good sales and review *manchiga ochindi* [was positive] . . . it reminds me of Indian soil. Made in India. Something made in India.

While such positive evaluations of "Made in India" as a symbol of Indian pride in the global context are fairly widespread among participant readings, what is worth emphasizing is also a sense, even if this is not exactly widely echoed in this study, that the images used to represent India need to be selected more carefully, given the fact that "others" (non-Indians) may be watching them. The following participant, who is a graduate student of classical dance, laments the fact that some of the dancers in the "Made in India" video are wearing what she considers to be objectionable ("sleeveless") costumes, as opposed to what she knows to be more authentic or accurate costumes for such dancers:

> But regarding the Kuchipudi [classical dance] they are not clear, the dress is not *pucca* [perfect] traditional way in which other girls are wearing. Because

when the layman abroad, they see, they think that this is a particular dress you're wearing in India but that's not true.

Despite this one exception, it is important that participants in general do not problematize the clearly orientalistic images used to represent India in this video about Indian greatness. It may be the case that these images, on the other hand, serve to reinforce the misperception that whatever Indian television audiences watch is also being seen by viewers around the world. On this note, it is also worth emphasizing that the orientalism of "Made in India" is by no means peculiar to this one video, and is a pervasive phenomenon on music television: numerous videos and promos exoticize Indian everyday life, and Indian working-class people in particular. The sort of "global" identity being sold by music television programs is therefore connected to an emerging self-perception as a global audience not so much in the usual terms of watching *Baywatch*, but instead in an assumption that becoming a global audience means that the rest of the world is watching Indian programs as well. The following comment by a young middle-class participant summarizes this perception:

> Like Star TV is okay [not surprising as an example of a global channel] but for example Zee TV. Basically it was Indian but now we get the feeling that that they are showing our programs to Europe, US, everywhere it's being shown.

The self-consciousness as a global audience is, however, inflected in numerous other ways as well. For instance, the following participant, talking in the context of the binational image of various Channel V VJs, notes that the "foreign accent" of some of these VJs may be understandable, given the presence of viewers outside India as well:

> If they're going to talk in English accent [or] Indian accent, I don't think Thailand people or Philippine people are going to follow it . . . because it's basically Asian channel, not Indian channel.

However, the same participant also downplays the extent to which television can "globalize" audiences:

> As soon as I switch off the TV it goes off. And I forget about everything and become Indian . . . so how you become part of the international audience? You are sitting in India and watching on Indian TV.

Thus, the "mythic" perception of global audiencehood is clearly one among others. However, the key issue is not so much whether those participants who "know" better may be more "resistive" than those who are not, but the whole question of what it means to be "in the know" in order to make meaning from music television discourses about globalization and national identity in the first place. Participants in this study were segmented not only in terms of their access to various kinds of global satellite television programs, but also in terms of their ability to engage with such discourses. Specifically, older middle-class participants, and working-class participants, did not seem to "get" the meaning of the various discourses about television and globalization (although they were familiar with the programs and the film songs and music videos in question). Although I would not reduce the distribution of cultural competences to their class (or age) backgrounds, it is worth examining the similarities and differences between those who assume a certain kind of prior knowledge in talking about (and talking to) certain discourses and those who do not.

One fundamental similarity that was apparent in the way participants talked about music television in this study was their emphasis on the relational and emotional aspects of the songs they watched. For instance, MTV-familiar viewers stressed these aspects of "Made in India," while working-class mothers stressed the same aspects about the regional-language film songs they watched. While this does not imply that "emotional" expression plays the same role given the material differences in access to privilege for these participants, it is clear that MTV viewers have not ignored such aspects of reception. However, working-class participants, and some middle-class participants, clearly do not find many other discourses surrounding these programs meaningful or perhaps even intelligible, while most young middle-class participants clearly engage with them in a meaningful and sometimes personally invested way. As I have argued elsewhere (Juluri, 2003), this difference may be described as one in which different sorts of authority to speak are claimed while speaking as an audience (see McKinley, 1997). Those who are in the know speak about their emotional experiences and relational values but speak from their modern, discursive authority as knowledgeable subjects. Those who are not in the know, speak about and perhaps from their *own* emotional experiences and relational values, but do not have the ability to claim any other kind of epistemic authority.

In other words, becoming a global audience – getting to be in the know so as to derive the full meaning and pleasure from music television in this context – may be seen as a process in which a certain set of experiences and values is increasingly marginalized for its epistemic authority, while the only source of epistemic authority becomes the discourse of music television – with all its attendant orientalistic premises. The outcome of such a process, arguably, is the naturalization of alien and imperialistic images into authentic representations; of Indianness, of the world even. Once a certain kind of representation becomes naturalized, not expressing one's self through such representations may become tantamount to not feeling or being that which is represented. For instance, 10 years ago, it was not considered commonsensical to advertise one's supposed Indianness (through songs, T-shirts, bumper stickers, and so on), but in the present discursive climate, not doing so may actually make someone appear un-Indian or unpatriotic – a condition eminently suitable for the fascistic thinking that has become "normal" common sense for many middle-class, educated Indians in recent years.

The problem with this phenomenon, however, is not so much only the appropriation of an arguably commendable epistemic universe (built around relational values and emotional experience) for the naturalization of an emerging social and political order, but the fact that the universalistic possibilities that may have existed for such an epistemic universe are increasingly marginalized. The process of becoming a global audience, in other words, represents a new and more dangerously widespread phase in what Ashis Nandy (1983) has described as the tension between definition and nondefinition since colonial times. The future of audience studies in India, not only as Indian audience studies, but as a broader globalist project, may be useful for demonstrating how the epistemic possibilities found in reception may actually represent another common sense, which is neither exclusively "Indian" nor "traditional," but rooted in both and yet capable of contemporary cosmopolitanism. The new cosmopolitanism, in other words, must come from neither the development/modernization desire to enlighten backward third-world populations despite their "cultural" baggage, nor from the orientalistic hybridity of MTV, but from a certain kind of a relational sensibility that needs to be claimed by scholars and others as the bedrock of the global condition and also as a possibility for an alternative globality.

Acknowledgments

I wish to acknowledge Sanjay Asthana for his help in mapping the Indian media-studies projects mentioned in this essay.

Notes

1 The work of the Bangalore-based Center for the Study of Society and Culture (www.cscsban.org), the New Delhi-based Media Foundation (www.thehoot.org), and the New York-based South Asian Journalists Association (www.saja.org) encompass a range of approaches and engagements with the media in India and south Asia.

2 Recent works on satellite television in India include Page and Crawley (2001), Melkote (1998), and selected essays in Brosius and Butcher (1999).

3 S. V. Srinivas of the Center is also engaged in a comparative study of spectatorship for Telugu cinema and Hong Kong action cinema. See www.cscsban.org.

4 MTV first appeared in India on the original Star TV line-up in 1991 and mainly featured Western pop songs. It was replaced by the Star network's Channel V in 1994, which pioneered the "Indian-Western" hybrid sensibility and found widespread success among urban middle-class viewers. MTV India started operations in late 1996, and quickly outdid Channel V in its "Indianization" strategies.

5 Despite a small market presence, Indian pop music mainly began to achieve visibility and commercial success in the post-satellite-television era. "Made in India" was the first pop album to achieve sales comparable to film albums. For an excellent overview of the Indian music industry, see Manuel (1993).

6 David McCaughan (1998: March 4–10) writes that Asian youth are in a process of "rebelling in" to the middle class, and do not see their generational identity in oppositional terms to that of their parents. In India, the "liberalization" age cohort is being especially targeted by market researchers for its ostensible uninhibited ability to express its national pride through consumption, according to media planner Rama Bijapurkar (1998: March 4–10).

7 Quoted in Hussain, 1997: Aug. 6–12.

8 In addition to mainstream Indian advertising, another source for such triumphalism is the internet. Young Indians frequently email each other lists of India's claims to greatness: these range from "India has never invaded another country" to the "inventor of Hotmail is an Indian." I have also observed that Indian students in the US now include statistics on the Indian armed forces during their cultural events.

References

Ang, I. (1996). *Living Room Wars: Rethinking Media Audiences for a Postmodern World.* New York: Routledge.

Appadurai, A. (2000). "Grassroots Globalization and the Research Imagination." *Public Culture* 12(1): 1–19.

Bijapurkar, R. (1998). A market in discontinuity. *The Economic Times* [online], available http://www.economictimes.com, accessed March 4–10.

Brosius, C. and Butcher, M., eds. (1999). *Image Journeys: Audio-Visual Media and Cultural Change in India*. New Delhi: Sage.

Butcher, M. (1999). "Parallel Texts: The Body and Television in India." In C. Brosius and M. Butcher, eds., *Image Journeys: Audio-Visual Media and Cultural Change in India*. New Delhi: Sage, 165–98.

Chadha, K. and Kavoori, A. (2000). "Media Imperialism Revisited: Some Findings from the Asian Case." *Media, Culture, and Society* 22: 415–32.

Chen, K. (1998). "Introduction: The Decolonization Question." In K. Chen, ed., *Trajectories: Inter-Asia Cultural Studies*. New York: Routledge, 1–53.

Dickey, S. (1996). "Consuming Utopia: Film Watching in Tamil Nadu." In C. Breckenridge, ed., *Consuming Modernity: Public Culture in a South Asian World*. Minneapolis: University of Minnesota, 131–5.

Gibson, T. (2000). "Beyond Cultural Populism: Notes Toward the Critical Ethnography of Media Audiences." *Journal of Communication Inquiry* 24: 253–76.

Hussain, S. (1997). "V'Jaying On." *The Economic Times*, Aug. 6–12, p. 8.

Juluri, V. (1998). "Globalizing Audience Studies: The Audience and its Landscape and Living Room Wars." *Critical Studies in Mass Communication* 15: 85–90.

Juluri, V. (2003). *Becoming a Global Audience: Longing and Belonging in Indian Music Television*. New York: Peter Lang.

Mankekar, P. (1999). *Screening Culture, Viewing Politics: An Ethnography of Television, Womanhood, and Nation in Postcolonial India*. Durham, NC: Duke University Press.

Manuel, P. (1993). *Cassette Culture: Popular Music and Technology in North India*. Chicago: University of Chicago Press.

McCaughan, D. (1998). "Hanging Out? That's Cool!" *The Economic Times* [online], available http://www.economictimes.com, accessed March 4–10.

McKinley, E. (1997). *Beverly Hills 90210: Television, Gender and Identity*. Philadelphia: University of Pennsylvania Press.

Melkote, S., ed. (1998). *International Satellite Broadcasting in South Asia*. New York: University Press of America.

Nandy, A. (1983). *The Intimate Enemy: Loss and Recovery of Self under Colonialism*. Delhi: Oxford University Press.

Nandy, A. (1998). "A New Cosmopolitanism: Toward a Dialogue of Asian civilizations." In K. Chen, ed., *Trajectories: Inter-Asia Cultural Studies*. New York: Routledge, 142–9.

Natrajan, B. and Parmeswaran, R. (1997). "Contesting the Politics of Ethnography: Towards an Alternative Knowledge Production." *Journal of Communication Inquiry* 21: 27–59.

Nightingale, V. (1996). *Studying Audiences: The Shock of the Real*. New York: Routledge.

Page, D. and Crawley, W. (2001). *Satellites over South Asia: Broadcasting, Culture, and the Public Interest.* New Delhi: Sage.

Radhakrishnan, R. (1994). "Postmodernism and the Rest of the World." *Organization* 1: 305–40.

Rajagopal, A. (2000). "Hindutva at Play (Interviewed by Darryl D'Monte)." *Frontline* 17. Available at http://www.the-hindu.com/frontline.

Roach, C. (1997). "Cultural Imperialism and Resistance in Media Theory and Literary Theory." *Media, Culture, and Society* 19: 47–66.

Sinha, D. (2000). "Info-Age and Indian Intellectuals: An Unfashionable Poser." *Economic and Political Weekly* 4188–94.

Stromer-Galley, J. and Schiappa, E. (1998). "The Argumentative Burden of Audience Conjectures: Audience Research in Popular Culture Criticism." *Communication Theory* 8(1): 27–62.

Tomlinson, J. (1991). *Cultural Imperialism: A Critical Introduction.* Baltimore, MD: Johns Hopkins University Press.

Vasudeva, S. and Chakravarty, P. (1989). "The Epistemology of Indian Mass Communication Research." *Media, Culture, and Society* 11: 415–33.

10

From Variety Shows to Body-Sculpting Commercials: Figures of Audience and the Sexualization of Women/Girls

Irene Fang-chih Yang

In recent years, two events have caught the attention of the public in Taiwan, both revolving around the role of media and their effects on teenagers and children. The first media event concerns the indecent content in TV variety shows; the second, a controversial TV commercial using a young girl to promote body-sculpting products. I want to use these two events as points of intervention. First, as the terms of the debate regarding these two events are framed within the passive/active dichotomy regarding the role of audience, I want to highlight how these two figures of audience are produced out of particular conjunctural and epistemological constraints. This focus on the politics of knowledge production enables us to understand how "audience" is used for certain purposes; and intellectuals, in producing these figures, need to be aware of the effects of their articulation of "the other." Second, as the debate is caught between two opposite interpretations of the phenomenon of female sexualization in popular media, I attempt to offer a new line of reading variety shows, through an engagement with the gendered public sphere, in envisioning an alternative space for feminism. I argue that feminists need to expose male physicality in problematizing the "abstract(ed)" male public sphere (Deem, 1996: 512), and variety shows offer such a possibility. However, this reading should be accompanied by a critique of the class/gender politics involved in drawing the boundary between high and low culture.

To achieve these ends, I will first introduce the two events; second, I will discuss the figures of audience produced among public intellectuals in their response to the events; then I move on to a discussion of the conjunctural and epistemological constraints which condition the production of audience. Finally, I come back to the debates and further engage with the issues raised in these two media events in order to situate the "avenue of escape" that I propose. Naming these two cultural debates on media effects as "events" is to highlight the "multiplicities of 'historical determinations, concepts, individuals, groups, social formation,' all of which coexist 'on a single page, the same sheet.'" Using Deleuze, Probyn points out that " '[e]vent' in this way therefore compels us to think about the conjugation of forces: individuals, concepts and theories that at any time enfold the past within the present, constraining or enabling action" (Probyn, 2000: 48–9). Hence, in conceptualizing these two media debates as "events," I want to put an emphasis on the explication of how relations of the past, present, and future are designated and conjugated, especially with regard to how the forces outside as well as inside the academic field conjugate in the figures of the audience. Let me now turn to the first event, the moral panic created around variety shows.

Media Event I: Variety Shows

Since 1997, media celebrities, cultural critics, media scholars, and feminists have begun to construct a moral panic around variety shows, targeting Jacky Wu, the most popular variety-show host, for bringing about the nation's moral decay, and therefore to call for state censorship. The pivotal moment in framing this panic occurred when the famous news anchor, Lee Yan-chiu, in May 2000 accused Jacky Wu of corrupting our teenagers' morality. Identifying herself as a mother who spoke for all mothers of the nation, Lee's accusation was passionately endorsed by mainstream media and media critics. Many criticisms centered around two themes. First, the sex and violence scenes in variety shows have corrupted our children and teenagers. Criticisms such as these abound in news magazines, electronic news, and print news: "save our children" (Feng, 2000); "give our children more educational variety shows, not shows that contain sex and violence" (Jiang, 2000); and "Our TV programs . . . have ruined our next generation and have created a lot of social problems. Faced with the increasing juvenile crime and social ills, can we afford not to supervise our media?" ("Special Report," 2000). The other focus concerns how variety shows objectify women and how the show-hosts sexually harass and hence traumatize female guests/entertainers and girls. For example, "In order to raise the ratings, variety shows have used voyeurism as their selling point. They not only use the camera to forefront young girls' breasts and lower body parts, but also make sexist comments on their bodies" (Chang, 2000).

This wave of attacks on variety shows led to state intervention as well as the transformation of the variety genre itself. Faced with criticisms from all sides, the Information Bureau took action to censor many shows, including the cancellation of "Taiwan Red" (*Taiwan Hung Bu Rang*). The government also penalized "a truckload of variety shows" for featuring "inappropriate" material ("Information Bureau," 2000). In addition, the five major networks responded to this wave of criticism by forming the "Self-censorship on TV Production Treaty." Some variety-show producers took the side of the moral majority and claimed to make "healthy shows" for our teenagers. In doing so, they replace the older host-centered shows with shows featuring many younger, "innocent-looking" teenagers as hosts (Yang, 2002).[1]

Media Event II: Body-Sculpting Commercials

In the wave of attacks on variety shows, the Awakening Group (the leading feminist activist group in Taiwan) held a workshop, inviting media scholars, feminists, state legislators, graduate students, and variety-show producers to evaluate/supervise variety shows. Though a consensus was largely forged among these critics in condemning variety shows, one feminist speaker at the workshop, Josephine Ho, spoke against the consensus. She pointed out that the audience was not as passive as the mainstream critics assumed, and that the moral discourse launched against variety shows should be read as a matter of class bias. Moreover, the exposure of sexual matters and sexual minorities in variety shows opened up possibilities for society to change its conservative attitude toward sex. Despite this alternative viewpoint, which, according to workshop participants, gained much popularity, this viewpoint did not make much of an inroad into public debate.

When a body-sculpting commercial, entitled "Jin-Hua's secret for making herself look like a child again" (*Jinhua de mimi – huan lao huan tung shu*), featured a 14-year-old girl as its main protagonist, *China Times* published an article on "Childlike Women and Stupid Men? – Should Children be the Spokespersons for Body-Sculpting Products?" (Chang & Huang, 2000). This article triggered a cultural war and the terms of the debate also took up the issues left from the debate on variety shows. On one side of the debate, notions of exploitation (of young girls), male voyeurism, girl victimization, and adult male pleasure are highlighted. In emphasizing these notions, critics also foreground the power of media, operated through the logic of patriarchal capitalism, in setting up norms of beauty which have adverse effects on both teenage girls and old women. On the other side of the debate, notions of agency, resistance, appropriation, and *bricolage* are accentuated. Teenagers are seen to appropriate consumer products as a way of making their bodies sexy – a process of self-formation that coincides with the rise of modernity.[2]

Figures of Audience

Two types of audience figure in these debates on media effects. The first figure constructs the audience as passive (male) children/teenagers or TV zombies, while the second figures the audience as active, possibly sexually deviant, (male) teenagers who fight against the establishment. Allor (1996) contends that the notion of audience as passive/active should be conceptualized as a general, unified, abstract theory which is created within certain conjunctural and epistemological constraints. Seiter (1996) further argues that, as discursive constructs, how the audience is utilized and talked about produces material effects and therefore should be analyzed within the field of social effectivities. I argue that the first figure is created, circulated, and legitimated in public discourses to create a moral panic around variety shows as a form of ideological displacement, and this displacement uses gender civility as its organizing rhetoric to forge a national consensus around a class-based moral order. The second figure is produced and distributed among a certain section of intellectuals to create and legitimize a "new" and "liberated" transnational subject of consumption (of Western scholarship). I will now turn to the first figuration of the audience.

> We as a society are much concerned about the sensational, controversial TV programs in Taiwan; in particular, we believe that the worst kind is to be found in our variety shows. Their taste for indecency has gone out of control. Some of its audience might argue that television is for entertainment only, there is nothing serious about this. However, television programs play a central role in our popular culture. In contemporary society, the monstrous TV is used as a babysitter and a learning machine for our children and teenagers; it plays an important role in shaping the values and the behavior of our children and teenagers. (Editorial, June 2, 2000)

Variety shows are full of "young beauties" and "spice girls." They are all in their teens, wearing bikinis or tight clothes, revealing their bodies in public. The male hosts investigate the girls' bodies as if they are weighing up a piece of meat in the market. Worse yet, the camera crudely exploits and invades their bodies by making their breasts and buttocks the center of attention. (Wu, 1999)

The audience figure here is a child or a teenager, usually male, who consumes variety shows that feature "sexually deviant" material (enacted through the body of girls) and who therefore is facing the danger of becoming a bad future citizen. The essence of the nation here is constructed through the rhetoric of gender civility, and variety shows are constructed as threats to the nation because of their gender incivility. In constructing male children and teenagers as the audience-subject and exploited girls as the object of consumption, a moral panic is framed within the boundary of gender and nation.

Tavener (2000) points out that historically the creation of the division of high/low culture has helped to denigrate low/popular culture and to "authenticate the middle class moral order." (In)civility is at the heart of class struggle and should be conceptualized as the expression of an "important fury at corroded leader-class values and standards" and a "flat-out rejection of leader-class claims of respect" (Demott, quoted in Tavener, 2000: 67). Precisely because civility functions as class distinction, incivility in the public sphere should therefore be seen as a form of resistance against bourgeois decorum and popular media/talk shows, one of the very few public outlets available for the working class, outlets offering a space for the expression of their voices. Seen in this light, feminists' and mainstream critics' attacks on variety shows as violating gender civility can be seen as maintaining a class-based moral order.

It is here I want to address the second figure of the audience. In pointing out the class bias in the moral critique of variety shows, Ho (2000) argues that the audience is not as passive as the mainstream critics assume, and that instead one should see the audience as active. Ka Wei-bou further elaborates this notion of an active audience in his analysis of the body-sculpting commercial. In arguing against the disappearance of teenagers (in the sense that adults speak for and about them), Ka contends:

Within the global communication network, our teenagers today can borrow cultural and desiring codes from London or Shinjuku as resources for their self- and body-formation. This [commodified] body can be used to fight against the disciplinary body that our education system and parents try to shape. It is within the space created through the conflicts and struggles between the commodified body and the disciplinary body that teenagers can exercise their own autonomy. In other words, the trend toward the fashioning and sexualization of the body is an effort made by teenagers to search for their autonomous selves. These images of commodified, sexualized bodies may be said to be another form of discipline, but teenagers are using their commodified body to fight against the sexual repression/conservatism that their teachers and parents impose on them. And their autonomy expands within this conflictual space. (Ka, 2001a and b: 23)

Drawing from Western cultural-studies scholars such as Mica Nava, Dick Hebdige, John Fisk, and Paul Willis, Ka argues that sites of consumption of transnational commodities should be seen as sites of empowerment, points where teenagers can exercise their agency. Identifying himself as a "young and wise" (*qing chun rei zhi*) radical sexual liberationist, Ka contends that feminists who disapprove of the eroticization (which is articulated as exploitation by many feminists and leftists) of girls in popular media "lag behind cultural studies scholarship by twenty years" (2001b: 12). In doing so, he relegates these feminists and critics to the realm of tradition, as expressed through his derogatory use of the term "aging feminists."

As mapped out, the construction of the audience as passive/active in these two debates is articulated to other vectors, including gender, sexuality, nation formation, moral order, class, and consumerism.[3] In the debates, feminists are caught in an either/or dilemma. On the one hand, if one stands against variety shows, then one is accused of engaging with the practice of class distinction/formation by excluding the working class and sexual minorities from participating in the public sphere in the name of morality. On the other hand, if one sides with variety shows, one ignores the role media play in the formation of gendered subjectivities as well as the problem of consumerism promulgated by transnational capitalism. How do feminists get out of this trap? How do we create other avenues? Here, I want to work through the figure of the audience again in order to address the conjunctural and epistemological constraints which ensnare Taiwanese feminists in this double bind.

Similar to the audience as figured in the United States, Allor (1996) argues that constructions of the audience as passive or active underline public discourses about relations between media and the people. The first figure conceptualizes the audience as situated at "the end point and guarantee of the stability (or instability) of the citizenry or the social itself." The second figure frames the relationship between people and media as "enacted practice and experience" (1996: 211). However, "we produce these figures (these concepts) within epistemological regimes that condition the ways in which we structure the engagement between concepts and empirical analyses. Our work, then, is conditioned by the more general discourses figuring the audience (representation and enacted agency) and by the specific logic of enquiry and interpretive rules of particular research traditions" (ibid.). As our work is always conditioned by the double set of determinations – conjunctural and epistemological – it is important to map out these conditions and see how the audience figures are produced within these constraints.

Conjunctural Conditions in the Production of Audience Figurations

I identify two vectors of convergence at this historical moment which condition the production of the figure of the passive audience: the first vector concerns the production of a media crisis, thereby calling for media reform; the second involves the liberalization/globalization of TV, which has changed the local environment for media production. The production of a media crisis has to be situated within Taiwanese democratic movements, the rise of media-watch groups, and the joining of the WTO in 2002. The rise of television in Taiwan as a commercial system is inseparable from its political history. When the KMT party took over Taiwan, they immediately saw media, particularly television, as an ideological tool for political mobilization. Consequently, the three major networks, TTV, CTV, and CTS, set up in the early 1960s and early 1970s, were owned by the provincial government, the KMT party, and the military.[4] While these three networks took the form of commercial TV, the board of directors and the major positions in the networks were all appointed by the KMT government and were all senior KMT members. With ownership controlled by the KMT party and the censorship of any speech that endangered "national" security (read as the security of the KMT party), it was very difficult for the opposition party to survive. Hence, "Remov[ing] the KMT party, the provincial government, and the military from the three networks" (*dang zheng jun tui chu san tai*) became one of the main concerns for the oppositional party and an important agenda in the democratic movements in the early 1990s. Approaching TV from the perspective of political economy, scholars from Cheng She (an organization) examined KMT involvement in the constitution of ownership and explored the relationships between ownership and control.[5] The reports of these investigations have become foundational texts in calling for media reform.[6]

In addition to the agenda to eliminate political influence in the current broadcasting system, the legalization/liberalization of cable TV in 1994, according to these scholars, has added rampant commercial influences to the existing problem, thereby contributing to the further deterioration of the public sphere. Believing that media should be a public forum, Cheng She, along with media scholars and cultural critics, endorsed the establishment in 1999 of MediaWatch, the first nongovernment-controlled media-watch group.[7] Other media reform groups have also emerged, such as "Communication Students Fighting Alliance" (*Chung bo xue sheng do zhen*). Composed mainly of university students and professors, this campaigning alliance argued that TTV and CTS should be made public so as to eliminate political control and commercial influence.

The election of the first DPP president in March 2000 marked the success of Taiwan's democratic movements, ending 50 years of KMT rule. Before the election, some media scholars helped the DPP party to draft a white paper on media reform as part of their election campaign package. With the successful shift of power to the DPP party, media reformers saw a chance to push for their agenda. MediaWatch issued their first electronic newsletter immediately after the new government was elected, hoping to "protect freedom of speech, maintain media justice, promote media self-regulation, and guarantee people's right to know" (Editorial, April 28, 2000).

In addition to civil groups pushing for media reform, the new government also found itself in need of a communication policy, as it was preparing to join the WTO in 2002. At a conference called "2001 Communication Forum," sponsored by the Government Information Office, Premier Zhang Jun-hsuing declared that the conference's aim was to "produce information which helped the government to set up future communication policies in order to reshape a liberalized, nativized, and internationalized communication environment" (Liao, 2001). At the conference, media scholars discussed the necessity of meeting international standards if Taiwan were to survive the competition of joining the WTO: "Faced with the overflow of Japanese and Korean drama into Taiwan, Taiwan needs to upgrade its media programs in order to compete in the international environment . . . it is necessary to close the gap between nativization and globalization" (W. M. Lin, 2001).

The convergence of these forces made variety shows the target of a reform campaign. With the liberalization of cable TV in 1993, variety shows have become the "most local" shows made in Taiwan as well as the emblem of commercialism at its worst. These two dimensions of variety shows – local/low standard and rampant commercialism – typify the concerns of media reformers as well as the government's impetus for media reform. In calling for media reform, public intellectuals used the images of teenagers and children as members of passive audience to address the devastating media effects.[8] I will now turn to a more detailed analysis of the site of media production of variety shows in order to explain why the use of teenagers and children as figures for the audience makes particular sense at this historical moment.

The major change in the field of TV production was the legalization of cable TV in 1993. The first illegal cable service was documented in 1979, and by 1985 there were already 230,000 households receiving illegal cable service; by 1991 the number jumped to 540,000 households. Ninety percent of the programs broadcasted during this time were imported from Japan and the United States and their audiences were largely upper middle-class professionals (Feng, 1995). The legalization and privatization of cable services in 1993 did not change this situation; instead, it made Japanese programs and American programs more available and it further stratified the audience according to their economic value. According to the Broadcasting Law in Taiwan, cable TV is required to produce 25 percent and network TV 75 percent of local programs. As a result, many cable channels do not make their own programs, but show imported programs from other countries. Hence, in addition to "special" channels such as Discovery, National Geographic, CNN, and HBO, which feature American programs and Jet Wei-lai and Guo-Hsing channels which both broadcast Japanese programming, many "variety" channels also buy foreign-made programs because it is a lot cheaper than producing their own. Moreover, the audiences who watch these imported channels tend to be more valuable to the industry because of their socioeconomic status (Yang, 2002).

While there is a tendency for transnational communication conglomerates such as HBO to take over many of the Taiwanese cable channels, local channels such as Sunli have also proliferated as a result of the legalization of cable TV. The increase of local channels in cable TV brought about an increasing demand for locally produced shows; and because talk shows and variety shows are cheap to produce, there is a great demand for variety shows. However, the growing demand for these shows has also created tougher competition for commercial sponsorship. Moreover, with the invention of the remote control, which makes it more difficult to predict the audience's loyalty, and the proliferation of different media such as the internet, many advertisers have cut down their financial support for variety shows. The recent economic recession makes this problem worse. As a result, many producers have cut the budgets for variety shows.

The liberalization of cable TV also brought about a changing definition of audiences for variety shows. Before cable service, variety shows were conceptualized as family entertainment not only because of the use of TV as a domestic medium but also because variety shows were made for family viewing. As a result, the different segments of variety shows aimed to include as many topics as possible to encompass large audiences, while they were usually scheduled on weekend evenings. However, with the advent of cable also came the practice of niche marketing. Unlike serial dramas, which tend to imagine a regional, Mandarin-speaking audience, or HBO, which tends to imagine an international audience, variety shows, with their low-budget production, appeal to local audiences. Because of the stratification of audiences for different types of programs, Taiwanese variety shows find their niche in teenagers. But this doesn't mean that only teenagers watch variety shows. According to *Broadcaster*, variety-show audiences tend to be economically disadvantaged – they tend to be housewives with no income, the unemployed, teenagers, and old people.[9] This also points out one aspect about TV viewing – that TV has become an entertainment for those who lack access to other leisure activities, such as KTV (karaoke TV) or playing with computers. In any case, among this socially and economically disadvantaged group, teenagers have come to be seen as the most desirable audience because of their relatively high spending power and their potential as future consumers. According to *Advertising Magazine*, children and teenagers in Taiwan possess the highest annual spending power in Asia, and their weekly allowance ranks third in Asia, next only to Hong Kong and Singapore. Hence it is no surprise that most of Taiwan's variety shows target teenagers as their audience (Yang, 2002).

The shift to teenagers and children as target consumers is not specific to TV or variety shows: the recent explosion of girls' magazines also indicates this trend. A brief look at Taiwan's daily news (both in print and electronic) demonstrates that teenagers are constructed as either consumers or delinquents. On the one hand, the media are dominated by "social" news such as how (male) teenagers (especially on motorbikes) kill innocent people, destroy cars, and rob stores; how they are caught by the police selling bootleg CDs, VCDs, and illegal drugs.[10] On the other hand, in the economic, entertainment, and cultural editions, there is the rise of consumer information for teenagers, such as stories titled "New Department

Stores Creating Special Sections for Teenagers" (2001); "You Can Enjoy the Hottest New Cell Phone for Only a Few Hundred Dollars per Month" (2001); and "When Hollywood Discovered Children's Books" (2001). It is within this general shift in our culture towards viewing teenagers as both consumers and delinquents, as well as the polarization of a middle-class, transnational audience and a culturally and economically disadvantaged local audience, that variety shows emerge as the target of a moral panic. As I point out here, the creation of a moral panic through the use of media crisis (or ill effects) has the purpose of justifying a comprehensive media reform, with the aim not only of making TV a public sphere for training in and practicing of citizenship, but also to help the government cope with the effects of joining the WTO. I have so far mapped out the conjunctural vectors which condition the production of a moral panic and the figurations of the audience as teenagers and children who are victims of popular media. Despite the emphasis here in explicating the construction of the figure of the passive audience, it is necessary to call attention to the fact that the figure of the active audience – a teenager who is able to appropriate cultural commodities imported from London, Tokyo, and New York – should also be situated within the trend of current commercialism to locate teenagers/children as consumers. Now I will turn to the site of academic research and investigate the epistemological constraints which condition the production of the figures of the active and passive audiences.

Epistemological Constraints on the Production of Audiences

Engagements with relations between people and media can largely be located within Communication Studies and Cultural Studies in Taiwan. Of course, these two are not mutually exclusive; however, the debates on variety shows and body-sculpting commercials can be broadly mapped out as polarized into an argument between audience as active versus audience as passive, with communication scholars taking up the latter notion and cultural studies the former. I will discuss the current paradigms in these two fields, which condition the production of these two figures.

The institutionalization of communication studies in Taiwan is a response to the need of the industry in training people to use new communication technologies. Hence, within communication departments, the majority of the courses offered are for professional training. In an environment where the purpose of education is to produce results that are conducive to the development of the industry and the strengthening of state power, it is no wonder that communication research in Taiwan has been dominated by the positivist paradigm since the 1960s and the main concerns within this paradigm are audience research and mass-media studies (Xyu & Chen, 1996).[11] Within the positivist paradigm, researchers tend to locate active audiences within an individualistic, psychological model, ignoring the context of audience consumption. Typical of this research is Su and Chen's (2000) article on "Global or Local? Research on Taiwanese Youth's Television Viewing Behavior." By asking the audience to fill out surveys, the authors aim to "explain the relationships between Taiwanese youth's television viewing, their motivations and attitudes" (Su & Chen, 2000). In addition, the notion of passive audiences also underpins this positivistic paradigm in studying media effects. The framing of research questions, such as "Exploring the Influence of Variety Shows' Use of Slang on Teenagers" (Chen, 2000), already assumes the power of media on teenagers.

The notion of a passive audience is also assumed in most of the critical feminist work in communication studies. As Good (1995) points out, with the influence of positivism on media studies, most research on women and media before the eighties did not engage with feminist criticism. In the 1980s, with the establishment of the Awakening Group, usually identified as the second-wave women's movement in Taiwan, some research began to recognize and discuss the inequality between men and women. However, because the research done in this era was still dominated by the positivist paradigm, issues of (patriarchal) power and ideology were elided. Before the lifting of martial law in 1987, the Awakening Group sporadically published articles that criticized media stereotyping of women. With the lifting of martial law, feminist movements gained much support, for they were recognized as part of the democratic reform in Taiwan. In addition to the growth and diversification of feminist movements in the early 1990s, women's studies centers were established to encourage research on women. Within media studies departments, under the influence of newly hired feminist media scholars, students began to use ideological analysis, semiotic analysis, and discourse analysis to investigate how women were represented and explored the ideological ramifications of female images in commercials, advertisements, and popular media texts (Good, 1995).[12] This particular way of looking at media images and women was taken up in popular media as these students graduated to become journalists and editors. Consequently, the feminist language of female stereotypes/exploitation and the male gaze has become the vernacular in talking about gender inequality.

The translation of cultural studies into the Taiwanese academy in the late 1980s and 1990s does not have much impact on communication studies because the discipline is already deeply rooted in the positivist paradigm (Xyu & Chen, 1996). Despite sporadic articles on introducing and engaging with theories/concepts of audience within the global village,[13] little work was done in the area of ethnographic audience studies. However, outside communications departments, cultural studies is growing rapidly, particularly in English and Sociology departments. However, as Liu (2000) points out, despite the proliferation of cultural studies and the institutionalization of cultural studies through the establishment of cultural studies centers and departments in the Taiwanese academy in the 1990s, most of the publications on cultural studies are "translations," defined as translation/introduction/application of cultural studies theories produced in the West. As much as cultural studies is about intervention into particular contexts, not much work in this area engages with specifically Taiwanese contexts (except in the area of gender/sexuality studies). In the words of Liu, "there are a lot of translations of cultural studies work, but there is a lack of [local] cultural studies work" (2000: 14).

It is within this context that theories of the audience emerged out of particular locations and have become the received "truth" for some cultural-studies scholars in Taiwan. Within feminist cultural studies, the notion of an active audience arose as a response to: (1) use and gratification theory which individualizes the politics of media reception, (2) Marxist critical theory (especially that of the Frankfurt school), which assumes the audience to be passive and associates passivity with the feminine, and (3) Althusserian ideological analyses which take the audience to be passive recipients of dominant ideology. In the spirit of political intervention, feminist cultural-studies scholars such as Seiter, Radway, and Ang, use "ethnography" to investigate the context of audience reception. Their notion of an active audience is, however, an ambivalent one which should be seen only through its contextuality. However, when it is translated into Taiwan, as shown in Ka's quote earlier on the figure of the active audience, the context disappears; instead, the audience as active becomes a general, abstract theory which is used for academic classification. Worse yet, cultural studies is constructed as a theory of the active audience and is used to argue against both the "backwardness" of feminist theory which criticizes the sexualization of young girls in the media, and Marxist class critique which insists on problematizing consumer culture brought about by transnational capitalism:

> With regard to the discussions on consumption, popular culture, and youth subculture, Cultural Studies have long ago disputed the elitist position inhabited by the Frankfurt School/critical theory. But recent mainstream media criticisms have totally neglected [the advances made in] contemporary Cultural Studies. They have simply used terms such as "capitalism/ patriarchal structure/objectification/commodification/media brainwashing/ commercial hypnosis" as big theories to criticize some new phenomena which threaten to disturb or change the status quo. . . . In fact, these mainstream media criticisms seem to just pick up some jargon and play with it, they have not caught up with any of the development in Cultural Studies within the past 10 to 20 years. (Ka, 2001b: 12)

This quote is quite revealing, for it points out one danger in Taiwan's academic standard – that we have to "catch up" with Western theories rather than produce our own, that the more in tune with Western theories we are, the more modern/advanced/substantive our work is. Within this environment, it is not surprising that the two debates about media and people are very much framed along the dichotomous axis of activity and passivity – a dichotomy produced within an administrative paradigm (with its roots in Enlightenment philosophy) which conceptualizes communication as a model of transmission (Carey, 1992). My mapping here of the dominant paradigm, shaped by positivist science, in Taiwanese communication departments, feminist ideological analyses of media images, and cultural studies aims to explain that the terms of the debate used in overvaluing or devaluing variety shows are framed within epistemological constraints imported/translated from the West. In unproblematically assuming the audience to be either passive or active, we lose sight of the context we are facing and the effects of our own critique. Now I will turn to the debate again and highlight the associated eviction of the politics of knowledge production.

Revisiting the Debate

As I point out, the figure of the passive audience is used to create a moral panic which justifies comprehensive media reform. Hall and Tavener contend that moral panics are ideological displacements. Moral panics are ideological frameworks that define the meaning and moral significance of concrete events and behaviors; they "displace complex social issues of political importance onto the terrain of culture and attempt to resolve them through a discourse that attributes a moral dimension to culture" (Tavener, 2000: 68). What Hall (1978) and Tavener (2000) point out is that moral panics are sites of conflict – they are the sites in which material inequalities are implicated and masked, and in which hegemony is affirmed and secured. But in terms of the framing of moral panics on variety shows, what gets displaced and what gets proscribed as appropriate behavior? Likewise, what is gained and what is lost in articulating the figure of the active audience in countering this moral panic?

Hartley (1998) makes the argument that in adults' panicking over the eroticization of girls in popular media, it is the girls' interests that get elided. The attack on or defense of variety shows through the rhetoric of defending children's and teenagers' well-being produces similar effects of evicting their real interests. On one side of the debate, there is an emphasis on depicting popular media as having monstrous power over teenagers. If one reads this together with the image of teenagers as juvenile delinquents in daily news, a causal relation between the media and teenage crimes can be established; consequently, attention is shifted to media reform, but the structural problems which cause teenagers to commit crimes, such as unequal access to education, commodity culture, health information, and so on, are ignored. On the other side of the debate, Ho and Ka's construction of teenagers as active as an attempt to address their agency not only matches capitalism's need to incorporate teenagers and children into consumer groups but also elides structural inequalities which shape teenagers' access to agency and mobility. In celebrating consumption as offering teenagers tools for exercising their agency, understood as their resistance against parents and school, issues of unequal access to commercial culture was discounted. Moreover, the relationship between teenagers and parental/school authority is essentialized as if there are no contradictions between the interests of the parents and the interests of the school authority, or no complicities between teenagers and parents/authority. In any case, both accounts ignore the fact that in the heat of their debate on media effects on teenagers and children in the name of defending their interests, the government, without making much noise in the media, passed a bill for a drastic cut in funding for children's welfare programs (Luo, 2001).

Another key issue raised in the debates concerns the notion of the public sphere and its gender/sexuality/class implications. On the one hand, the sex and violence which characterize variety shows are seen by the media reformers as an exemplar of the public sphere's contamination by commercialism. On the other hand, the eroticization of girls' bodies or women's sexy bodies in variety shows is seen by some as opening up the public space to minority groups, including working-class and sexual minorities. Both arguments are predicated on the dichotomous notion of passive/active audiences.

These contradictory ways of interpreting the phenomenon of sexualization in popular media should be conceptualized within a contemporary capitalist-democratic system. This is a problem inherent in the definition of the public, a problem that has also haunted the British broadcasting system (the BBC) since its inception. The state sees media as a public space for the training of citizens through a model of cultural/moral cultivation; however, the norm of civility is class based. As a result, public TV, with its aim to serve all citizens, tends to lose its subject of cultivation (Hall, 1986). The contradiction between the ideal public and commercialism, between the norm of a middle-class, male public sphere and the inclusion of women and teenagers in commercial media, is manifested in the debate on variety shows. As Hartley points out, "the democratization of the public sphere through the popular media was historically not merely *accompanied by* feminization and sexualization, but has been *conducted through the media* of feminization and sexualization, using this semiotic genre to communicate with the vast, unknowable, but sovereign and comfort-seeking readerships of modernity" (1998: 48, original emphasis). Because of the inherent contradiction of media as carrying both a "communicative" (democratic) function and a "truth-seeking" (governmental) function, the media both produce sexualization and denounce the very phenomenon they produce. These two contradictions are resolved through setting up the boundary between high/low culture, with the designation of the former category as "hard news" (informational address), associated with masculine seriousness, while the feminine triviality of "soft news" is relegated to the latter (Holland, 1998).

The division between serious news and soft news is not only laden with hierarchically structured, gendered value but is also embedded in class politics. The division between high/low culture should be located within processes of class formation (Hall, 1986; Tavener, 2000; and Bourdieu, 1984). The condemnation of popular TV such as sleazy talk shows displaces class issues, for the condemnation itself is predicated upon the norm of bourgeois civility in the public sphere (Tavener, 2000 and Birmingham, 2000). In analyzing variety shows in Taiwan, it is important to pay attention to the unequal access to transnational cultural commodities such as the HBO and Discovery channels and "local" variety shows, the asymmetrical values attached to these two types of shows, and their relationships with class formation. In general, those who have access to HBO mostly belong to the new professional managerial class whose identities and sense of belonging transcend the confines of the nation-state, while those who are bound to the "local" or to watch "local" shows tend to be the most disadvantaged groups.

Taking these critiques into account, it becomes urgent that we retheorize variety shows, that we produce a new way of looking at variety shows without being trapped in the two opposite positions. How do we, as feminists, change the representations/treatment of women in variety shows without imposing bourgeois taste on the working class or teenagers? How do we theorize the opening up of popular media to traditionally marginalized groups such as sexual minorities/women/girls while at the same time critiquing the exploitation/objectification of women?

Producing Avenues of Escape

I want to rethink the issue of sexualization/eroticization of women and girls in popular media without being trapped in the mainstream critique of exploitation/objectification of women/girls or the "Cultural Studies" critique of celebrating this sexualization. Central to the debate is the notion of media as a public sphere. While the media reformers believe that the public sphere should be equally accessible to all identity groups, they also believe sobriety to be the appropriate style of public address. The opposing camp, on the contrary, believes that visibility of any marginalized group should be read as a form of democratization, of disrupting the status quo.

Many feminists have pointed out the gendered dimension of the public sphere (e.g. Landes, 1998; Deem, 1996; Holland, 1998). The male public sphere is constituted through the eviction of the male body:

> The political sphere has been constituted through the "naturalized" historical link between masculinity, political agency, and speech. Thus the recognition of the "historical antinomy between women and public authority" has been particularly important for feminism . . . The abstract(ed) body of the bourgeois white male, imbued with rational speech, came to stand in for the representativeness of the political. Logics of abstraction account for the invisibility of the male body and the simultaneous visibility of those groups traditionally associated with the body, affect, and desire. (Deem, 1996: 512)

The male public sphere conducted through the rendering invisible of the male body and the constant presentation of women's/girls' bodies, particularly through the use of the camera to create them as being sexually different from the normative male, constitutes no moment of democratization. Even at the most radical moment for the opposing camp, when variety shows feature "betel nut girls" or transvestites,[14] the show host's and the camera's focus still produce these marginal groups as spectacles for the consumption of the male audience. The "sexual radicals'" attempt to bring marginal sexualities to the political in their discussion on variety shows, however, reinforces the norm of masculine heterosexual desire and female desirability as they are premised upon the hypereroticization of the female body (hooks, 1994). As a result, "[b]y reinforcing sexual difference, the nature of the democratic discursive space is brought into question" (Holland, 1998: 28).

Holland argues that if sexual difference is always presented in a way that highlights sexual inequality, as in variety shows featuring women's/girls' bodies for heterosexual male pleasure, the negotiation of the line between feminization (as an attempt to broaden the male public sphere) and sexualization is closed off. "A politics of sexual fantasy which opens up a gap between women and men by reinforcing men's 'sex-right' over women's bodies continues to imply a political allegiance which ultimately undermines democratic participatory rights, and which continues to link the feminine with the trivial" (Holland 1998: 31). Hence, it is still necessary, at least in contemporary context, to keep critiquing the power inequality embedded in the popular media's re-presentations of sexualized women and girls as the media attempt to include a larger audience.

However, if the public sphere is predicated on the eviction or abstraction of the male body, the exposure of the male body in the political imaginary constitutes a moment of danger for the maintenance of the façade of a "gender-neutral" public sphere. Variety shows offer us such an opportunity for making the male body visible in the public sphere, and it is along this line of reading variety shows that a new discursive space for feminism can be opened up.

The "vulgarity" in variety shows provides an escape route. Deem specifies the liberating potential of scatology: "Scatological rhetoric is indecorous discourse which, through the lushness of bodily excess, deterritorializes language, pushing it to its extremes" (1996: 523). Decorum functions as distinction and exclusion for "the very substance of bourgeois subject [and citizenship] is constructed through sanitized modes of address" (p. 527). On the one hand, masculine speech excludes women from participation in the public sphere (as women's speech is relegated to the genre of the complaint or nagging); on the other hand, scatology exposes male physicality as it belongs to the domain of the male. In this sense, scatology exposes the hypocrisy of rational male speech, opening up a space for women's speech in the public sphere.

> Scatological language is the property of the male: locker-room talk happens away from women and the political. The female is denied access to the scatological precisely because the scatological speaks the male. The physicality of the male is betrayed through scatological performance despite his best efforts to totalize himself through the abstraction of language. This practice actually turns language back upon itself and shows that the physical, the scatological, is the habitat of the male. . . . Classifying scatology, the catalogue of male physicality, as obscene and improper, is a strategy seeking to distance the physical threat from man's fragile fantasy of abstract completion. (Deem, 1996: 530)

In this line of reading, Jacky Wu's (variety-show-host) "vulgarity" should be conceptualized as making private locker-room talk visible in the public sphere, as exposing male physicality; hence, threatening the invisibility of the male body which underwrites bourgeois decorum. The focus on how women's or girls' bodies are objectified produces unintended ill-effects of reinforcing the image of female passivity, of women as noncitizens and male teenagers as the subject of "nation." Instead, if we look at how, in talking vulgarly about women's bodies, the primary male host also reveals his own physicality; or if we focus on how female guests or other female co-hosts talk back and redirect our attention to the male body, the possibility of the male phallus shrinking to male penis is created, especially when the phallus/penis is exposed in the public for laughter.

In fact, these moments of reducing male power by exposing male physicality are not rare. Instead, they have become part of the generic traits of variety shows. Female co-host Ah-bao, when interacting with the main hosts, Hu-gua and Jacky Wu, constantly makes fun of their body sizes, their faces, and even their pretentious sexual prowess. Similarly, Tao-zi, the female host in *Notes on Love* (*Lian ai jiang yi*), often expresses her sexual desire for the male body and asks men to "take off your pants" and "wag your butt for me." These moments create avenues of liberation, not only in the sense that they expose male physicality through male hosts' vulgarity, but also through women's participation in scatology, in undermining the speech mode traditionally associated with the male.

However, this reading should be accompanied by a critique of the high/low culture distinction in maintaining a class-/gender-based social order through the domain of culture. While variety shows have been relegated to the domain of the low, it is necessary to refocus our attention to how this "lowness" is created out of particular social and economic relations. As my previous analysis indicates, it is with the liberalization of media and the rise of the new "transnational" professional middle class that variety shows are relegated to the local/low and that BBC and Discovery channels are overvalued as the proper address of the (male) public sphere. Without such a critique which links the discursive space to material inequalities, a rereading of variety shows as exposing male physicality and as women's participation in scatology remains ineffective, for it does not challenge the "triviality" associated with variety shows.

Notes

1   There are many factors which contributed to the change of the variety genre, including the liberalization of cable TV, the scarcity of major variety-show hosts in Taiwan as the result of an increasing need for variety shows, the economic recession, and the public's intervention, including the critics' attacks outlined here (Yang, 2002).

2   The first position was largely articulated by people from MediaWatch, such as Chang Jin-hua, Huang Hao-rong, and people from the left, Lin Shen-jing and Wang Li-xia. The second position was articulated mostly by Ka Wei-bou. Of course I am simplifying the debate, particularly on the issue between left politics and sexual politics (between Lin and Ka). I am also excluding Chang Jin-hua's later article which uses Bourdieu's notion of "field" and "habitus" to go beyond the passive/active audience dichotomy, largely because the circulation of that article is limited to a small number of readers. Also, that article was published much later, in 2002, and should be read not as part of the debate, but as a way to escape the dilemma created by the debate.

3   This list is of course not exhaustive. Some issues are excluded, such as the one on "left" politics as debated between Lin and Ka in *The Left* and the issue of freedom of speech raised by Ho. These issues in the list are foregrounded in the circulation of public discourses and have also put feminists in a dead end as each is caught within their own logic of intelligibility.

4   Despite the fact that the three networks were opened up for private investment, the provincial government, the KMT party, and the military (all controlled by the KMT party) owned more than half of the stock in each of the network.

5   Cheng She is an organization consisting largely of male intellectuals and scholars, with the aim of offering timely social critique for social justice.

Members of Cheng She take turns publishing articles on different social, political, and economic issues in *China Times* once every week.

6 For example, the classic book on unveiling the relationship between KMT involvement in Taiwan's broadcasting business is *Deconstructing Broadcasting Media (Jie go guang bo mei ti)*, published by the Cheng She in 1993. I thank Zi Jun-jie for providing me with this information.

7 Media-watch groups have existed in Taiwan since the establishment of the "Association for News Supervision " (*Xin wen ping yi hui*) in the 1960s. However, as Lin points out, these organizations were all controlled or sponsored by the KMT party; they did not fulfill their role to supervise the media (C. J. Lin, 1999).

8 For example, in the "2001 Communication Forum" conference, Feng invoked several quotations from newspapers to address how commercialism, exemplified through their wide coverage of media violence and sex, had negative impact on society as a whole, especially the moral standards of our teenagers and children.

9 According to *Broadcaster*, a trade journal, 52.4% of variety-show audiences are women. In terms of age, only 23% of the normal viewers (as opposed to heavy viewers) are between 13 to 19 years old. People from age 20 to 39 constitute 52.3% of variety-show viewers, while people with no income constitute 33.6% (Y. L. Lin, 2000: 54–8). It is reasonable to infer from these numbers that housewives (women, people with low education, and low or no income), not children and teenagers, constitute the majority of variety-show audiences.

10 News such as this dominated our everyday reading of newspapers. I will only list a few here: "Police Caught Teenagers Possessing Rave in a Pub in Kaohsuing" (*China Times*, 5/12/2001); "Teenagers Were Caught Selling Bootleg CDs in MRT station" (*China Times* Evening News, 28/12/2001)); and "Preventing Teenagers from Motor-bike Racing" (*China Times*, 23/12/2001).

11 According to Xyu and Chen (1996), between 1961 and 1992, 62% of research done in communication studies belonged to the positivist paradigm. And more updated surveys indicate that 70% of research belongs to this category.

12 Good (1995) identifies some research as recognizing the audience's active status, such as Huang's *Decoding Variety Shows' Gender Discourse* (1994); however, audience's resistant reading is allowed only when polysemy exists within the texts. Hence, in this work, despite Huang's recognition of possible alternative readings of comedy skits in variety shows, the overall tone tends toward the ideological closure inscribed in the text in producing a gendered subject.

13 For example, Chang, Wei-chiang's article on "Audience and News Reading," published in Research on Journalism 1997.

14 From "Workshop on Evaluating/Supervising Variety Shows" by Josephine Ho, 19/8/2000.

References

Allor, Martin (1996). "The Politics of Producing Audiences." In J. Hay, L. Grossberg, and E. Wartella, eds., *Audience and Its Landscape*. Boulder, CO: Westview Press, 209–20.

Birmingham, Elizabeth (2000). "Fearing the Freak: How Talk TV Articulates Women and Class." *Journal of Popular Film and Television* 28(3): 133–9.

Bourdieu, Pierre (1984). *Distinction: A Social Critique of the Judgment of Taste*, tr. Richard Nice. Cambridge, MA: Harvard University Press.

Carey, James (1992). *Communication as Culture*. New York: Routledge.

Chang, Jin Hua and Huang, Hao-rong (2000). "Childlike Women and Stupid Men? – Should Children be the Spokespersons for Body-Sculpting Products?" *China Times*, Dec. 18.

Chang, Jin Hua (2000). "Media Belong to the Public Sphere and Should be Subjected to the Order of the Law." *China Times*, May 25.

Chen, Man-xian (2000). "Exploring the Influence of Variety Shows' Use of Slang on Teenagers." Retrieved March 8, 1999, from http://ccs.nccu.edu.tw/db/ccs-20/輔大 /12.htm.

Deem, Melissa (1996). "From Bobbit to SCUM: Re-memberment, Scatological Rhetorics, and Feminist Strategies in the Contemporary United States." *Public Culture* 18(3): 511–38.

Editorial (2000, April 28). *MediaWatch Electronic News*, 4. Retrieved Oct. 20, 2001, from http://www.mediawatch.org.tw.

Editorial (2000, June 2). *MediaWatch Electronic News*, 6. Retrieved Oct. 20, 2001, from http://www.mediawatch.org.tw.

Feng, Jian-sun (1995). *The Political Economy of Broadcasting Capital Movement* (*Guang Dian Zi Ben Yun Dung De Zhen Zhi Jing Ji Xue*). Taipei: A *Radical Quarterly in Social Studies Research* Series in Taiwan.

Feng, Jian-sun (2000, Nov. 23). "Save Our Children and Support Public Television." *MediaWatch Electronic News*, 11. Retrieved Oct. 10, 2001, from http://www.mediawatch.org.tw.

Good, Yu-Jane (1995). "The Production of Gender Knowledge in the Domestic Communication Academy." *Studies on Journalism* 51. Retrieved Oct. 15, 2001, from http://www.jour.nssc.edu.tw/Mcr/005/01.asp.

Hall, Stuart, et al. (1978). *Policing The Crisis: Mugging, the State and Law and Order*. London: Macmillan.

Hall, Stuart (1986). "Popular Culture and the State." In T. Bennett and C. Mercer, eds., *Popular Culture and Social Relations*. Milton Keynes: Open University Press, 22–49.

Hartley, John (1998). "Juvenation: News, Girls and Power." In C. Carter, G. Branston, and S. Allan, eds., *News, Gender and Power*. New York: Routledge, 47–70.

Ho, Josephine (2000). "Evaluating Variety Shows: An Outline for the Workshop on Evaluating Variety Shows." Talk presented at the Evaluating Variety Shows Workshop, sponsored by the Information Bureau, the Awakening Group, and *Tomorrow Times*, held at National Taiwan University, Aug. 19.

Holland, Patricia (1998). "The Politics of the Smile: 'Soft News' and the Sexualization of the Popular Press." In C. Carter, G. Branston, and S. Allan, eds., *News, Gender and Power*. New York: Routledge, 17–32.

hooks, bell (1994). *Outlaw Culture: Resisting Representations*. New York: Routledge.

Huang, Li-ying (1994). *Decoding Variety Shows' Gender Discourse*. Unpublished dissertation, Graduate Institute of Journalism, Chinese Culture University.

"Information Bureau's Sticks Have Shown Effects" (2000, June 2). *MediaWatch Electronic Newsletter*, 6. Retrieved Oct. 15, 2001, from http://www.mediawatch.org.tw.

Jiang, Tsung-ming (2000). "Give Our Next Generation a Clean Television Culture." *United Daily News*, Aug. 29, p. A28.

Ka, Wei-po (2000). "Aging Media Criticism, Low IQ Feminism." *China Times*, Dec. 23.

Ka, Wei-po (2001a). "The Young and Wise Left? The Old and Idiotic Left? (Part I)." *The Left* 16: 19–34.

Ka, Wei-po (2001b). "The Young and Wise Left? The Old and Idiotic Left? (Part II)." *The Left* 17: 10–28.

Landes, Joan (1998). "The Public and the Private Sphere: A Feminist Reconsideration." In J. Landes, ed., *Feminism: The Public and The Private*. Oxford: Oxford University Press, 135–63.

Liao, Qiu-yi (2001). "Communication Forum Held in Kaohsuing to Welcome the New Century." *Taiwan News*, Dec. 16, p. A3.

Lin, Chao-jen (1999). "Some Blind-Spots in Contemporary Mediawatch Organizations." *Studies in Journalism* 60. Retrieved Nov. 1, 2001, from http://www.jour.nssc.edu.tw/Mcr/005/01.asp.

Lin, Yang-ling (2000). "A Study on Variety Show's Audience's Behavior." *Broadcaster*, Feb., pp. 54–8.

Lin, Shen-jing (2001a). "Young and Wise Ka Wei-po?" *The Left* 15: 13–17.

Lin, Shen-jing (2001b). "Ka, Wei-po, the Left Who Pretend to be Cute?" *The Left* 18: 21–4.

Lin, Wei-ming (2001). "Joining the WTO, Taiwan's Media Should Live Up to International Standards." *Taiwan News*, Dec. 16, p. A3.

Liu, Ping-jun (2000). " 'Translation' of Cultural Studies: From England to Taiwan." *Studies in Journalism* 64. Retrieved Nov. 15, 2001, from http://www.jour.nccu.edu.tw/mcr/showIssue.asp?IssueID=0064.

Luo, Ru-lan (2001). "A Lack of Balance on the Budget on Social Welfare." *China Times*, Dec. 17.

"New Department Stores Creating Special Sections for Teenagers" (2001). *China Times*, Dec. 22.

Probyn, Elspeth (2000). "Shaming Theory, Thinking Dis-connections: Feminism and Reconciliation." In S. Ahmed et al., eds., *Transformations: Thinking Through Feminism*. New York: Routledge, 48–60.

Seiter, Ellen (1996). "Notes on Children as Television Audience." In J. Hay et al., eds., *Audience and Its Landscape*. Boulder, CO: Westview Press, 131–44.

"Special Report on the Establishment of MediaWatch Alliance" (2000, Sept. 23). *MediaWatch Electronic News*. Retrieved Oct. 12, 2001, from http://www.mediawatch.org.tw.

Su, Heng and Chen, Xue-yun (2000). "Global or Local? Research on Taiwanese Youth's Television Viewing Behavior." *Studies on Journalism* 64. Retrieved Oct. 15, 2001 from http://www.jour.nccu.edu.tw/mcr/showIssue.asp?IssueID=0064.

Tavener, Jo (2000). "Media, Morality, and Madness: The Case Against Sleazy TV." *Critical Studies in Media Communication* 17(1): 63–85.

"When Hollywood Discovered Children's Books" (2001). *China Times*, Dec. 23.

Wu, Tsui-jen (1999). Sex and Children on TV. *China Times*, Jan. 24.

Xyu, Wen-wei and Chen, Shi-min (1996). "The Current Development of Communication Studies." *Studies on Journalism* 53. Retrieved Oct. 10, 2001, from http://www.jour.nccu.edu.tw/mcr/showIssue.asp?IssueID=0053.

Yang, Fang-chih (2002). "Variety Shows: Exploring the Genre of the 'Most Local Show' in Taiwan." *Dong Hwa Journal of Humanistic Studies* 4: 295–329.

"You Can Enjoy the Hottest New Cell Phone for Only a Few Hundred Dollars per Month" (2001). *China Times*, Dec. 14.

Zhen, Rei-cheng, et al. (1993). *Deconstructing Broadcasting Media: Establishing a New Broadcasting Order*. Taipei: Cheng She.

11

*Recuperating Malay Custom/*Adat *in Female Sexuality in Malaysian Films*

Gaik Cheng Khoo

I

The sexual is deeply political in the Malaysian media, as played out in 1998–9 in the vast coverage of former Deputy Prime Minister Anwar Ibrahim's alleged acts of sodomy and corruption. That a discourse regarded as belonging to the private sphere – sexual activity – is used by the state to malign and politically undermine Anwar in the public eye, reflects how sexuality is a highly contested site in sociocultural, religious, and political terms in Malaysia. In fact, sexuality will continue to be a very important battleground in the current post-Anwar climate, where a conflict is waged between the imperatives of modernity, the greed of capitalism, and the growing Islamist right.

But first, some understanding of Malaysian cultural history and politics is necessary. Before the coming of Islam in the fifteenth century, the region that is now Malaysia derived its culture from Indianization when "a relatively limited number of traders and priest-scholars brought Indian culture in its various forms to Southeast Asia" (Osborne, 1995: 21). Indianization was absorbed and adapted by the locals into their own existing culture and became integral to Malay custom or *adat* (more on *adat* later). Today, modern Malaysia is a multiracial country run by the National Alliance, initially consisting of three major ethnic-based political parties headed by UMNO, the United Malays National Organization, which has been in power since independence in 1957. Under Prime Minister Dr. Mahathir's leadership, Malaysia has seen tremendous economic growth and increase in living standards in the last 30 years, achieving an annual GDP of about 8 percent from the late eighties until the Asian economic crisis in the mid-1990s. These changes concur with the National Economic Plan (NEP, 1971–90) which was a kind of affirmative action for the majority indigenous Malays (60 percent of the population) whose feelings of disenfranchisement had led, in May 1969, to violent racial clashes with the Chinese, who were long believed to have dominated the then new nation's economy. Under the NEP, the Malays were declared *bumiputera* (sons of the soil) and maintained linguistic, religious, and cultural dominance and rights over non-Malays. The NEP saw the burgeoning of a Malay middle-class who were educated in local universities or sponsored by the government to study abroad. The pace of modernization, outmigration of young female factory workers to the cities from rural areas, the move from a largely agrarian-based economy to high-tech and service industries, etc., combined with the rise of resurgent Islam, have led to cultural shifts and social displacement for the Malays.

In the November 1999 elections, Mahathir's National Alliance managed to win a majority government despite the public disenchantment with the obviously biased treatment of Anwar Ibrahim[1] and despite the opposition put up by Wan Azizah, Anwar's wife, to form a coalition with other opposition groups under the Gerak Keadilan banner (Movement for Justice). However, the most important outcome of this election is that "with or without Anwar, Islam is here to stay" (Maznah, 1999: 6) as reflected by the victory of PAS,[2] the Islamic Party, over the predominantly Malay state of Trengganu. Anwar represents the modernist, moderate Malay Muslim position, having been the charismatic student leader of the Muslim Youth Movement of Malaysia (ABIM[3]) who led a massive student protest in 1974 in solidarity with Malay farmers. When the secularist UMNO realized the strong influence of *dakwah* (Islamic proselytizing) groups over the lower-class Malays, it co-opted the revivalist Islamic movement by setting up Islamic institutions and also by recruiting Anwar in 1982. The latter's struggle for rural farmers' rights as ABIM leader gave UMNO a tinge of Islamic credibility and broadened its appeal for Malays who believe in social justice. Hence, when Mahathir eradicated his political enemy, Anwar, he achieved the very opposite of his goals – the strengthening of radical Islamic movements which will continue to intensify (Maznah, 1999: 6). Maznah Mohamad's post-mortem of the election results that "UMNO will try to counter radical Islam by becoming even more Islamic as a way of winning back the Malay heartland" (1999: 7) was supported by journalist and lawyer Karim Raslan a year later during his seminar "From Command Politics to

Civil Society?" given at the University of British Columbia (Nov. 14, 2000). He pointed to the government's sponsoring of the Restoration of Faith bill which calls for a year's jail sentence and gives the Islamic syariah court the power to determine what "apostasy" means. Raslan also sees inherent class differences among the Malays widening: for him, Anwar's political devastation has destroyed the link of trust between the lower-class (more religious) Malays and the secular elites who were more dependent on the patronage system[4] in place since feudal times and which was fostered by British colonialism.

This rather long foray into Malaysian politics is to contextualize the framework in which the contemporary discourse of gender and sexuality is defined and produced. For example, Nik Aziz Nik Mat, leader of the opposition party PAS, was recently quoted as saying that female contestants should be banned from Quran recital contests because they had to use "high melodic voices which 'may be an attraction to men' " (*The Asian Post*, Oct. 26–Nov. 8, 2000). Moreover, he had been criticized a month earlier for stating that women who wore skimpy attire encouraged men to commit rape. Such statements display the patriarchal dominance of an imported Arabicized Islam overshadowing the more liberal modes of Sunni Islam as traditionally practiced in Malaysia, especially the kind that acknowledges the critical role of women's labor in the growth of the Malaysian tiger economy.

In the face of such struggles for cultural and political hegemony and their intersections with multiple and varying discourses of modernity, I suggest that a small group of liberal, progressive (read "secularist") Malay filmmakers, writers, and journalists is responding to the mainstreaming of resurgent Islam and to potentially homogenizing westernization by consciously or unconsciously recuperating *adat* in the 1990s. Many progressive Malays view the impact of Islamic revivalism as repressive of Malay sexuality. Some of the filmmakers in this category include U-Wei Haji Saari, Adman Salleh, Mahadi J. Murat, Hishamuddin Rais, and woman filmmakers Shuhaimi Baba and Erma Fatima. A few sample names of writers and journalists who recuperate *adat* are Salleh Ben Joned, Karim Raslan, and Dina Zaman. The process of recuperating *adat* occurs simultaneously too in theater and the performing arts as attempts to discover, uncover, and recover the fragmented subject in a globalized postmodern Malaysia. But for this short essay, I will only focus on cinema.

There are various forms of reclaiming *adat* in Malay film, such as a showing scenes of traditional healing, and uniquely indigenous folk dances like the *kuda kepang* dance (in *Ringgit Kasorrga*), the Malay martial arts *silat* (*Amok*), holding traditional festivities like *puja pantai* (*Selubung*), all of which are deemed un-Islamic as they contain forms of Hinduism, magic, and spirit worship. Another aspect of *adat* is bilaterality in gender relations (which encourages women's power and autonomy) as well as more openness to sexuality: "In their homes, married women customarily held the purse strings, despite the Islamic emphasis on men's keeping and handling money. Most important, women's special knowledge and skills were used in cooking, childbirth, health care and the intensification of sexual pleasure" (Ong, 1995: 166). In her footnote, anthropologist Aihwa Ong goes on to say that the Malay *kampung* (village) women she interviewed saw Islamic beliefs about sexuality in a positive light[5]: "For instance, *kampung* women claimed that female circumcision (partial removal of the clitoral hood) increased a woman's sexual pleasure during intercourse. *Kampung* women use different techniques and tonics (*jamu*) to condition their bodies for enhancing erotic pleasure. Sex was considered essential to good health and a normal life and only viewed negatively when indulged in excessively or with an unsuitable partner" (1995: 188, n. 5).

The focus on sexuality by the *bumigeois*[6] is linked to the proliferation of ethical discourse on sexual conduct by the ideological state apparatus – the media – not to mention by political and religious leaders (of course, the most overt being the Anwar Ibrahim case). But even prior to the economic slowdown in 1997, space for sexual as opposed to political discourse was permitted as the state carefully cultivated a liberal, cosmopolitan image in order to encourage foreign investment. Global trends like the discourses around AIDS prevention have also opened up issues of sexuality as workers at Pink Triangle and the Malaysian AIDS Council in Kuala Lumpur set up awareness programs in the 1990s. I believe that the increasingly advanced level and pace of modernity and westernization in Malaysian cities paradoxically allows an opening up of discussion on the relation of sexuality to Malay *adat*. It enables Malay writers to recover the sensuality, earthiness, and sexuality in *adat* that are being repressed by the new Islamic hegemony, and one detects this preoccupation with sex even in writings that supposedly contain an Islamic-fundamentalist morality.[7] To reiterate, aspects of Malay *adat* regarded as traditionally tolerant (though still patriarchal) and more open to sensual or sexual matters than resurgent Islam thus share common traits with secular modernity.

The form of recuperating *adat* that I want to discuss in this chapter is the portrayal of female sexuality embedded in the image of the Malay woman (*perempuan*) wearing a sarung tied around her midriff (*berkemban*). Such an image evokes an earthiness and raw sensuality that is rooted in the imagery of the *kampung,* suggesting a kind of Malay essentialist femininity before the advent of urban modernity, and the period of *dakwah* (Islamic proselytizing) activism which dictated Muslim women cover themselves by wearing head scarves (*tudung*) and the *baju kurung,* a long sleeved loose-fitting blouse over a long skirt. This representation of native, female sexuality seems to emerge from male filmmakers[8] recuperating an essential Malayness or an essentialized ethnicity that is cathected onto the body of the gendered Other. Thus, in the process of reclaiming ethnic roots while resisting a homogeneous global modernity and fundamentalist Islam, an elision or sleight-of-hand of another kind occurs; privileging ethnicity in this case means sacrificing gender politics.

In fact, women's bodies are usually the ambivalent markers of cultural and socioeconomic changes: not only does her *berkemban* image recuperate *adat,* her western dress or fashion may reflect "loose" western values (or Westoxification) whether she is in typical hooker gear (e.g. Erma Fatima in *Bintang Malam*) or chic evening gowns (e.g. Nina Juren in *Lenjan*). Alternatively, by wearing the *tudung* and *baju kurung,* she embodies Islamic values and piety. This is notable, as representations of male characters are not so frequently encoded through fashion. Aihwa Ong has discussed "the ways in which competing state and Islamic resurgent discourses use women as symbols of motherhood, Malay vulnerability, and as boundary markers in their visions of Malaysian modernity" (1995: 163). In other words, women end up bearing the burden of nationalist, ethnoreligious representation in the (male) politics of modernity which usually places them at a socioeconomic and political disadvantage. At a discursive level, "Women . . . are deployed as metaphors for often conflicting aspects of modernity in popular, religious and official discourse" (Stivens, 1998: 93).

In the next section, I analyze a film auteured by U-Wei Haji Saari, *Perempuan, Isteri Dan . . . ?* (1994) as an example of a film that represents the image of the *perempuan berkemban.* I will then suggest that in contrast, women filmmakers like Shuhaimi Baba and Erma Fatima do not focus so heavily on female sexuality as part of the project of recuperating *adat.*

II

The woman in a sarung is perfectly embodied by Sofia Jane's character, sultry Zaleha, in *Perempuan, Isteri Dan . . . ?* (*Woman, Wife, and Whore*). This was a popular and controversial film in Malaysia, partly because of the provocative elision in the title brought about by opposition from local feminists, not to mention its topic of unleashed female sexuality. Sofia Jane plays a simple *kampung* girl turned prostitute by her jealous and vengeful jilted fiancé Amir, who is forced to take her back to his village as his wife after she tricks him into marriage. The narrative encourages the viewer to feel that it is Amir who has transformed the naive village girl, who believed she was eloping with a man who truly loved her, into a whore, and that additionally, it is prostitution which unleashes her sexuality, shaping all her consequent actions in the plot. The notion of unleashed female sexuality ties into my theory that 1990s Malay male filmmakers are responding to perceived Islamic trends which suppress female sexuality by recuperating *adat* and recognizing the latent power of female sexuality in Malay culture. On the other hand, though, there is ambivalence and uncertainty about how to deal with an *adat* that is offset by the modern liberal discourse of female emancipation. By the time Amir returns to collect her from the pimp, she has become a true "jalang," wearing a short Western dress and chain-smoking.[9] Amir, as the one responsible for releasing Zaleha's female sexuality, is unable to keep it in check. A conversation she has with her neighbor, Kak Maria, is telling. She describes how she feels after flirting with a lorry driver in a restaurant: "Don't you feel our blood rise? This feeling is difficult to imagine. How shall I say it? Surrender. I like it. It makes my blood hot. Can you feel it? Not knowing what will happen next, left to the circumstance at hand. Don't you?" Kak Mariah hesitantly adds, "Isn't that dangerous?" and Zaleha admits, "Precisely" [my translation]. These are the words of a woman who courts danger when exercising libidinal power. Embodying female sexuality and femininity, Zaleha exudes and projects this on the social gaze in her husband's village that defines her as "perempuan" (woman) and "isteri Amir" (Amir's wife).

Her sexuality figures largely in the diegesis of the film. This is a woman who tells her neighbor that she prefers to bathe in the river than using indoor plumbing, probably because she is an exhibitionist who is keenly aware of the many male heads she can turn being clad only in a sarung and sunshades. One hot night, she sits on a low stool in the kitchen facing an electric fan, her top shirt button undone. Using a metal plate, she fans into her sarung. The camera then cuts to a close-up of her uplifted face with eyes closed, a slight smile gripping her cigarette, looking either aroused or relieved from the heat. Meanwhile, the audience is aware of the presence of a peeping-tom, Tapa, spying at her through a hole in the outer wall of the house. Next, she levels her look straight into the camera as if she is aware of being stared at by Tapa (and the cinema spectator), still fanning herself and smoking. Contextually, this voyeurism reinforces the spectator's sense of forbidden pleasure and encourages us to suspect a sexual underlying meaning in her facial expression.

She is perfectly aware of herself as the object of the male gaze as she states candidly, "Kita orang perempuan, orang suka tengok cantik" ["We are women and people like to look at attractive women"]. She even encourages the other women to be proud of their bodies, "Kalau kita dah ada, kita tunjukkanlah" [which loosely translates into "if you have it, flaunt it"]. These occasions of boosting female pride occur at the seamstress's house, demonstrating that Zaleha's clothing expenses are utilized to "accessorize" and enhance her sexual appeal. It might be conceived as disempowering to cater to the male gaze, but in Zaleha's case, her sexual image is her only weapon of power – evident in the sway of her hips while walking, her eye contact with men, her flirtatious gestures. She attracts the attention of male onlookers even without trying. Totally comfortable with her body and sexuality, she immodestly speaks to the cloth merchant dressed only with a sarung tied around her midriff (*berkemban*), exposing areas of her body such as her shoulders and arms considered *haram* [not kosher] under Islamic law. Granted most women represented in the film do not wear the *tudung*, yet they are not shown "berkemban" either except when they are bathing and washing clothes at the river. She does not hesitate to carry out her heart's desires, whether it is eloping with her first husband, a town dandy, or having a secret tryst in the rubber estate with Tapa during a stormy afternoon. In her relationship with Tapa, she has complete autonomy and power in deciding when they meet. Unsurprisingly, then, she encourages a young village girl, Mina, to respond to the attentions of Bakri, a young man who has been trailing the girl around. She tells Mina to be direct, and as a result Mina willingly meets Bakri in secret for a sexual tryst. Unfortunately, the pair is caught by the villagers and punished. Thus, Zaleha triggers conflict among the villagers with her lack of concern for social propriety.

Just what are the consequences of unleashing female sexuality and feminine libidinal desires? What is Zaleha's impact on the community? First, she encourages conspicuous consumption among the women when she goes to Asiah, the local seamstress, to make some new clothes. Her trendy fashion sense infects the village women and, soon, Asiah is sewing full time and neglecting her cooking chores as she tries to cope with new orders. This incurs the wrath of her husband who demands to know why his wife has not prepared his dinner. But Asiah is not easily cowed like Maria, Zaleha's neighbor, who gets slapped by her husband in an earlier scene where he, too, wants to know why she has not prepared his dinner. Asiah confronts her husband in front of the other women and produces the money she has earned from taking in sewing. She tells him in Malay, "I've worked nonstop with my hands from this morning, do you know that? Here, here [she pulls out the dollar notes from her neckline], who do you think all this is for? Have you ever asked me where I get the money for the children's education? From this, this [she flings the money at him]! You don't realize anything!" [my translation]. Her husband is stunned into a shamed silence. While Zaleha herself does not have the skills to earn any income in a legitimate way and is forced to rely totally on her husband for money, she has created business for Asiah, unintentionally demonstrating that the only way for women in the village to earn any respect and power from the men is to become wage earners themselves.

Zaleha continually challenges the boundaries of the village mindset, and in doing so, exposes the repressive limits on women in the *kampung*. She persuades her neighbor, Maria, to accept the invitation from the truck driver and his friend to go to the cinema. She convinces her that they should not give up the opportunity as, after all, women are usually cooped up in the house.[10] While the complaint is uttered by a bored young woman, it also highlights that *kampung* women are restricted in terms of social and spatial mobility. It seems women are denied any interlude for recreation or levity; just as Zaleha succeeds in persuading a group of women who were washing clothes by the river to join her for a swim or to play some kind of girlish game in the water, a male passerby orders the women back to work.

If Amir has indeed unleashed Zaleha's feminine libidinal desires by forcing her into prostitution, he is totally at a loss as to how to control her except through the threat of physical violence. She, however, manipulates him without utilizing violence or her sexuality, knowing full well that she is no match for him in terms of physical strength and hypermasculinity (having witnessed his cold-blooded murder of her first husband) and understanding that he is immune to her physical attractions.[11] Her manipulation begins as early as the time he collects her from the pimp and humiliates her: he makes her sleep on the floor and refuses to let her share his bed, saying it is reserved for his wife and that she is only a prostitute. In response to his cruelty and in an attempt to regain some social standing, she tricks him into marrying her when they get "caught" for *khalwat* [close proximity] in the hotel in Golok, a border town infamous for its brothels and hasty marriages. Unknown to him, she tips off the religious office that there is an unmarried couple in their hotel room and the religious officers appear at their door. After the married couple return to Amir's village, her attempts to be a good wife fail as he refuses to play his part as a caring husband, thereby violating that reciprocal contract which is integral to bilaterality. Finally, when she has had enough of his abuse and finds another man who can satisfy her sexual desires (Tapa), she puts a spell or charm on Amir. This controversial scene, what is known as the *nasi kangkang* [straddled rice] scene, was censored because it was considered un-Islamic. It is an *adat* undertaken by menstruating women to gain control over straying husbands: standing with her legs apart over his rice bowl, she urinates on the rice, symbolizing the assertion of female power and dominance over the man who eats this charmed rice.

As a result of her spell, he becomes more generous and caring. For example, he gives his brother a generous bunch of fresh *buah petai* (a type of vegetable) for his family the day after he has been hexed. The spell weakens his constitution and he suffers from headache, fatigue, and pallor and sweats the following day. There is also heavy rain, "a type that does not bode well," as a man tells Amir: "Hujan macam ini, tak elok pula" [my translation]. As if to confirm these words, when he starts his truck in the downpour, he punctures a tire. The cross-cutting between scenes of Amir changing the tire in the rain and Zaleha's seduction of Tapa among the rubber trees juxtaposes emasculation and cuckoldry, reinforcing the overall sense of Amir's emasculation by Zaleha. To carry the metaphor of emasculation further, there is even a scene when a male villager slaughtering the calf teases the young uncircumcised boys about splitting a boy's penis into four if he, the butcher, were blind. Zaleha's hex domesticates Amir and he even returns home early to look for his wife, intending to spend more time with her. Another day, he decides to go home early to rest when he spies Zaleha outside the meeting-hall. And then he does something completely out of character: he hurries to the passenger side of the car and holds the door open for her to get in, smiling at her. This kind of deference towards his wife does not go unnoticed by his friends who are equally misogynistic in their treatment of women; thus far in the film, erring wives are slapped or reprimanded. For instance, Maria is slapped in public for returning late at night in a lorry with two male strangers and, secondly, Halim, Amir's older brother, does not intervene to prevent Amir from forcing the soup bowl to Zaleha's mouth and spilling soup all over her. Careful to preserve his younger brother's "face," his advice about letting bygones be bygones and being a better husband only comes when both their wives are out of earshot. In addition, Halim is also the man who yells at the women to return to work, i.e. to washing clothes, when he sees them having fun and playing in the river. If we include the close homosocial rapport Amir evidently has with the men in the village and their treatment of women, it would seem that Amir signifies the typical *kampung* male who outlines and prescribes the gender mores and conduct for women.

Zaleha's hex is so effective that she is able to safely reject Amir's sexual advances with the excuse that she does not feel well. The dialogue between the two here hints of irony and role reversal as he asks her to approach, "Mai sini" ["Come here"]. She is standing at the entrance of the bedroom and she answers in an incredulous tone, "Who? Me? You want me?" [my translation]. Suddenly finding herself in charge, she seizes the opportunity for vengeance and denies him his spousal "rights" to her body. After all, he has not performed his social role as a husband by caring for her, providing adequately for her, and fulfilling her sexual needs. (For example, when she first arrives at his village, she has no other dresses or clothes of her own apart from the one she is wearing. Consequently, she gets into debt with the cloth merchant because Amir has not given her any money for clothing. Moreover, they have not been having any sexual relations as husband and wife.) Unsound as it may seem, this is a valid argument that Malay Muslim men would be likely to make. The same men might claim that had Amir kept her sexually gratified, she would not have turned to Tapa, even though her reasons might have more to do with Tapa's kindness and simplicity.

Female sexuality or libidinal desires seems to be a popular theme in Malay 1990s cinema because, while being sensationalist in attracting audiences, it also reflects modernity and the liberal challenges posed by changing gender configurations. Nevertheless, it should be added that these are male projections; women filmmakers like Shuhaimi Baba and Erma Fatima seem more interested in exploring the fuller sense of female subjectivity (more later). In U-Wei Haji Saari's vision, as woman, wife, and whore, Zaleha symbolizes modernity and capitalism (but which, unconsciously perhaps, taps into female power in *adat*). Her cigarette-smoking which encodes the contagion of urban modernity marks her as rebellious, independent, and transgressive. In short, she epitomizes female sexual autonomy and sexual liberation which is good for some men, but not for others. Hence, female sexual activity has to be regulated by the patriarchy, as illustrated in hypermasculine acts of violence on intruding male strangers in the village such as the lorry driver and his friend, and the itinerant cloth merchant, Si Majeet, who is killed by Tapa. In both instances, the male villagers act aggressively and violently before giving their victims any opportunity for explanation. The adulterous Tapa, in turn, is slain by Amir. It is her presumption that she has such liberties that enrages and emasculates Amir. Zaleha also spends a lot of her husband's money – money that she does not have – on consumer goods and is able to create a high demand for Majeet's goods as well as Asiah's skills. One of the women comments that ever since Zaleha's arrival, the cloth merchant's trips to their village have become regular/more frequent. In keeping with the capitalist fashion industry, she advocates the modern and the *en vogue*, telling Kak Maria that "if you make a modern baju kurung, it would suit your skin" [my translation].

Deeply resilient and ever resourceful, she utilizes whatever talents and skills she may possess to survive. Her assets being her sexual charms and body, she uses both to full advantage by flirting and seducing men to get what she wants. Yet, her desires for material things seem to undermine a story that may be trying to deal sympathetically with the alienation and oppression of women. Her desires are for beautiful, fashionable clothes, jewelry, high-heel shoes – essentially the trappings of femininity that cater to her vanity and self-image. Even though some sense of female bonding develops around the shared interests in fashion and femininity, the issues are too shallow to guarantee any strong female solidarity in the village. For example, feeling as though their presence is intruding on a domestic argument, the women make their excuses and start leaving after Asiah's confrontation with her husband. Moreover, Zaleha's decision to try to make the best of the volatile situation that is her marriage is problematic. She may have tricked him into marrying her to gain herself some social respectability, to ensure that her past profession stays a secret, and to get back at Amir (who has to marry a woman he forced into prostitution). But there is a streak of recklessness in her, too, for wanting to marry Amir despite having witnessed his cruelty and egoism. Assuming she has no family or is too proud/ashamed to return to them, should she try to make her marriage to a cold-blooded murderer work? And to dispute with those viewers who might actually want it to work, why should she want any kind of sexual attention from him after all the abuse she has suffered in his hands? For a film that purports to represent the power of unleashed female sexuality, it seems all too eager to co-opt its heroine into the bourgeois fantasy of heterosexual marriage. Note how she plays wife to him by preparing him dinner and, in front of the neighbors, when she tells Maria that they will go shopping together once he gets back from work. She actually ends up going to the store alone as he has intentionally stayed out till late at night.

By killing her, Amir destroys the dominant symbol of female libidinal desires in the village. When she dies, most probably the spirit of female autonomy and libidinal agency and of feminine consumerism die with her, for she has been the agent of change, the symbol of the gender of modernity, all dolled up with no place to run to within the oppressive patriarchal structures of the *kampung*. She becomes an example to the other women that testing patriarchal boundaries will not be tolerated; and neither will emasculating female libidinal desires. In fact, these will be punished severely through hypermasculinity that seeks to empower men to reestablish their hegemonic control.

III

In contrast to the representation of the *perempuan berkemban*, Shuhaimi Baba and Erma Fatima's strong-minded, articulate, educated, and independent heroines imply that it is not necessary for their male counterparts to remind the Malay woman about her own "essential" pre-*dakwah* sexuality, or to free her from her own Islamicized sexual inhibitions and repressions. Rather, the female character's desires revolve around other crucial issues: career choices, emotional relationships with friends, family, and the potential romantic partner, and lastly, how to lead a productive, satisfactory life as a decent human being in a rapidly industrializing society. In all of Baba's films, *Selubung* (1991), *Ringgit Kasorrga* (1994), *Layar Lara* (1996), and *Mimpi Moon* (2000), striking a balance between rural and urban spaces which symbolize tradition/the past and modernity/the future is a key theme. Her female protagonists played by Deanna Yusoff in *Selubung* and *Ringgit Kasorrga* are both at home in the *kampung* setting as well as in the city.[12] While Baba continues with the notion of recuperating *adat* in her latest film *Mimpi Moon* by exploring the hitherto unknown properties of the sea cucumber, *gamat emas*, to heal the wounds of landmine victims, Erma Fatima's newer work, I think, mainly revolves around the formation of modern Malay identity and gender politics which may include sexuality but not be at the service of recuperating *adat*.

The sexual continues to be political in the Malaysian media. But what bears closer examination is how that discourse of sexuality is shaped or transformed and by whom. There are two articles posted on the malaysiakini website[13] that I would like to mention in closing which deal with female sexuality in the contemporary Malaysian film/entertainment industry. The first is Amir Muhammad's article "The State of Erma Fatima," which, in the course of discussing Erma's rising career as actor and director, mentions that her third feature, *Bulan Dan Matahari* [*Moon and Sun*], is "about a married man who decides that he is homosexual." Again, I think this supports my thesis that women filmmakers are not so much interested in dealing with the sole idea of uncontrollable female (hetero)sexuality as they are in exploring other more subversive issues related to modern Malay identity today. In fact, Erma Fatima's past film projects have included directing an award-winning telemovie, *Jangan* (1995), about "a Malaysian woman caught in a bureaucratic mess when she marries a Bangladeshi immigrant" (Amir). Film critic Amir Muhammad claims that *Jangan* was "so daring in its indictment of official hypocrisy that it was then banned from TV." Her second film, *Perempuan Melayu Terakhir* [*The Last Malay Woman*], he says, "clashed religious fundamentalism against the sexual awakening of a young woman."

Female sexuality is a hot topic for men across the politically and culturally conservative to liberal spectrum, attracting the attention of those who claim that women should stay at home and be covered as well as those who "defend" women's right to expression of their sexual fantasies and whatnot in the newspapers, in men's English-language magazines, and on the internet (in both the English and Malay languages). An example of this is Farish A. Noor's article "Sex and the Asian Woman" written in defense of young Malay R&B pop diva Ning Baizura's frank interview about her sexual fantasies in an English-language men's magazine, *FHM*. I problematize this and suggest, at the risk of destabilizing an already fragile solidarity with liberal heterosexual men of goodwill, to women themselves to reclaim their spaces for vocal expression. Indeed, Malaysian writer Sheryll Stodhard claims in the online version of music magazine, *Tone*, that *FHM*, "a milder Malaysian version of its almost soft-porn British progenitor, still unabashedly makes full use of its cover girls as selling tools for the sex slant of the publication here." What is worse is that instead of targeting *FHM* as sexually exploitive and sexist, the Malay media and English mainstream press as well as assorted politicians zoomed in on Ning for being sexually explicit. Ning Baizura's sexuality gets "exploited twice; once, by *FHM*, in a bid to cash in on her sexuality to sell magazines, and again, by other media who have cashed in on second-hand sex for their audiences" (Stodhard). As example, Stodhard refers to the August 6 issue of Malay tabloid *Mingguan Perdana* whose cover features "a headline quoting an Ustaz's exhortations that Ning is spiritually 'sick' and needs immediate treatment. [Yet] in the centrespread of the same issue, the newspaper lifts a shot of Ning in the same short black dress from *FHM* and re-sells it as their 'Poster *Mingguan Perdana*.'"

Lastly, I should point out that the narrowing of public discourse on the television screen when filtered through the new Islamic lenses already operates as more and more rural and working-class Malays gain access to film and video-making techniques.[14] While the film industry is largely run by and supported by the secularist elite, the growing interest in film and video production, and the proliferation of satellite and cable television as global media networks expand, will eventually lead to the desire for more and more self-representations from the young *dakwah* generation.

The acts of recuperating *adat* that I have described in this essay may indeed be tiny, tiny points of resistance, especially when we take into account the growing sense of Islam as the central pole of Malay identity in the current post-Anwar climate in Malaysia. And perhaps in that light, it is all the more vital and necessary to highlight these little precious points of resistance just as secularist cultural producers, writers, and journalists so often write appealing for tolerance, open-mindedness, and striving for commonalities – "the ethics and values of our shared humanity" (Martinez, 1999: 11) – in a multiracial nation.

Afterword

For me, writing about Malaysian culture and film from Vancouver, British Columbia, has often been a somewhat alienated process. Information garnered from the internet can never make up for my not being physically present in Malaysia, for having one's research be shaped by current Malaysian political and cultural discourse and the multiple local insights from Malaysian academia and popular cultural activists. I was made more conscious of this aspect in the summer of 2001 when I returned to Malaysia. In a conversation with two young, cynical Malaysian journalists (both of whom used to write for the mainstream press) about malaysiakini.com providing a great alternative media perspective to the other state-controlled presses, I was informed that the online journalists could have conducted a more thorough investigation before preparing their story about the outbreak of racial violence in Petaling Jaya in March 2001 (July 9, 2001). Being here in Vancouver, my only source of information about events in Malaysia comes through the internet. After all, not every magazine has been put online or has an up-to-date website. For example, Malay-language media such as pop magazines, some journals, the FINAS (Film Development Board of Malaysia) newsletter, and comics have no internet equivalent. Thus, I was quite relieved and gratified to learn that my interpretations of U-Wei and Shuhaimi Baba's works, formulated during the thesis-writing stage in Vancouver over the late 1990s, were not inaccurate upon talking to U-Wei himself and film animator Hassan Muthalib (July 6, 2001).

Having said that, at the same time, there are advantages to being a researcher on Malaysian culture who is based abroad at a time when the Malaysian government has threatened to censor any academic criticism of government policies through expulsion (for university students) and job termination (for its faculty members). Malaysia-based academics nowadays are lamenting more and more about the difficulty of conducting cutting-edge research or producing radical criticism of the nation-state within Malaysia without facing terrible repercussions. Moreover, Vancouver, situated in British Columbia on the edge of the Asian Pacific Rim, is significant first as a cosmopolitan city with a large Asian population. It is home to *The Asian Post*, a fortnightly paper started by Malaysian immigrants which used to focus substantially on southeast Asian news. During the Anwar debacle, the paper's coverage (then *The Southeast Asian Post*) was more in-depth and comprehensive than that in the daily *Vancouver Sun*. Secondly, the University of British Columbia and the University of Victoria form two important points on the North American academic circuit of Southeast Asian Studies on the west coast. Hence, Malaysian academics and writers such as Maznah Mohamad, Shamsul A.cB., and Karim Raslan have stopped by to give talks at both BC universities.

Unfortunately, when the funding from the Ford Foundation runs out for the North West Consortium for SE Asian Studies (NWCSEAS), and as the pioneer Canadian Southeast Asianists retire and are not being replaced due to federal and provincial funding cuts to universities, not to mention the academic shift away from area/regional studies to Global Studies, being an institutionally independent scholar of southeast Asia in BC will become more and more an isolating experience and career.

Notes

1   Deputy Prime Minister Anwar Ibrahim was removed from office for allega-
    tions of sexual misconduct, specifically sodomy (a sin for Muslims), as the
    government-controlled newspapers were loudly proclaiming in their head-
    lines in September 1998. Anwar believes his removal from office is motivated
    by a political conspiracy by Mahathir and his cronies to preserve their own
    positions of power and wealth. After a trial which critics have called "an
    absolute travesty of justice" (Rajendra, 1999: 10), he was found guilty of cor-
    ruption and sentenced to 6 years' imprisonment. A later trial added another
    9 years' sentence for sodomy. For more details and analysis of the Anwar case,

see *Aliran Monthly*, May 1999. Up-to-date information is readily available on the internet by typing in Anwar Ibrahim's name.

2   PAS's political agenda has always been total islamicization of the state, which, unsurprisingly, is opposed by the ethnic Chinese (26% of the population), who are mostly Taoist/Buddhist, and the Indians (7%), who are predominantly Hindu. The PAS leadership consists of conservative Muslim *ulama* or clergy.

3   ABIM's motto since its inception in 1969 has been "Islam first, Malay second" (Shamsul, 1999: 8). The formation of ABIM signaled the beginning of the *dakwah* movement in Malaysia.

4   Critics see the patronage system within UMNO functioning in the form of cronyism, nepotism, and corruption.

5   This shows the integration of Islam and *adat*. Many anthropologists studying Malaysia find the dichotomy between *adat* and Islam that Malaysian anthropologist Wazir Jahan Karim makes problematic. Her point is to valorize *adat* as being more fair to women than contemporary revivalist Islam, which she views more as an arabicization that threatens to transform Malay culture and to purge *adat*. See her book *Women and Culture: Between Malay Adat and Islam*. My position is that while some aspects of *adat* seem more liberal to women and women's equality, this is not to say that the culture is not patriarchal. Moreover, as capitalism, urbanization, and development continue to expand, those very aspects of *adat* that give women power as farmers and landholders are eroding. Ong discusses, for example, how "population growth and land scarcity have affected gender relations and peasant householding" so that "the *adat* practice of awarding equal land shares to sons and daughters has been superseded by the Islamic Shafi'i law dictating that sons be entitled to claim shares twice those of their sisters" (1995: 164).

6   Malay middle class.

7   Shahnon Ahmad, a Malay writer whose works have become more religious over the years, is a prime example. He was a member of Al Arqam, a radical Islamic group which got shut down by the government in the early 1990s. Earlier, Shahnon had worked and studied at the Australian National University in Canberra from 1968 to 1972. He lost his poet laureate status after the publication of his novelette *Shit@PukiMak@PM* (1999) a political satire of Mahathir's corrupt regime. "PukiMak" is an obscenity referring to one's mother's vagina.

8   The *perempuan berkemban* is also featured in *Amok* (Adman Salleh, 1994), and *Panas* (Nurhalim Hj. Ismail, 1998).

9   Malay cinema encodes a woman who smokes usually as a prostitute or, at least, as someone aspiring to have the same privileges as men.

10 "Ini kita perempuan asyik duduk di rumah saja."

11 He warns her after they get married that despite her official status as legal wife, it does not change his feelings towards her: "Although we are married, you are

still dirty and don't think you are now clean" [my translation]. His murder of her first husband is treated as almost incidental, the murder scene does not recur in flashbacks, and there is no discussion or internal reflection about it by any of the characters.

12   For a brief analysis of *Layar Lara*, see "Recuperating Malay Custom/*adat* in the Malaysian New Wave: Responses from the Work of Woman Filmmaker Shuhaimi Baba," in *Women Filmmakers: Refocusing* (2002, University of British Columbia Press). A short discussion of Erma Fatima's teledrama appears in "What is it to be a Man? Hypermasculinity in Contemporary Malaysian Cinema," *West Coast Line reZonings 2* 34(2) (2000): 43–60. For an in-depth discussion of *Selubung*, see chapter 4 of my dissertation, "Gender, Modernity and the Nation in Malaysian Literature and Film (1980s–1990s)."

13   Since the Anwar affair, Malaysians have begun to turn to the internet as a more reliable news source. Malaysiakini.com, launched on Nov. 20, 1999, aims to provide unbiased and responsible news, analysis, and feature stories "in the spirit of inquiry with truth being the sole criterion of investigation" (editorial policy).

14   When I was doing fieldwork in Malaysia in 1998, I had the opportunity of catching the preview of a television drama entitled *An-Nur* at FINAS, the National Film Development Corporation Malaysia, which houses a film academy as well. Made by a young male film student, the tone was heavily moralistic, as highlighted by, first, the Quranic quote in the beginning of the film, the thunderous nondiegetic music, and the content whereby the young couple is finally punished for premarital sex. The title of the film refers to surah 434, a line in the Quran which highlights men's superior position over women. The film's ending with the adulterous couple being given a hundred strokes of the rotan each is an intertextual reference to a classic *purba* (drawing from Malay history/mythology) film, P. Ramlee's *Semerah Padi* (1956). But given the different era and social climate, *An-Nur* reflects a less forgiving, *dakwah* perspective unlike Ramlee's conclusion in which "having survived the ordeal, the couple is reinstated into society as a legitimately married couple via a traditional ceremony" (Kueh, 1997: 27).

References

Amir Muhammad (2000). "The State of Erma Fatima." Oct. 11; www.malaysiakini.com.

"Call to Ban Women in Koran Contest" (2000). *The Asian Post*, Oct. 26–Nov. 8, p. 17.

Farish A. Noor (2000). "Sex and the Asian Woman." Sept. 23; www.malaysiakini.com.

Khoo, Gaik Cheng (1999). "Gender, Modernity and the Nation in Malaysian Literature and Film (1980s–1990s)." Unpublished doctoral dissertation, University of British Columbia.

Khoo, Gaik Cheng (2000). "What is it to be a Man? Hypermasculinity in Contemporary Malaysian Cinema." *West Coast Line reZonings 2* 34(2) (2000): 43–60.

Kueh Siaw Hui, Adeline (1997). "The Filmic Representations of Malayan Women: An Analysis of Malayan Films from the 1950s and 1960s." Doctoral dissertation, Murdoch University.

Martinez, Patricia (1999). "More than Meets the Eye." *Aliran Monthly*, Dec., pp. 10–11.

Maznah Mohamad (1999). "UMNO and Its Partners In the New Malaysia." *Aliran Monthly*, Dec., pp. 2–7.

Ong, Aihwa (1995). "State Versus Islam: Malay Families, Women's Bodies, and the Body Politic in Malaysia." In A. Ong and M. Peletz, eds., *Bewitching Women, Pious Men: Gender and Body Politics in Southeast Asia*. Berkeley: University of California Press, 159–94.

Osborne, Milton (1995). *Southeast Asia: An Introductory History*. Australia: Allen and Unwin.

Perempuan Isteri Dan . . .? (1994). Dir. U-Wei Haji Shaari. With Sofia Jane Hisham and Nasir Bilal Khan. Berjaya Fp.

Rajendra, Cecil (1999). "An Absolute Travesty of Justice." *Aliran Monthly*, May, p. 10.

Raslan, Karim (2000). "From Command Politics to Civil Society?" Centre for Southeast Asian Research, Institute of Asian Research, University of British Columbia, Vancouver, Nov. 14.

Shamsul A.B. (1999). "Ringgit, Sex and the Internet: Economy, Politics and Culture in Contemporary Malaysia." Centre for Southeast Asia Research, Institute of Asian Research, University of British Columbia, Vancouver, March 3.

Stivens, Maila (1998). "Sex, Gender and the Making of the New Malay Middle Classes." In K. Sen and M. Stivens, eds., *Gender and Power in Affluent Asia*. New York: Routledge, 87–126.

Stodhard, Sheryll (2000). "Sex and Morality Ning Baizura." *Tone* 1 (Sept.); http://www.toneonline.com/media/00000116t. jpg.

Wazir Jahan Karim (1992). *Women and Culture: Between Malay Adat and Islam*. Boulder, CO: Westview Press.

12

The Formation of a Queer-Imagined Community in Post-Martial Law Taiwan

John Nguyet Erni and Anthony J. Spires[1]

Introduction

In 1996, the first popular lifestyle magazine catering to young Chinese-reading gays and lesbians appeared in Taiwan. *G&L Magazine* was launched only nine years after the end of almost half a century of martial law, during which such a visible cultural production would not have been possible. The magazine was granted permission by the Taipei City government to publish in 1996, and its premiere issue arrived in bookstores in June of that year. Glossy, colorful, and designed with a dual cover featuring images of men on one side and women on the other, the magazine carries with it a vibrantly celebratory tone (figure 12.1). "G&L" signifies more than gays and lesbians; it doubles as a shorthand for a number of multiplying nominations appropriate for its celebratory attitude (e.g. the premiere issue also names the magazine as Glory & Liberty, Gentlemen and Ladies, George & Louis, Gina & Lisa, etc.). Compared to the drabness of other "underground" queer publications or queer-friendly magazines of earlier times (e.g. *Girlfriend* [*Nupengyou*] and *Teacher Zhang Monthly* [*Zhang Laoshi Yuekan*]), *G&L*'s design concept projects positive self-affirmation cloaked in commercial vigor.[2]

"The World's First Chinese-Language Gay and Lesbian Magazine" is how *G&L* proclaims its global appeal. In 2000, its circulation reached 40,000. Besides selling in Taiwan, Japan, Canada, and the US, the magazine achieves one-third of its sales in Hong Kong.[3] In April 2003, the magazine's English name was changed to *Gamma* (issue 42), while its Chinese title remains the

Figure 12.1:   Cover of *G&L Magazine*

same (*Re Ai*). Many bookstores are too squeamish about putting the magazine on obvious display, except for the large chain, Eslite Bookstore. A favorite hangout for young queers, Eslite places a big pile of the magazine out in the open to attract its 22- to 28-year-old readership. If young gays and lesbians in Taiwan were bound in "darkness" (*heian*) under authoritarian rule, the arrival of this glossy magazine signals the freedom of "sunny" (*yangguang*) visibility. For many of them, the evocation of what appears to be a common and simplistic metaphor of sunlight/darkness in fact serves to contextualize the significance of *G&L* within a fundamental frame for understanding power in the everyday life of Taiwanese society.

In this chapter, we offer a critical reading of *G&L* within the parallel contexts of the politics of "traditional culture" (*chuantong wenhua*) and the politics of an emerging identity-based consciousness around sexuality in contemporary Taiwanese society. We reviewed all of the issues in the first two years of the magazine (from June 1996 to October 1998), as well as relevant newspaper and magazine coverage of homosexuality in Taiwan during the same period. We coded the magazine exhaustively under the following categories: feature stories, essays, editor's letters, family issues, activism, literary works, educational events, erotic materials, counseling, HIV/AIDS, non-AIDS health issues, international news, and advertisements and promotions. Additionally, we interviewed the current Editor and staff of *G&L* in the summer of 1998.

In an effort to understand the historical and social formation of gay and lesbian experience under capitalism, recent investigations of queer consumer culture in the West have addressed a variety of complex and inter-related issues, the most important being the political paradox in the relationship between gay identity politics and experience of commodifica-tion. Perhaps because, as Rosemary Hennessy notes, "queer spectacles often participate in a long standing history of *class*-regulated visibility" (1995: 66; emphasis added), theories *about* gay consumerism fall prey to the same ten-dencies to valorize class difference as the privileged term of analysis. In any event, analyses of queer consumerism assume interdependence between queer identity and class experience or consciousness, thus contributing to an underestimation of other forms of social and ideological positioning for queers. Yet in the case of *G&L*, we shall argue that the merging of the economic trend of the so-called global gay consumerism with the political opportunity for charting a new sexual movement in a newfound liberal democracy, has enabled an opportunity to work out the relationship between gay and lesbian visibility and the cultural politics of family-centeredness in Taiwan. We shall suggest that *G&L* evinces not a class pol-itics, but family politics, that underwrites queer consumption of popular culture in Taiwan. The convergence between consumerism, politics, and family life underscores a certain tentativeness about queer identity in *G&L*. Queer identity is tentative less because it has entered into commodity rela-tions (an inevitable price of modernity itself) than because it is the result of a delicate attempt to reconfigure traditional culture, especially matters of filial piety. Despite its (rightful) attempt to celebrate queer visibility, *G&L* provides its young readers with an approximating social and politi-cal ideal fit for an emerging visibility of homosexual culture in Taiwan.

This chapter is not a study of the gay and lesbian social movement in Taiwan *per se*; rather, it focuses on a highly visible and widely consumed cultural product in order to discern how it illustrates, animates, and helps to shape readers' emerging identities in this historical moment of Taiwan's history.[4] It has two parts. In the first part, we discuss briefly the political changes in Taiwan since the late 1980s and the rise of queer visibility in various social and cultural formations among Taiwanese youth during the same period. In the second part, we examine *G&L* with respect to questions of relational life, family, and queer consumption. The range of private and public issues covered in *G&L* offers a prism for looking at various images and narratives of (tentative) queer identities in Taiwan. We conclude by exploring the theoretical implications of *G&L* for queer-visibility politics in an Asian context.

A brief note on the terminology used in this chapter. The nomenclature "gay and lesbian" is not entirely accurate for the targeted readers of *G&L*, or for the public discussion of queer visibility in Taiwan. While the terms homosexual, lesbian, gay, bisexual, and transgender do exist in Mandarin equivalents, they all fall under one popularly used name: *tongzhi* (meaning "same aspiration" or "comrade"). It is this spirit of "sameness" which in theory forges a unified "gay" community and movement. Through appropriating the meaning of comradeship from the political vernacular of the PRC, "*tongzhi*" is a creatively ironic usage deemed necessary for a repressed group. In addition, the idea of "coming out," an interesting discourse in itself as it is understood in Taiwan, has been translated as *xianshen* (to "let the body appear," or to "reveal one's self") or *chugui* (to "come out of the closet").

The term "queer" that is popular in current American discussion has been translated in Taiwan as *guaitai* ("strange creature") or *kuer* (for its rhyme with "queer"). It is important to note that we use "queer" only to echo what has already been accepted, localized, and commonly used among Taiwanese *tongzhi*. While we do not believe "queer" is the most widely used term there, we use it to highlight an emerging attitude of defiance observable among young gays and lesbians in Taiwan (and Hong Kong). We also use it heuristically to connect with the existing literature of "queer theory," which has been increasingly adopted and appropriated by gender and sexuality studies in Taiwanese universities. Above all, we agree with Adam et al. (1999) that the impact of international diffusion of terms such as "queer" has been most impressive "in the situation of a sudden change in political opportunities, such as the opening of the political system in the transition from dictatorship to democracy" (p. 369).

Contexts

The reinvention of Taiwan

Rapid social changes occurred in Taiwan during the 1990s and beyond. 1992 saw the first real legislative elections in over 40 years, the result of which replaced many mainland-elected old Nationalist Party supporters with younger, Taiwan-born, well-educated representatives intent on democratizing Taiwan. In 1996, the country held the first direct Presidential election, while the National Assembly began revising the nation's Constitution toward a more democratic and fair legal and political system. Since the lifting of martial law in 1987, the country has gone from an authoritarian regime controlled by one family – Chiang Kai-shek and his son Chiang Ching-kuo – to a multiparty system designed to make the government more representative of and accountable to the people of Taiwan. More recently in early 2000, the new elections produced for the first time a new President, Chen Shui-bian, who did not come from the longtime dominant KMT party.

Economically speaking, Taiwan has enjoyed prosperity sustained by a vast and stable middle class. According to the World Bank, income inequality in Taiwan is the lowest of nine Asian nations.[5] Taiwan's foreign reserves of US$83.5 billion have helped it weather the east Asian economic crisis that began in 1997, as has it high domestic savings rate (Chen, 1998).[6] It is important to note that political struggle faced by marginalized groups in Taiwan must be considered within this context of relative economic stability and prosperity. Queer political struggle in this context is thus largely a middle-class struggle for visibility. (Queer consumption takes this middle-class context as self-evident.)

The changes in politics and the relaxation of the KMT government's control of the media signaled an unprecedented opening for a plurality of voices in Taiwan. Women's struggles, the rights of the disabled, concerns about the environment, and gay and lesbian issues all thrust themselves or were thrust into the new public sphere. These new voices, which were previously ignored, are articulated not in the American political language of majority versus minority, but in a discourse about power which distinguishes them as "weak groups" (*ruoshi tuanti*) who have been formally distanced from the traditional, patriarchal power center.

The rise of queer visibility in Taiwan

While the activities of Taiwan's gay and lesbian community in this newfound political consciousness have only recently begun to receive scholarly attention (e.g. Chang, 1998; Ding & Liu, 1998; Gian, 1998; Patton, 1998; and Yang, 1999), the issue of homosexuality entered into public discourse in the early 1990s with the establishment of Gay Chat at National Taiwan University. In March 1993, Gay Chat became the first officially registered and recognized gay student organization on a Taiwanese university campus

(Han, 1995). The news of its establishment quickly spread throughout mainstream newspapers and television and inspired students on university campuses around Taiwan. By November 1995, there were 10 other gay and lesbian student groups at other universities, although they were still mainly "underground" organizations (not officially registered with school authorities). From the beginning, then, these student-centered *tongzhi* organizations gave the gay and lesbian movement in Taiwan a definitively youthful character.

Outside the university setting, the attention afforded homosexuality in the national media during the mid-1990s was nothing less than remarkable. Despite the persistent homophobia in the emerging discourse about homosexuality and AIDS,[7] there were encouraging signs of an opening social and cultural space for queers in Taiwan. There has been a tremendous increase in gay-related publications of both "underground" and public varieties. In electronic media, the explosive growth of the internet and interuniversity networks created opportunities for BBS chat sites targeted to and supported by gays and lesbians. By May 1996 there were at least 7 MOTSS (Member of the Same Sex) BBS sites under university-student operation. Even the government's Office of Education had an "experimental" site open (Li, 1996). Furthermore, the explosion of books, articles, and films depicting homosexuality is too extensive to document here.[8]

In 1994, Nu Shudian, a women-, feminist-, and lesbian-oriented bookstore in Taipei, joined Eslite Bookstore in bringing news of the homosexual community to gays and lesbians and the wider Taiwanese reading public. In January 1999, another small gay and lesbian bookstore, Jing-jing, opened its door for business in Taipei. Eslite's *Chengpin Yuedu* (*The Eslite Reader*), a monthly book review, regularly brings attention to gay-related publications that also appeal to a wide variety of readers. Addressing gay issues since 1984 is *Zhang Laoshi Yuekan* (*Teacher Zhang Monthly*), a magazine which, like *Chengpin Yuedu*, appeals to a wide audience with its coverage of many social issues (see Lin, 1996).

G&L is capitalizing on this unprecedented visibility and has become the most popular glossy magazine among Chinese *tongzhi* readers today. Broadly, the cover stories in *G&L* span the public and private trajectories of queer life in Taiwan. The main concerns that receive feature treatment range from broad public issues (such as gay consumer culture, sexual harassment of gays, the Chang De Street police harassment incident,[9] World AIDS Day, gays in the military, and gay marriage) to more personal issues of identity (such as coming out to family, aging, self-love, transvestism, and so on). Besides the featured cover stories (which comprise about 5 percent of a given issue), the magazine is organized into five broad domains: (1) promotional materials for consumer goods, for celebrities (both local and Western), and a whole host of cultural activities (about 30 percent); (2) gay and lesbian international news (10 percent); (3) materials on gay relationships in a format akin to "Dear Abby" and in the personal ads format (10 percent); (4) gay and lesbian fiction and other literary writings (15 percent); and (5) erotic photographs (30 percent). Through this variety of materials, G&L projects a gay cosmopolitanism that not only flatters its young urban readers, but also provides a central guide for readers to seek each other out, to build their identities, and to pursue their desires in a still conservative society.

As a means of developing subcultural knowledge for the readers, the lifestyle pages of G&L work as a shopping-mall-in-print that points the readers to the emerging local gay life in Taiwan while simultaneously connecting them to the international gay scene. The regular sections on gay-relevant films, music, books, fashion, restaurants, clubs and bars, tanning salons, gay saunas and hot springs, gay travel, and so on, mark out the social territory for spending, urban, young queers. The centralization of these consumption choices appears in pages known simply as "The Gay Map." Of course, this Map animates queer desires in commercial terms. The magazine also encourages queer consumption of international cultural goods, such as music (e.g. there are pages profiling Melissa Ethridge, k. d. lang, RuPaul, Elton John), theater (e.g. there are reviews of Jeffrey, Angels in America), films (e.g. reviews of Go Fish, The Birdcage, For a Lost Soldier, Lilies, Bent, The River, and many others). In short, a hip gay world is delivered by the magazine through a coalescence of local and imported queer tastes (figure 12.2).

G&L also devotes a great deal of attention to books. In Taiwan, a thriving reading culture exists, which is supported by a 95 percent literacy rate and a highly educated population (US Department of State, 1997). Knowing that queer literature is an indispensable part of queer consumption, G&L routinely publishes book reviews, excerpts, and featured essays about the queer literary scene. Moreover, like many Western and Japanese queer magazines, G&L publishes a good quantity of male and female semi-nude photographs and recycles them in advertisements for seductive swimwear, tanning salons, and bars. Interspersed with the promotional materials on books, these titillating images offer another kind of "reading" material.

Figure 12.2:   The hip world of *G&L Magazine*

A Critical Reading of *G&L*

Consuming passion: tongzhi *relationships and affect*

In a discussion with us about the origin of *G&L*, Michael Chiao, the former Editor, placed the magazine as part of an early beginning (*qibu*) of the gay and lesbian movement in Taiwan (Interview, 1998). Basic visibility rather than complex political assertions, he reasons, is the first step toward antidiscrimination of gays and lesbians. But, as we shall see, the kind of visibility constructed in the magazine is anything but basic.

What comes across strongly in *G&L* is the way the magazine attempts to represent a strong collective social desire for affirmation through the promotion of what can be called Chinese "queer affect" (*tongzhi de qinggan*). Especially in the early issues, the magazine focuses on building a community of desire through shared emotional experiences of isolation, secrecy, fear of coming out, and frustration in facing family pressures, as well as positive experiences of cruising, hooking up, clandestine romances, and narratives of various sexual longing and excitation. Affect (*qinggan*) has a double meaning here: it embodies both "*ganxing*," or sensibility, and its reverse "*xinggan*," which means sexiness. In this way, *G&L* offers space to tell the various stories of the yearning, and slightly sentimentalized, *tongzhi* as well as space to construct his/her positive sex appeal. There are articles filled with instructions on how to look and feel sexy and how to cruise (or "fish" in local usage). There is a section devoted to publishing readers' letters, poems, and short essays about their same-sex emotional and sexual experiences. There is another section called "Mommy Bear Box" in which a mommy-bear figure answers readers' heartfelt letters about love, anxiety, or confusion.[10]

Not surprisingly, many pages are devoted to gay relationship issues. In general, there are two notable observations about *G&L*'s coverage of gay romance. First, it tends to rehearse a parental voice, which substitutes for relationship advice that readers are not likely to obtain from their own parents. As we mentioned before, a regular feature of the magazine is a relationship advice column called "Mommy Bear Box," in which readers can pose questions about sex and romantic yearnings and receive answers from a kind and supportive mommy bear. Second, in "counseling" readers about their romantic affairs, *G&L* advocates a definition of desirability stemming from a certain sexual bashfulness. De-sexualization goes a long way, as it were, in developing and maintaining a "healthy" and desirable image of oneself in relationships.

In an article entitled "From Dating to Commitment," the author debunks the various myths of romance by issuing a universal call for rationality and pragmatism. This form of advising strongly echoes parental rhetorics. For instance, the reader is warned not to believe in sappy romantic movies or novels that profess love at first sight. Considering only the so-called "chemistry" between two people is not enough: "This type of romantic expression of love is great entertainment, but not necessarily applicable to real life situations" (Bi, 1997: 46). "Chemistry" and rational judgment are contrasted over and over again; perhaps this is to mimic the rhetorical form of parental nagging. As a result, romance enters into *G&L* largely as a discourse of surrogate parenthood, as a family training for sense, rationality, and emotional maturity. The practice of sexual modesty is clearly echoed in readers' construction of personal ads. In discussing the culture of personal ads in Taiwan, Lin (1997) explains that in comparison with the more sexually explicit language in American personal columns, ads in Taiwan are much more likely to be "full of a romantic, artistic flavor" (p. 119). According to him, the personal ads by gay men and lesbians in Taiwan are not very different, since ads by both genders share a similar tone that is not centered in sexual excitation, but on expressions of emotional longing.[11]

Expressions of coy modesty are coupled with a sentimentalized language of desire. This works to deemphasize the physical side of queer romance. For instance, in an article about "fishing" (*diaoren*), used in Taiwan to mean "hooking up with someone," the emphasis is again placed on developing the skills of being demure as part of one's sex appeal. Even in the supposedly erotic photographs of young gay couples published in the magazine, the emphasis is on the models gazing longingly into each other's eyes, holding hands, sharing a lazy Sunday afternoon together, or strolling in a pleasant autumn day in the garden, and so on. This kind of alluring image centering on a heavily affective appeal to idyllic couplehood is, we suggest, far more powerful in the construction of romantic discourse for queer readers in Taiwan than the appeal to explicit sexual display commonly seen in many American, European, and Japanese magazines. The downplaying of the sexual self in fact appeals to young Chinese readers, because it works on a reserved sexual ethic *assumed* to be a part of their cultural sensibility.

Tongzhi *lifestyle as a familial problematic*

Behind *G&L*'s appeal to sexual modesty in fact lies a broader and more underlying concern having to do with relationship of *tongzhi* with their families. In Taiwan, like their heterosexual counterparts, the overwhelming majority of unmarried young *tongzhi* live with their families. Sharing living space with one's grandparents, parents, and siblings, and performing family duties define the typical character of life before (expected) marriage (see Chen & Chen, 1997). On the social scale, this explains a total lack of such things as "gay neighborhoods" in Taiwan. As a result, *tongzhi* are reliant on a gay market that is never entirely able to disarticulate from family life. This makes the formation of gay and lesbian identities – especially in matters of coming out – an egregiously complex struggle. We suggest that the editor and writers of *G&L* are fully cognizant of this dimension. From practices of "reserved" sexuality to the problem of coming out, we see how *G&L* outlines a contour of gay life that is quite firmly connected to the figure of the parents.

In the spring of 1997, a gay university student was interviewed on a variety show in Taipei about his sexual orientation. When this program aired, talk shows had already delved into the subject of homosexuality for at least a year. The controversial aspect of the interview was that the young man's mother was brought onto the show, with no idea of what was going to happen. It was on this show that the son came out to his mother. Visibly shaken, the mother then burst into tears. After the show was aired, there was public outrage about the commercialization of the subject of homosexuality on television for the sake of ratings. In the gay and lesbian community, controversy erupted over the son's insensitivity to the feelings of his mother and his irresponsibility in "bringing family matters into the open." MOTSS BBS sites were full of fervent and mostly negative commentaries about the event.

This controversy inspired *G&L* to carry a six-page feature article entitled "How to Come Out to Your Parents" in its June 1997 issue. Offering itself as a resource for counseling young *tongzhi* on the process of coming out to their families, the feature article contains a checklist of considerations to make before coming out. The advice of "thinking about possible consequences" tops the list, while "don't demand immediate acceptance" appears in a section on the "dos and don'ts of coming out" (see W. Li, 1997). Indeed, the specter of the closet is still a part of what *G&L* reminds their readers of from time to time. "The More Dangerous, the More *G&L*: Twenty Ways to Hide Your *G&L* Magazines," a special report in the December 1996 issue, offers a list of lighthearted suggestions for concealing the magazine from the family. Besides the most obvious method of hiding it underneath the mattress, the reader also learns how to conceal the magazine inside the vacuum cleaner, underneath the cat-litter box, and beneath the Buddha figure on the family altar table. The tongue-in-cheek tone aside, the need to conceal is not to be taken lightly.

By and large, in articles about coming out, *G&L* constructs the family space as the sanctuary of well-established traditional values, including filial expectations and roles. The parents, the central figures embodying traditional family values, are portrayed as unimaginative, uptight, but ultimately benevolent. For instance, in one article, we learn of one mother's extreme agony upon discovering that her son is gay. She writes about her disappointment, shame, and even thoughts of suicide. As a mother, she worries about her son finding a meaningful relationship, contracting AIDS, and most of all, not creating children in order to carry on the family name (Jiang, 1996: 88–9). In another article, a father similarly expresses shame, but frames his son's homosexuality as "*bu zhengchang*" (abnormal) and describes the need for him to change as in "turning away from evil" (*gaixie guizheng*) (An & Jiang, 1996). Both articles serve to remind readers of the possible agony coming out to one's parents may cause. Moral considerations of filial duties therefore become a part of what the magazine appropriates for and sells back to the reader.

However, in affirming this traditional morality, *G&L* nonetheless expands the standard understanding of filial piety to a possible reconciliation with homosexuality in the family. This becomes clear because these stories of family agony often offer closure in the form of parental acceptance. In "He is Gay, and He is My Son," the mother reaches a turning point in her struggle with her son's homosexuality when she reflects on inadequacies of her own marriage:

> Thinking about myself, in other people's eyes I am lucky because I have a husband and a son. But besides loneliness and worry, what else have I gotten from my marriage? Since my son is definitely not getting married, looking at this from another angle, isn't he escaping the miseries of a bad situation anyway? Why should I worry about what others say? After this realization, I made peace with myself. (Jiang, 1996: 89)

Conveying parents' concern for their children's happiness becomes a way to articulate how the rules of filial piety can be rewritten to accommodate homosexuality. This mother expresses her wish for her son's future:

> I once asked myself, "If one day my son settles down with one partner, and they want to live with me, could I accept it?" My answer was that I would be willing to accept it. And I would take care of his partner the same way I take care of my son. Because no matter how old my son is, I want to see him often and be able to cook good meals for him, wash his clothes for him. This is all that any mother really wants. (Jiang, 1996: 89)

In "Son, I Just Want You to be Happy," an 82-year-old grandmother best explains how traditional hopes for children and grandchildren – marrying, bearing offspring, and taking care of elders – can still be maintained for gay children:

> If he's together with a boy in the future, I hope the boy is obedient, gentle, thoughtful, knows how to show deference to his superiors, and respects his elders. If the two of them can live a really happy life together, I would be willing and happy to live with them as one family. It would be like having another grandson. If they decide to adopt a child, I can help take care of it, too! If things work out that way, I will be really happy, too. (An & Jiang, 1996: 93)

Reconciliatory scenarios such as this offer the possibility for *tongzhi* to refigure and reevaluate their relationship with their families and with their sense of family duties (albeit through practices of the traditional domestic role for women). Ultimately, this provides hope to the readers.

Taking a step further, and in an attempt to localize an increasingly visible debate in the West concerning family rights for gays and lesbians, *G&L* began to cover gay marriage in 1998. Implicitly, its treatment of gay marriage works toward a redefinition of "family," not through compromise within their family of origin, but through the construction of "success stories" of independent gay households. The August 1998 issue features a story entitled "Marriage? Gayrriage?" It employs comparative stories to describe the two main marital possibilities for gays and lesbians in Taiwan. The first possibility draws on the experience of Hsu You-sheng, a famous gay author who in November 1996 held the first public gay wedding in Taiwan. News of his wedding created a media explosion around the topic of homosexuality and gay marriage. The picture presented is one of "Sunny Gayrriage" (the English subtitle for the article on Hsu) in which openly gay couples are shown as healthy, happy, and, in Hsu's case, contributing to a positive change in society's view of gay relationships. Juxtaposed against this idealized form of same-sex marriage is the second possibility of a more troubling kind: that of gay men in "fake" marriages. Presented under the heading of "Closet Marriage," this second form of marriage for gays is depicted through three interviews with gay men who are married to women. The stories they tell convey entrapment, frustration, and, most of all, regret. Married for three years, one 36-year-old gay man exclaims: "If I could do it all over again, I would not choose to be in this marriage" ("Marriage? Gayrriage?", 1998: 27). Another man interviewed strongly opposes this practice: "No matter what the reasons are, even pressure from parents and society, there is never a good reason to enter into this kind of marriage. I think people have to face themselves. These pressures [from family and society] can be avoided" (p. 28). A third man simply advises the readers: "If you absolutely have to get married, you must not reveal the truth to your spouse" (p. 30).

Facing family pressure is by no means unique to Taiwanese queers. Most of us have had to confront it. What is unique is how *G&L* carefully inscribes the pleasures and anxieties of being gay as a problematic *of* the family. Eager to show its readers how to live a happy gay life (e.g. through the utopic story of Hsu), *G&L* is equally eager to ask them to be considerate of the potential agony gay life causes both to their family of origin and to their own families formed through "closet marriages."

The question of coming out (*xianshen*) indeed directs *tongzhi* to the centrality of the family. "You can only truly come out if you're an orphan" has sometimes served as a common joke in this regard. This is why the effort to reimagine traditional culture (*chuantong wenhua*) so that homosexuality can be accepted is a compelling and welcomed idea. Another way in which coming out is dealt with is through collective activism. In recent years we have witnessed the practice of "collective coming out" (*jiti xianshen*) by Taiwanese queer activists. It is a practice staged largely to the media on university campuses as a human rights protest. In order to protect individual anonymity, *tongzhi* who come out collectively have put on Chinese opera masks in front of the media (figure 12.3). The masks signify that their action situates queer identity precisely between "in" and "out": not exactly out, but not exactly staying in the closet either. What is being signified is that in Taiwan, *tongzhi* are caught between the family and the state, between claiming a stake for themselves in the newly democratized order of Taiwan politics and feeling uncertain as to whether this new order will include a space for them or not.[12] Bound by constraints in the family, and not yet recognized as a meaningful voice by the state, Taiwanese *tongzhi* do not see how the *individual* coming out heralded by the West can work for them.[13] Local scholar Chu Wei-cheng (1998) has called it a case of "cultural indigestion" (p. 40).

Figure 3

Figure 12.3: *Tongzhi* coming out collectively

In the above, we have tried to show *G&L*'s main preoccupations as a new queer magazine in a newly democratizing public sphere. We have suggested that *tongzhi* culture is constructed by *G&L* through an articulation of queer affect and a rearticulation of family life and filial duties. Yet an important question remains: how are queer affect and family politics, in turn, mediated by the larger process of commodification? In other words, how is queer experience in Taiwan filtered through a consumerist ideology?

Just another "gay marketing moment"?

Critical analyses of commodified queer experience that are available from the West tend to be strongly underpinned by class concerns. Since John D'Emilio's (1983) groundbreaking essay on the relationship between capitalism and gay identity, Western analysts have largely focused on class difference as a central problematic in their consideration of queer consumption. Amy Gluckman and Betsy Reed's important book, *Homoeconomics: Capitalism, Community, and Lesbian and Gay Life* (1997), places an implicit emphasis on the same, to an extent that differences between gay male and lesbian consumption and among diverse racial groups are examined as differences subsumed in class politics. For lesbians and gay men in the US, the onset of the "gay marketing moment" signals an increasing recognition of the interaction – and elision – among identity, commerce, and politics. Yet more than anything else, this recognition of gay commercial visibility has brought home an important fact: visibility does not apply evenly to all gay people. In the US, the impressive demographics, profligate spending habits, and high levels of discretionary income boasted of the gay community by marketing organizations and appropriated by conservative political voices have produced a new mythology of gay affluence, which of course turns out to be a class-based mythology (Badgett, 1997). Accordingly, critical analyses of this new cultural mythology rightfully emphasize the politics of class in order to illuminate underlying conflicts in the phenomenon of gay consumerism. Moreover, implicit in such class-based analyses is a rather common assumption about queers' relationship to the nuclear family. The presupposition is that capitalism (and some social-insurance or welfare safety net) provides an escape route for queers to exist *apart from* their families. Conceptualized as being independent from familial constraints (including pressure to marry and procreate), queers, especially queers who engage in popular consumption, are placed in a society and economy whose distinguishing feature is class stratification. In Taiwan, it is unclear how relevant this kind of individual-based and class-based analysis is. In this section, we extend our analysis of *G&L* by asking: What makes queer experience in Taiwan, even in a consumerist environment? Is class difference a major force in the commodification of Taiwanese *tongzhi* identities?

To be sure, class differences exist in Taiwan, especially in the urban/rural divide. Yet it does not follow that Taiwanese society has a strong class consciousness. In fact, the KMT's economic policies have been directed against the creation of stratified class experiences. As Taiwanese scholar Tu Wei-ming (1996) has argued in "Cultural Identity and the Politics of Recognition in Contemporary Taiwan":

> An important feature of the "Taiwan miracle" . . . is the absence of a sharp increase in inequality, despite extraordinarily rapid growth. Much of this . . . can be attributed to the role of the government. Through subsidies, taxation, trade policies and other remedial measures, the KMT leadership seems to have dampened economic pressures to polarize the society. (1996: 1137)

To understand the formation of *cultural identity* as it is shaped – and "imagined" – by acts of consumption, it is important to note the distinction between a politico-economic logic and a consumption logic. Broadly speaking, the former stresses various forms of economic practices, including labor relations and modes of production and consumption, as the basis of ideological experience. Social life is abstracted into economic life. The same conceptual abstraction also exists in a cultural logic of consumption, for it stresses that both the producers and consumers of culture acquire their (commodified) experience and identities through various modes of representation, fetishization, reification, etc. (see Goldman, 1992). With consumption logic, then, social life is abstracted into "discourse." It is not our purpose here to delineate the validity of each approach. Instead, in the present analysis of queer cultural visibility in Taiwan, we want to highlight the role of consumption logic in the formation of an emerging identity politics. Specifically, we are concerned that a certain preferred analytic approach that may be suitable in other contexts may not apply to the present one. We maintain that the "cultural" in queer cultural consumption as it appears in the pages of *G&L* has a strong ideological association with traditional "familial culture."

Thus, the primary concern of *G&L* in its attempt to animate a "*tongzhi* lifestyle" in Taiwan is about how to have the pleasures of the body in commodity terms *vis-à-vis* the family space. This often means either shielding those pleasures from the family (e.g. "The More Dangerous, the More *G&L*:

Twenty Ways to Hide Your *G&L* Magazines," *G&L* 1996) or making them visible so as to intervene into traditional family constraints (e.g. "Mom, Dad, He's My Other Half: How to Introduce Your Lover to Your Family," *G&L* 1997). In *G&L*, the "*tongzhi*" becomes a dual construct: a pleasure-seeker in the form of a free, imaginative, adult consumer, and a curious, somewhat melancholic person in the form of a family member (more specifically, a child). Put in another way, the magazine can be seen as providing an understanding of homosexuality emerging as an interesting process of hybridizing a new market-liberated identity and one that is articulated into a hegemonic familial tradition. In this way, *G&L*'s participation in the rapid proliferation of sexual discourses in Taiwan helps to outline the homosexual as a democratic invention on the one hand (a sort of new cultural citizenship constituted by market ideology) and a familial reinvention on the other hand (as a resource to engage with, and possibly change, traditional Chinese gender and sexual systems). Such is the "everyday-ness" of being gay in Taiwan, a notion that entwines the commercial and the familial.

In contrast with the economic life of gays and lesbians in the US detailed by D'Emilio (1983), Faderman (1991), Gottlieb (1984), Matthaei (1997), Valocchi (1999), and others, the development in Taiwan of a labor force autonomous from the family sphere provides partial economic autonomy for queers without *cultural* autonomy from family responsibilities. Industrial modernity in Taiwan does not agitate cultural traditions – the former in fact works in conjunction with the latter.[14] This has produced contradictions for young queers whose identity increasingly relies on reworking the lines that intersect economics and culture. One of the consequences of this contradiction is the creation of differences between gay men and lesbians (which, by the way, is also prevalent in the US).

In general terms, the sexual division of labor in the Chinese family positions men firmly in the heterosexual framework, making marriage a fundamental definition of family duty as well as masculine personhood. For women, however, the patriarchal pressure to serve the family, ironically, allows a space for homosocial relationships. Filial duties in some sense alleviate women from the pressure of marriage; so long as they take care of the family, singlehood is a more permissible identity for women than for men.[15] Under this particular perspective, Taiwanese gay men generally experience a more salient tension between economic independence and the cultural constraints of family duties than lesbians do. This difference would in turn result in a divergence of consumer desire between the gay male and lesbian readers of *G&L*.[16]

In *G&L*, gay male desire is visibly configured around the tabooed male body repressed by heterosexual masculine and family ideals. In fact, in their letters to the editor, many male readers demand to see more male images showing more open nudity. They also frequently request more information about how to obtain sex in public commercial sites. The challenge to the repression of erotic desires is facilitated by gay men's relative economic freedom. Lesbian desire, on the other hand, is configured around the consumption of female homosociality and the homoerotic feelings that can flourish in it. Some lesbian readers in fact complain about the nude photographs of women in the magazine. They reason that since images of nude women are widely available in the dominant male culture (e.g. *Playboy*), a queer magazine like *G&L* should devote more space to female-to-female relational issues. They argue that the female body need not become a focal point of lesbian consumption because it is not a tabooed or repressed object in the patriarchal erotic imagination. The difference in consumption between gay men and lesbians, therefore, does not appear to be mitigated by class distinctions (which seems to be more evident in the US), but rather by their different ideological positions in traditional patriarchy and the gender hierarchy supported by it.

In sum, in asking what kind of consumer identity *G&L* promotes for its readers, we have suggested moving away from a class-based analysis for understanding the commodification of Taiwanese queer identity. Rather, we have argued that family ideals continue to shape male and female *tongzhi*'s different desires and tastes in cultural consumption. Seen in these ways, queer consumerism in *G&L* (and other similar cultural products) must be seen as something that is situated between the market and the national imagination of traditional family morality. Consumption stages the necessary conflict between economic liberty, the promise of which is reinforced by newfound democratic pluralism, and persistent cultural constraints in the name of the traditional social order. More importantly, we want to show that *in G&L, a cultural "logic of consumption" bypasses economic concerns in order to enable a reworking of family life for its tongzhi readers.* This logic of consumption generates a community of desire that is weakly, if at all, tied to class politics.

Conclusion

Western theories of identity politics, particularly those developed in cultural studies and cultural sociology in recent years, conceive of the social sphere as the site of multiple, intersecting political struggles in which a critical sense of visibility matters, especially as it proffers the possibility for social transformation (see e.g. Erni, 1996; Gilroy, 1993; Hall, 1992; Seidman, 1993). Yet making identity visible is both about contesting history and about the remaking of the social sphere. The former question calls for a political challenge of historical relations of domination that have produced various forms of "otherness" through erasure of cultural memory and historical violence. The latter question about rearticulating the social sphere attends to the strategies and tactics of "difference," of how difference disrupts the normative surface of everyday life. Works that address sexual minorities on how they disrupt gender and sexual categories and practices, for instance, contribute to the resignification of the social sphere, especially the media (e.g. Clark, 1993; Doty, 1993; Doty & Creekmur, 1995; Fejes & Petrich, 1993).

The rapid political transformation in Taiwan in the post-martial law era presents a particularly relevant context for a discussion of identity politics of visibility. The political possibilities opened up by the proliferation of previously invisible groups demonstrate the problematics of "otherness" and "difference" briefly outlined above. "Weak groups" (*ruoshi tuanti*) represent both outcasts marked and marginalized from the center of power, and a social category whose meaning depends entirely on its relation to, its difference from, other categories. In this chapter, we have largely drawn on a theory of difference in order to examine whether and to what extent gay cultural consumption can resignify homosexuality and disrupt notions of normalcy in Taiwanese society. We have analyzed such resignification and disruption in relation to, and not outside of, "heteronormativity" (Warner, 1993) and capitalist formation.

In the West, queer visibility today is a highly contested term. Recently, this negotiation of the relation between queer cultural visibility and consumerism has been manifested in many different ways in the US.[17] Yet how we struggle with visibility depends on how we conceptualize queer marginalization. In the US, the social and political subjugation of sexual minorities emanates from specific historical formations producing various discourses of stigmatization. Religion, class, race, and biomedical science are the primary discourses that mark queerness as deviant from "the normal." The situation in Taiwan is quite different. Confucianism, or alternatively, "traditional culture" (*chuantong wenhua*), is the ideological backdrop regulating social and political life in Taiwan. It is against the weight of a set of traditional conservative cultural norms that the emerging political consciousness of the Taiwanese *tongzhi* must be understood.[18] The stigmatization of queers in Taiwan therefore must be understood in its own context. Rather than the religion-based, class-inflected, or medically pathologized definitions of homosexuality in the US, queers in Taiwan are marginalized through their fundamental deviation from the (heteronormative) traditional family-centered social order deeply informed by Confucianism. In this way, significant social change for queers in Taiwan requires a disruption of that traditional social order.

In *G&L*, the marshalling of gay cultural sensibilities in an effort to rethink the family space in fact exposes the arbitrariness of "traditional culture" and helps to reconfigure it into a more cosmopolitan mode. Here, the link between family and sexual alterity is made possible, where homosexuality finds a possible space of existence, even constituting a modernizing factor. The magazine forges a new intersection between gay sexuality and the Taiwanese nation-state implied by the strong "family tradition," even when this intersection is found within the framework of consumer culture. This peculiar condition renders young Taiwanese *tongzhi* a kind of social emblem for a new Taiwan. Collectively referred to as "*xinxing renlei*" (the "newly rising humanity"), the youth of the 1990s and beyond are well educated, hip, fashionable, and informed about the outside world. Yet they are still wrangling with their financial dependence upon their parents and with their ideological relationship to traditional family life in a rapidly changing society. Tu Wei-ming (1996) has argued that the whole of Taiwanese society today is confronting the generational cleavages between old and new times. *G&L*'s emphasis on the split between the family and individual economic and sexual freedom must therefore be understood in the context of these larger changes. As a cultural production making a specific mark at this historical moment, *G&L* projects *tongzhi* as "glossy subjects" whose commodified visibility tests the limits of a society poised for a new sexual imaginary.

Notes

1 This project benefited from a research grant from the Center for the Study of Media & Society, Gay and Lesbian Alliance Against Defamation (GLAAD), New York, and a grant by the George M. Camp Fund, Department of Sociology, Yale University. The authors express their gratitude. In addition, a different version of this essay has appeared in *Sexualities* 4(1), 2001.
2 A comment on our use of the *hanyu pinyin* romanization system in the chapter. It should be noted that *G&L*'s reporting and advertisements are virtually without exception written in Mandarin-style Chinese. That is, the mag-

azine uses conventional Mandarin grammar and vocabulary so as to reach as broad a range of Chinese speakers as possible, including people in Taiwan, Hong Kong, and (potentially) mainland China. Our use of *hanyu pinyin*, which is based on Mandarin pronunciations, is in keeping with the magazine's own Mandarin usage. Moreover, while other romanization systems exist (e.g., Wade-Giles, the Yale system, etc.), the PRC-propagated *hanyu pinyin* has become the most widely used and recognized system in the world, taught in American universities, Hong Kong, Singapore, and even recently in many of Taiwan's language schools. We therefore hope that using the system to represent Chinese characters will allow us to reach the broadest possible range of English readers who may also be readers of Chinese. Moreover, while Mandarin is based on the Beijing dialect and has been politicized in Taiwan due to its propagation by the KMT, there is no "indigenous" form of romanization that we find suitable for an international reading audience. Various branches of Taiwan's own central government utilize at least three different systems, a situation that only further complicates any effort to find a "Taiwanese" romanization system for Mandarin.

3   For the first year and a half, *G&L* had no competition in the market. In fact, sales were so steady that its parent company, Re Ai Publishing Company, began producing a second magazine named *Glory* in January 1998. *Glory* targets only gay male readers, a result of male readers' demands for an all-male magazine. The company has no plans to produce a comparable spin-off for its lesbian readers, which in essence duplicates the blatant imbalance of coverage of gay male and lesbian concerns in *G&L* itself. Also in January 1998, a second gay and lesbian glossy named *Together* was published in Taiwan. But, according to former *G&L* editor Michael Chiao, since the sales figures of *Together* are four to five times less than that of *G&L*, it does not constitute major competition.

4   There are only a handful of studies on gay and lesbian social movements in the Asian context. Examples include Gian (1998) and Ni (1996), both of whom discuss the questions of "agency" and "community" in such a movement in Taiwan, and Zhou (1997) who gives an "anticolonial" reading to the formation of queer identity politics in Taiwan, Hong Kong, and China. For a study of Japanese gay and lesbian movements, see Lungsing (1999). As for studies of images of *tongzhi* on Taiwanese television, see Lin (1999). See also Lungsing (1995) for an analysis of a Japanese gay magazine called *Barazoku*. His analysis focuses only on personal ads in the magazine (particularly those ads looking for "marriage" by gay men in Japan).

5   According to the World Bank (1998), Taiwan scored a Gini coefficient in 1995 of only 31.7.

6   Taiwan in the 1990s was one of the Newly Industrialized Countries (NICs) in the east Asian region. Once a recipient of American aid in the 1950s, Taiwan now contributes economic and disaster relief aid to its Asian neighbors, as well as being a major foreign investor in countries such as the Philippines, China,

and Malaysia. Enjoying an average annual growth rate of 6.6 percent between 1991 and 1995, Taiwan is now a leading producer of high-technology goods (US Department of State, 1997). More recently, the country's strong economy indicates its ability to cope with the devastating earthquakes that began on September 21, 1999.

7   The government's refusal to allow Magic Johnson to enter Taiwan in October 1995 due to his HIV-positive status attracted much media attention (Tian, 1996). As late as 1996, the blame for AIDS was still placed on homosexuals. The national government's Health Department "educated" Taiwanese to believe that "[h]omosexuals are the only high risk group. They are self-destructive and will live painfully and die painful deaths."

8   Some notable examples include Ang Lee's internationally acclaimed *The Wedding Banquet* (1993), Zhuang Huiqiu's *Chinese Homosexuals* (1996), *Nupengyou* ("Girlfriend," a bimonthly magazine started in 1994), Zheng Meili's *Nuer Quan* ("The Girl's Club," 1997), Li Zhonghan's *Wode Airen shi Nanren* (1998), Zhou Huashan's *Post-Colonial Tongzhi* (1997), and *G&L Magazine*. The debut of *G&L*, as reported in the mainstream magazine *The Journalist*, signified the movement of homosexuality from the fringes of media to mainstream visibility.

9   In July 1997, about 40 to 50 gay men were detained on Chang De Street – just outside the "gay park" in central Taipei – photographed, and threatened with exposure to their families. This police harassment incident was widely reported in the Taiwanese gay and straight media and caused an explosive debate about gay civil rights in Taiwan. Only one and a half years after the Chang De incident, a squad of policemen on December 1998 raided AG Club, a gymnasium and sauna well-known for its gay clientele in downtown Taipei. They also arrested two men found caressing one another in a small, private compartment and proceeded to force them to re-pose their caress so that their photographs could be taken as evidence to support the police charge of "obscenity in public" (see IGLHRC, 1998).

10 Beginning in the October 1988 issue, "Mommy Bear" was replaced by "Big Sister Bear." Using a family reference continues *G&L*'s focus on the family. The idea of the big sister also resonates well with gay culture in Taiwan, since the big sister/big brother figure (*ganjie, gange*) brings with it the status of "*guolairen*" (someone who's been there). Their advice on love and sex is therefore especially appreciated.

11 Some typical examples he cites (which are also found throughout *G&L*'s personal columns) are: "Hoping for a true feeling, a true love"; "If you also believe in destiny, let us fulfill ours"; "Waiting to share my world with you, and yours with me"; "Looking for a shoulder to rest my head on"; and so on.

12 This uncertainty takes form in the pages of the October 1998 issue, in which two of the three major parties' candidates for Taipei mayor are interviewed about their positions on gay issues (see "Chen Shuibian," 1998). The DPP can-

didate, incumbent mayor (and now newly elected President) Chen Shuibian, responded favorably to the questions posed regarding the political and civil rights of Taiwanese *tongzhi*, yet he declined to answer to these questions: (a) "Mayor Chen, you once said you do not 'oppose' homosexuals but neither do you 'encourage' them. Could you explain that statement?"; (b) "If you discovered that your son or daughter were gay, how would you deal with the situation?" (p. 18). Particularly given his status as the incumbent mayor, Chen's failure to respond to these two questions did not alleviate the anxieties *tongzhi* feel about their status in Taiwanese politics. His lack of response to the question posed in the family context also heightens the schism between the public and private spheres.

13   The practice of "collective coming out" indeed stages an important step toward the formation of a queer space of citizenship. As Chang (1998) explains, "In a place like Taiwan, where the family structure is compact and personal space extremely limited, the individual coming out adopted by lesbians and gays in places such as the United States never appealed to their counterparts in Taiwan. Collective coming out, on the contrary, satisfies local sexual dissidents' longing for "speaking out" in public and tactfully avoids their being tracked down at the same time" (p. 289).

14   For more discussion of the relationship between cultural tradition and economic prosperity in Chinese societies, see Tu et al. (1992: 74–90) for the insightful observations made by Thomas Gold, Tu Weiming, Benjamin Schwartz, and others.

15   For ethnographic evidence of the relative freedom of lesbians, see Ke (1996). We feel it important to also note, however, that this position is strongly refuted in the more extensive ethnographic research of Zheng (1997).

16   *G&L* has a serious imbalance of coverage of gay male interests and lesbian interests. This is an issue that has troubled the staff of *G&L* from its inception (Interview, 1998). Many of the magazine's readers feel dissatisfied with the share of attention lesbians receive. Antagonism between gay male and lesbian readers arises often in the letters to the editor and is reflected in lower sales to women (which may or may not be due to the imbalance of coverage mentioned here). The perceived lack of attention to lesbian issues is repudiated by some male readers, who feel that women's photos are, in their words, "disgusting" and do not want to have "their" magazine "include so much about lesbians." Yet in reality, the magazine devotes a much smaller amount of space to lesbian photos, stories, and concerns than what gay men receive. Moreover, and perhaps more importantly, the vast majority of advertisements in *G&L* are geared solely to promoting services and goods to gay men. The perception is that lesbians do not constitute a market worth targeting.

17   Take briefly, for instance, three sites that have shown us the political ambivalence of queer visibility:

- in AIDS fundraising events, which was first iconized in the use of the Red Ribbon, and then embedded in product endorsements, "pride" events, and celebrity-driven charity activities;
- in the practices of Queer Nation, whose tactics of infiltrating public sites of consumption aimed at reterritorializing them for queers, but which also fed the public's appetite for the shocking, the spectacular, and the freaky-exotic (see Hennessy, 1995);
- in the "Ellen phenomenon" on American primetime television, which served up the figure of middle-class, white, and explicitly depoliticized lesbianism as the model of queer acceptability.

In each of these cases, visibility remains an ambiguous tool for affecting social change. Moreover, once the images of gays and lesbians are sufficiently fetishized as "lifestyles," they can be packaged and sold back to gay and lesbian consumers as ostensibly "liberatory" goods.

18 The ideological underpinnings of Taiwanese society today cannot be done full justice in this chapter. For an illuminating discussion of the interaction between Confucianism and *chuantong wenhua* and the ways they play out in the political, social, religious, and economic realms of Taiwan today, see Tu et al., 1992.

References

Adam, Barry, Duyvendak, Jan Willem, and Krouwel, Andre (1999). "Gay and Lesbian Movements Beyond Borders? National Imprints of a Worldwide Movement." In B. Adam, J. W. Duyvendak, and A. Krouwel, eds., *The Global Emergence of Gay and Lesbian Politics: National Imprints of a Worldwide Movement.* Philadelphia: Temple University Press, 342–77.

An, Keqiang and Jiang, Diantai (Aug. 1996). "Haizi, Wo Zhi Yao Ni Huode Kuaile! Yige *Tongzhi* Jiaren de Zhenshi Shengyin" [Son, I Just Want You to Be Happy! True Voices of A Gay Man's Family Members]. *G&L Magazine* 2: 92–3.

Badgett, M. V. Lee (1997). "Beyond Biased Samples: Challenging the Myths on the Economic Status of Lesbians and Gay Men." In Amy Gluckman and Betsy Reed, eds., *Homoeconomics: Capitalism, Community, and Lesbian and Gay Life.* New York: Routledge, 65–72.

Bi, Ming (Aug. 1997). "Zai Shuo 'Wo Ai Ni' Zhi Qian de Zhunbei Gongzuo: From Dating to Commitment" [How to Prepare Before saying "I Love You": From Dating to Commitment]. *G&L Magazine* 8: 44–9.

Bureau of Statistics (1997). "The Republic of China on Taiwan 1997 Statistics." Taiwan Bureau of Statistics, Directorate-General of Budget, Accounting and Statistics, Executive Yuan. (A brochure.)

Chang, Hsiao-hung (1998). "Taiwan Queer Valentines." In Kuan-Hsing Chen, ed., *Trajectories: Inter-Asia Cultural Studies.* New York: Routledge, 283–98.

Chen, Chien-jen (1998). "How Has Taiwan Withstood Asia's Financial Crisis?" Government Information Office, Republic of China.

Chen, Mickey C. and Chen, Ming-Hsiu (Producers and Directors) (1997). *Not Simply a Wedding Banquet* [Film]. Third World Newsreel.

"Chen Shuibian vs. Ma Yingjiu: *Tongzhi* Zhengjian Da Leitai" [Chen Shuibian vs. Ma Yingjiu: Fighting in the Ring about *Tongzhi* Politics] (Oct. 1998). *G&L Magazine* 15: 16–19.

Chu, Wei-cheng R. (1998). "Coming Out Or Not: Postcolonial Autonomy and / Gay/ Activism in Taiwan." *Taiwan: A Radical Quarterly in Social Studies* 30: 35–62.

Clark, Denae (1993). "Commodity Lesbianism." In Henry Abelove et al., eds., *The Lesbian and Gay Studies Reader*. New York: Routledge, 186–201.

D'Emilio, John (1983). "Capitalism and Gay Identity." In Ann Snitow et al., eds., *Powers of Desire: The Politics of Sexuality*. New York: Monthly Review Press, 100–17.

Deng, Wenling (April 1997). "*Tongzhi*, Rang Wo Qiaoqiao Nide Chaopiao!" [*Tongzhi*, Let Me See Your Money!]. *G&L Magazine* 6: 32–3.

Ding, Naifei and Liu, Jen-ping (1998). "Reticent Poetics, Queer Politics." *Working Papers in Gender/Sexuality Studies* 3 & 4: 109–55.

Doty, Alexander (1993). *Making Things Perfectly Queer: Interpreting Mass Culture*. Minneapolis: University of Minnesota Press.

Doty, Alexander and Creekmur, Cory, eds. (1995). *Out in Culture: Gay, Lesbian, and Queer Essays on Popular Culture*. Durham, NC: Duke University Press.

Erni, John (1996). "Eternal Excesses: Toward a Queer Mode of Articulation in Social Theory." *American Literary History* 8(3): 566–81.

Faderman, Lillian (1991). *Odd Girls and Twilight Lover: A History of Lesbian Life in Twentieth Century America*. New York: Penguin.

Fejes, Fred and Petrich, Kevin (1993, Dec.). "Invisibility, Homophobia, and Heterosexism: Lesbians, Gays and the Media." *Critical Studies in Mass Communication* 10(4): 395–422.

Gian, Jia-shin (1998). "Taiwanese Lesbians' Identification Under the Queer Politics Since 1990." *Taiwan: A Radical Quarterly in Social Studies* 30: 63–115.

Gilroy, Paul (1993). *The Black Atlantic*. London: Verso.

Gluckman, Amy and Reed, Betsy (1997). *Homoeconomics: Capitalism, Community, and Lesbian and Gay Life*. New York: Routledge.

Goldman, Robert (1992). *Reading Ads Socially*. New York and London: Routledge.

Gottlieb, Rhonda (1997). "The Political Economy of Sexuality." *Review of Radical Political Economics* 16: 143–66.

Hall, Stuart (1992). "The Question of Cultural Identity." In Stuart Hall, David Held, and Tim McGraw, eds., *Modernity and Its Futures*. Cambridge: Polity Press.

Han, Guodong (1995, Nov.). "*Tongzhi* Chulie: Daxue Xiaoyuan Tongxinglian Tuanti Saomiao" [Gays Come Out: Gay Groups on University Campuses]. *Dangdai Qingnian* [*Contemporary Youth*], pp. 11–13.

Hennessy, Rosemary (1995). "Queer Visibility in Commodity Culture." *Cultural Critique* 29: 31–76.

Hsu, You-sheng (April 1997). "Dajia Dou Yao Tao *Tongzhi* de Hebao" [Everybody Wants the *Tongzhi* Wallet]. *G&L Magazine* 6: 34–5.

IGLHRC (International Gay and Lesbian Human Rights Council) (1998). "Taiwan Policemen Raid Gay Gymnasium in Taipei." IGLHRC Action Alert, Dec. 22.

Interview with Michael Chiao (Editor of *G&L*) (1998, Aug. 6). In Taipei, by Anthony J. Spires.

Jiang, Yue (June 1996). "He is Gay, and He is My Son." *G&L Magazine* 1: 88–9.

Ke, Lisi (1996, Oct. 1). "Nannan Nunu Zhu Chao Zhuan'an: *Tongzhi* Jiating Xiezhen" [2 Men, 2 Women Building Nests: True Stories of Gay Families]. *Zhang Laoshi Yuekan* [*Teacher Zhang Monthly*], pp. 76–80.

Lee, Ang (Director) (1993). *The Wedding Banquet* [Film]. Samuel Goldwyn Company.

Li, Ming (Aug. 1997). "Ba Ma, Ta Shi Wode Ling Yiban: How to Introduce Your Lover to Your Family" [Mom, Dad, He is My Other Half: How to Introduce Your Lover to Your Family]. *G&L Magazine* 8: 120–3.

Li, Wen (June 1997). "Ruhe Xiang Fumu Kaikou Shuo: Wo Shi!" [How to Come Out to Your Parents]. *G&L Magazine* 7: 20–5. (Translated from Eric Marcus, *The Male Couple's Guide.*)

Li, Yanfu (1996, May 8). "Wanglu Kongjian, '*Tongzhi*' Changsuoyuyan." *Zixun Zhuankan* [*Infoweekly*], http://udn.com.tw/service/pcnews/infoweekly.

Li, Yixue, et al. (June 1996). "Taiwan *Tongzhi* Xiaofei Wenhua: Guke Zhishang, *Tongzhi* Wansui" [Taiwan *Tongzhi* Consumer Culture: The Customer First, Long Live *Tongzhi*]. *G&L Magazine* 1: 19–28.

Li, Zhonghan (1998). *Wode Airen Shi Nanren: Nantongzhi de Chengzhang Gushi* [*My Lover is a Man: Growing Up Stories of Gay Men*]. Taipei: Zhang Laoshi.

Lin, Hongzheng and Song, Zihao (Oct. 1996). "Shierge *Tongzhi* Diao Ren Shu: How to Go Fishing?" [12 Ways to Catch Someone: How to Go Fishing?]. *G&L Magazine* 3: 100–5.

Lin, Liyun (1996). "Women Zhijian: Ji Yige Nutongxinglian Tuanti" [Between Us: A Record of a Lesbian Organization]. In Huiqiu Zhuang et al., eds., *Zhongguoren de Tongxinglian* [*Chinese Homosexuals*]. Taipei: Zhang Laoshi, 211–15.

Lin, Xianxiu (June 1997). "Zhengyou Qishi Toulu le Shenma Qishi?" [What do Personal Ads Reveal?]. *G&L Magazine* 7: 118–21.

Lin, Yu-ling (1999). "The Gender Politics of Transvestite Shows on Taiwanese TV." Paper presented at the Fourth International Conference on Sexuality Education, Sexology, Trans/gender Studies and LesBiGay Studies, Chungli, Taiwan, May.

Lungsing, Wim (1995). "Japanese Gay Magazines and Marriage Advertisements." In Gerald Sullivan and Laurence Wai-teng Leong, eds., *Gays and Lesbians in Asia and the Pacific: Social and Human Services*. New York and London: Haworth Press, 71–87.

Lungsing, Wim (1999). "Japan: Finding its Way?" In B. Adam, J. W. Duyvendak, and A. Krouwel, eds., *The Global Emergence of Gay and Lesbian Politics: National Imprints of a Worldwide Movement*. Philadelphia: Temple University Press, 293–325.

"Marriage? Gayrriage?" (Aug. 1998). *G&L Magazine* 14: 20–35.

Matthaei, Julie (1997). "The Sexual Division of Labor, Sexuality, and Lesbian/Gay Liberation: Toward a Marxist-Feminist Analysis of Sexuality in US Capitalism." In Amy Gluckman and Betsy Reed, eds., *Homoeconomics: Capitalism, Community, and Lesbian and Gay Life*. New York: Routledge, 135–64.

Ni, Jia-chen (1996). "Discourse and Agency in Lesbian and Gay Movement in Taiwan." Paper presented at the First International Conference on Sexuality Education, Sexology, Trans/gender Studies and LesBiGay Studies, Chungli, Taiwan.

Patton, Cindy (1998). "Stealth Bombers of Desire: The Globalization of "Alterity" in Emerging Democracies." *Working Papers in Gender/Sexuality Studies* 3 & 4: 301–23.

Seidman, Steven (1993). "Identity and Politics in a "Postmodern" Gay Culture: Some Historical and Conceptual Notes." In Michael Warner , ed., *Fear of a Queer Planet: Queer Politics and Social Theory*. Minneapolis: University of Minnesota Press, 105–42.

Tian, Liqing (1996, Dec. 12). "Wu Qishi de Weilai: Aizi Fangzhi de Tuidong yu Kunjing" [A Future Free of Discrimination: Dilemmas in and Promotion of AIDS Prevention and Treatment]. *Zhang Laoshi Yuekan* [*Teacher Zhang Monthly*], pp. 95–9.

Tu, Wei-ming (1996). "Cultural Identity and the Politics of Recognition in Contemporary Taiwan." *The China Quarterly* 148: 1115–40.

Tu, Wei-ming, et al., eds. (1992). *The Confucian World Observed: A Contemporary Discussion of Confucian Humanism in East Asia*. Honolulu: The East–West Center.

US Department of State (1997). " Notes: Taiwan, November 1997." Bureau of East Asia and Pacific Affairs, Nov. 22 (http://www.ait.org.tw/twbgnote.htm).

Valocchi, Steve (1999). "The Class-Inflected Nature of Gay Identity." *Social Problems* 46(2): 207–24.

Warner, Michael, ed. (1993). *Fear of a Queer Planet: Queer Politics and Social Theory*. Minneapolis: University of Minnesota Press.

World Bank (1998). http://www.worldbank.org/poverty/eacrisis/sector/employ/before2.htm.

Yang, Chung-chuan (1999). "Internet and Gay Civil Right Movement in Taiwan." Paper presented at the International Communication Association, San Francisco, May.

"Yue Weixian, Yue Reai: Ershige Shoucang Reai Zazhi de Fangfa" [The More Dangerous, the More *G&L*: Twenty Ways to Hide Your *G&L* Magazines] (Dec. 1996). *G&L Magazine* 4: 98–9.

Zheng, Meili (1997). *Nuer Quan: Taiwan Nutongzhi de Xingbie, Jiating, yu Quannei Shenghuo* [*The Girls' Club: Taiwanese Lesbians' Sex, Family, and Life on the Inside*]. Taipei: Nushu Xilie (Fembooks).

Zhou, Huashan (1997). *Hou Zhimin Tongzhi* [*Postcolonial Tongzhi*]. Hong Kong: Hong Kong Tongzhi Publishing Company.

Zhuang, Huiqiu (1996). *Zhongguoren de Tongxinglian* [*Chinese Homosexuals*]. Taipei: Zhang Laoshi.

Index

Index

Index

Index

Index

Index

Index

Won, Yongjin, 117, 120, 124
Wong Kar-wai, 29, 32
WTO, 189, 190, 193
Wu, Jacky, 184, 201

Yan-chiu, Lee, 184
Yao, Souchou, 13

Yoon, Sunhee, 122
youth, 122, 244

Zee TV, 177
Zhang Laoshi Yuekan (*Teacher Zhang Monthly*), 230
Zhou Huashan, 246